Designspark Mechanical 4.0 Basics Tutorial

Tutorial Books

Contents

Introduction

Designspark Mechanical helps you to design and modify product concepts without having to learn sophisticated traditional CAD software.

This tutorial book provides a systematic approach for users to learn Designspark. It is aimed at those with no previous experience with CAD. However, experienced CAD users may also find this book useful for them to learn Designspark. The user will be guided from starting a Designspark session to constructing parts and assemblies. Each chapter has components explained with the help of various screen images.

Scope of this Book

This book is written for students and engineers who are interested to learn Designspark Mechanica for designing mechanical components and assemblies.

This book provides a systematic approach to learning Designspark. The topics include Getting Started with Designspark Mechanical, Basic Part Modeling, Constructing Assemblies, Sketching tools, and Additional Modeling Tools.

Chapter 1: Introduces Designspark Mechanical 4.0. The user interface, terminology, and mouse functions are discussed in this chapter.

Chapter 2: Takes you through the creation of your first Designspark model. You construct simple parts.

Chapter 3: Teaches you to construct assemblies. It explains the Top-down and Bottom-up approaches for designing an assembly. You construct an assembly using the Bottom-up approach.

Chapter 4: In this chapter, you learn the tools needed to create 2D sketches.

Chapter 5: In this chapter, you learn additional modeling tools to construct complex models.

Chapter 1: Getting Started with Designspark Mechanical 4.0

In this chapter, you learn some of the most commonly used features of Designspark Mechanical. Also, you learn about the user interface.

In Designspark Mechanical, you create 3D parts and use them to create 3D assemblies.

Designspark Mechanical is a Direct Modeling Software. Most of the CAD systems allow you to do feature-based modeling. In feature-based modeling, you create individual features that are combined to build a part. These features are saved in the model-history, and you can edit them whenever you want.

Direct Modeling is different from feature-based modeling. In direct modeling, you are not required to consider the model history, design intent, features, and parent child-relationships. Instead, direct modeling helps you to create models easily. In addition to that, you can manipulate existing models without considering how they were created. Designspark makes it easy for first-time users to create and modify models easily.

In Designspark Mechanical, you create a sketch and convert it into a 3D object. A sketch is a 2D profile and can be extruded, revolved, or swept along a path to create models.

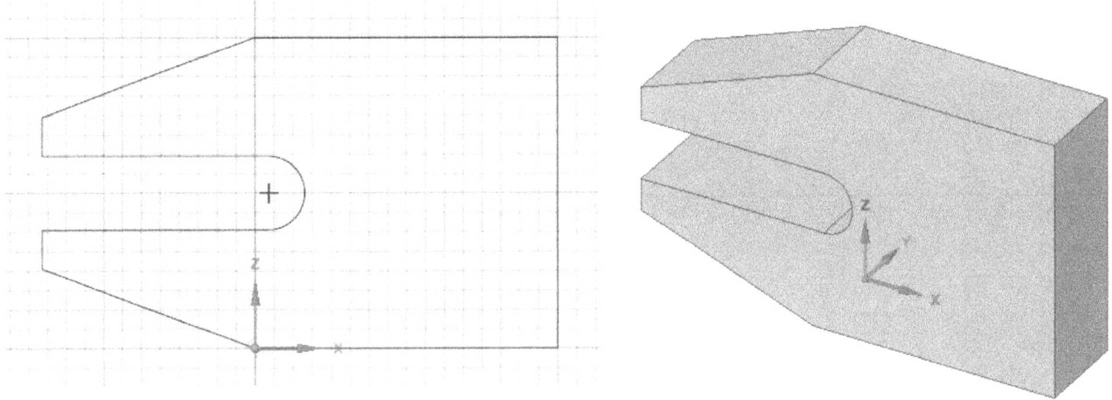

Starting Designspark Mechanical 4.0
1. Click the Windows button on the taskbar.
2. Scroll down to the **D** section.
3. Click **DESIGNSPARK MECHANICAL 4.0**.
4. Click **File** menu > **New** > **Design**.

Notice the essential features of the Designspark Mechanical window.

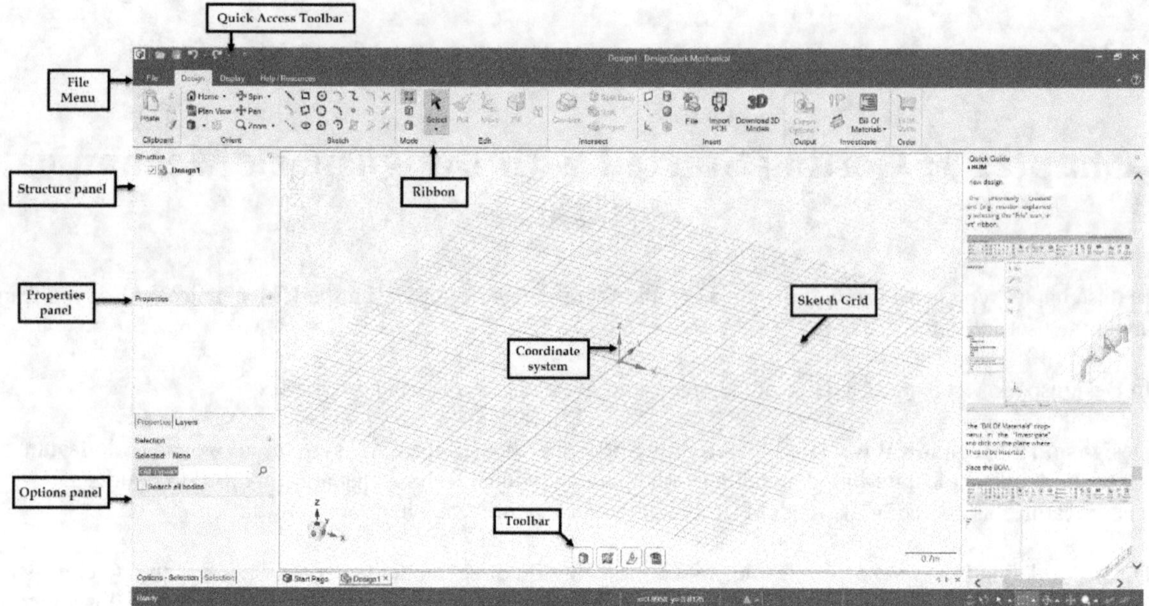

User Interface

Various components of the user interface are discussed next.

Quick Access Toolbar

The Quick Access Toolbar is located at the top left corner of the window. It consists of the commonly used commands such as **Save, Undo, Redo,** and **Open.**

File Menu

The **File Menu** appears when you click on the **File** icon located at the top left corner of the window. The **File Menu** consists of a list of open menus. You can see a list of recently opened documents under the **Recently Documents** section.

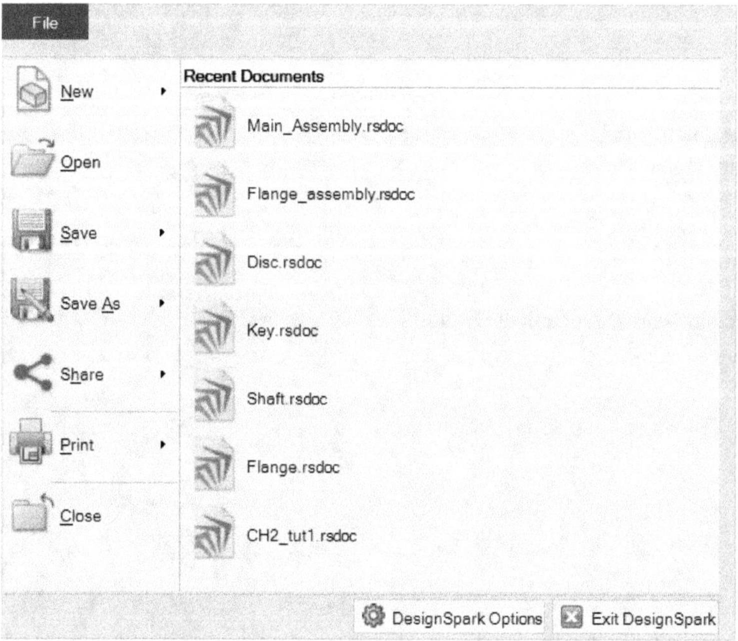

Ribbon

A ribbon is a set of tools, which are used to perform various operations. It is divided into tabs and panels. Various tabs of the ribbon are discussed next.

Design tab

This ribbon tab contains the tools to construct 3D features.

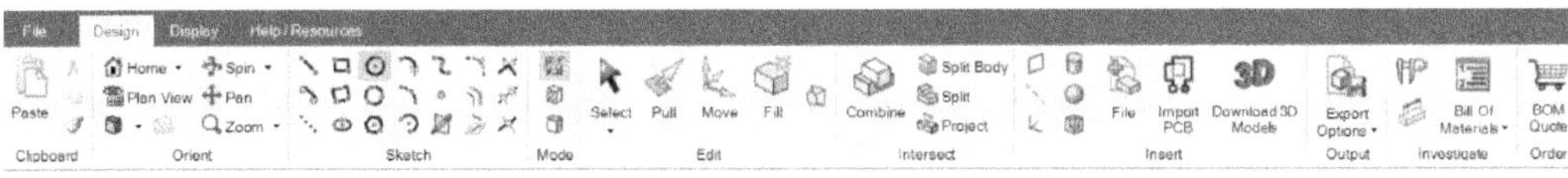

Display tab

This ribbon tab contains the tools to modify the display of the model and user interface.

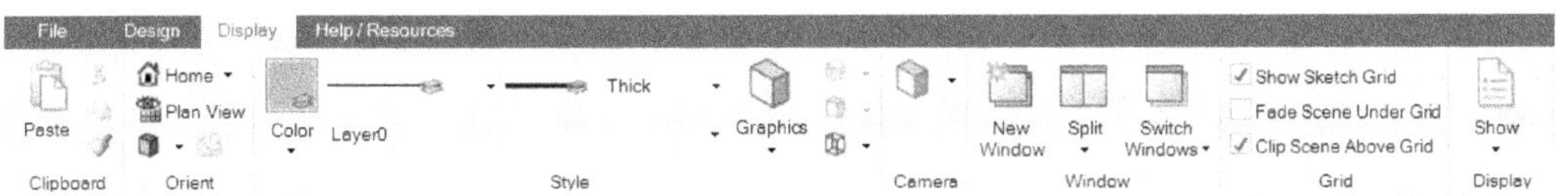

Help/Resources tab

This ribbon tab has the tools to access various help resources.

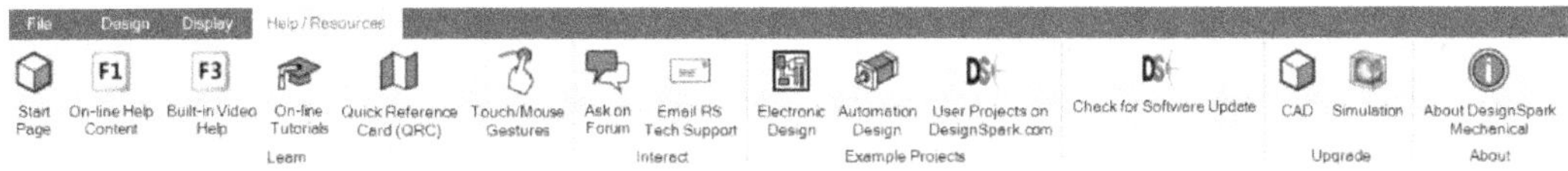

Status bar

The Status bar is available below the graphics window. It displays the prompts and the action taken while using the tools.

The Structure panel

It contains the list of solids, surfaces, curves, and planes created in the graphics window.

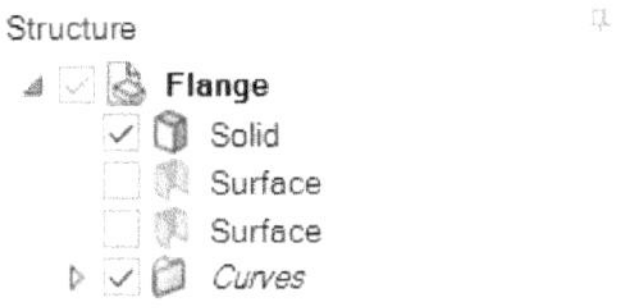

The Properties panel

The **Properties** panel lists the properties of a selected object.

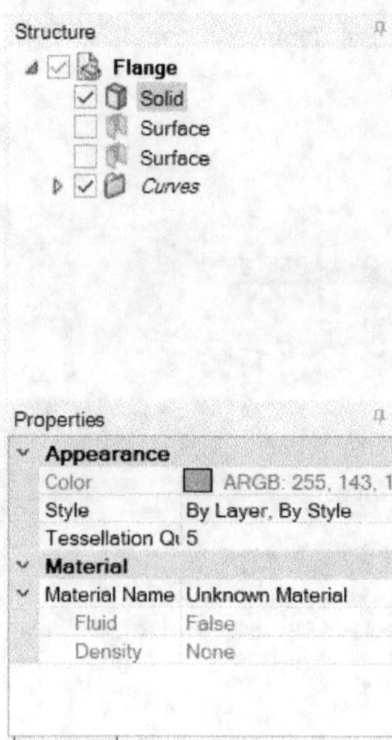

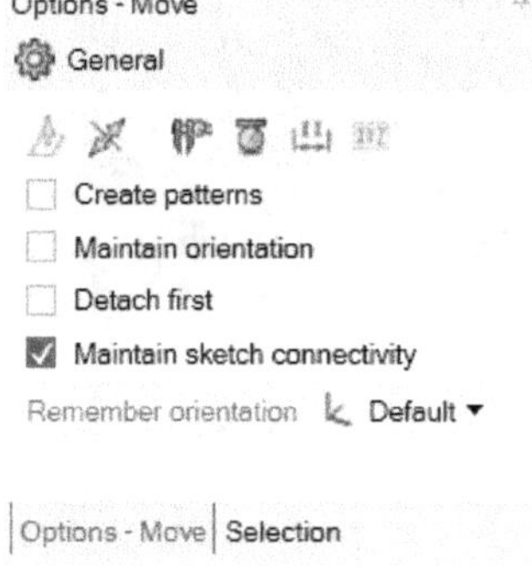

The Options panel

The **Options** panel lists the options of the active tool. For example, if you activate the **Move** tool, the **Options** panel displays the options related to the **Move** tool.

Mouse Functions

Various functions of the mouse buttons are discussed next.

Left Mouse button (LMB)

Click the left mouse button (LMB) on an object to select it.

Middle Mouse button (MMB)

Click and drag the middle mouse button to spin the model.

Right Mouse button (RMB)

Click this button to display the shortcut menu.

You can change the mouse settings on the **Navigation** page of the **Designspark Settings** dialog (click **File** menu > **Designspark Settings** button).

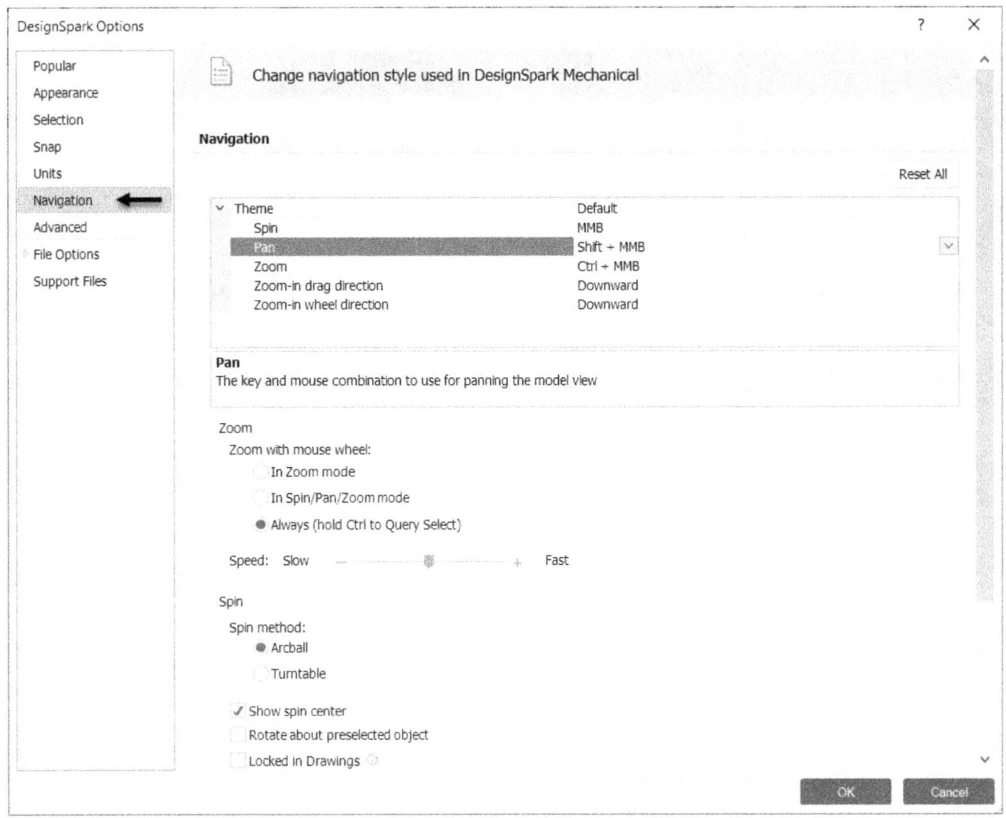

Chapter 2: Part Modeling Basics

TUTORIAL 1

This tutorial takes you through the creation of your first Designspark model. You create the Disc of an Oldham coupling:

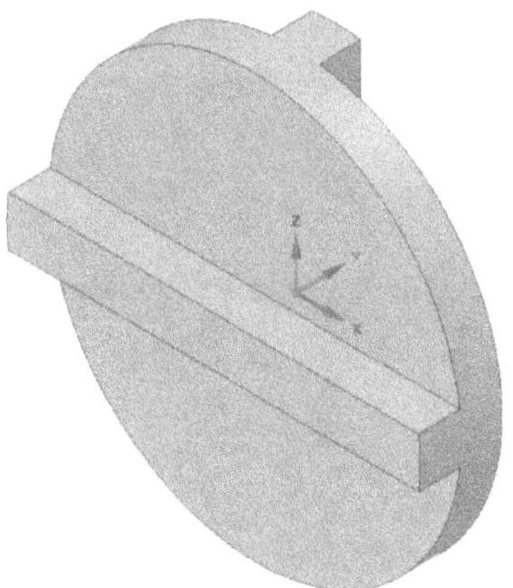

Creating a New Project

1. Start **DesignSpark** by double-clicking the **DesignSpark** icon on your desktop.
2. Click **File > New > Design**.
3. Click the **File** menu > **DesignSpark Options** button; the **DesignSpark Options** dialog appears.

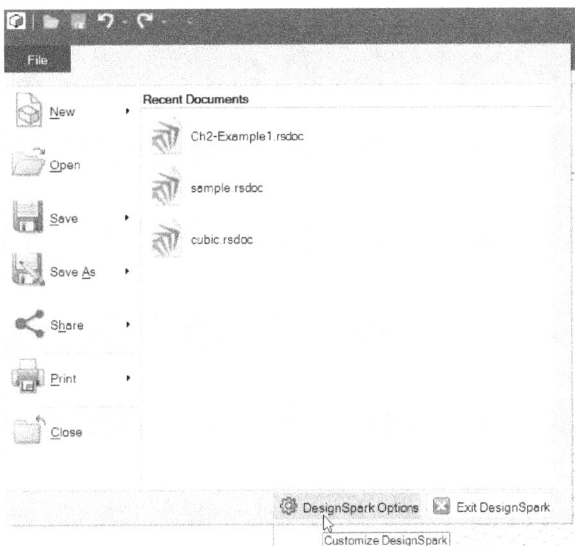

4. On the dialog, click the **Units** option on the left pane.
5. Select **Units settings for > All New Documents.**
6. Select **Type > Imperial**.
7. Select **Length > Inches** under the **Units** section.

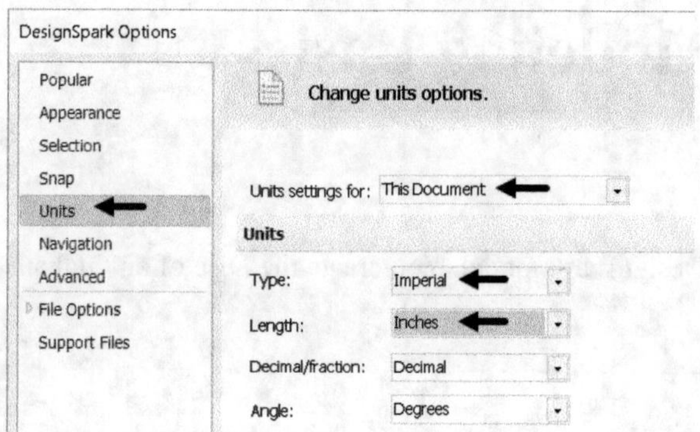

8.   Click **OK** on the **DesignSpark Options** dialog.

Starting a Sketch

1.   To start a new sketch, click **Select New Sketch Plane** on the Mini Toolbar at the bottom of the Design window.

2.   Place the pointer in the first quadrant of the coordinate system.
3.   Click to select the **XZ** plane.

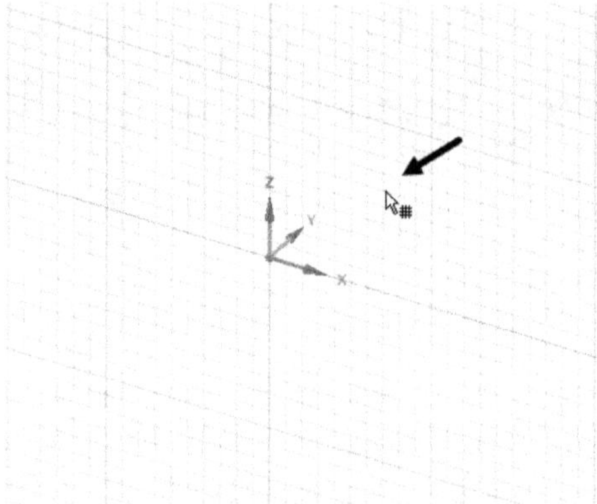

4.   Now, click **Design > Orient > Plan View** on the ribbon to change the orientation to the sketch view.

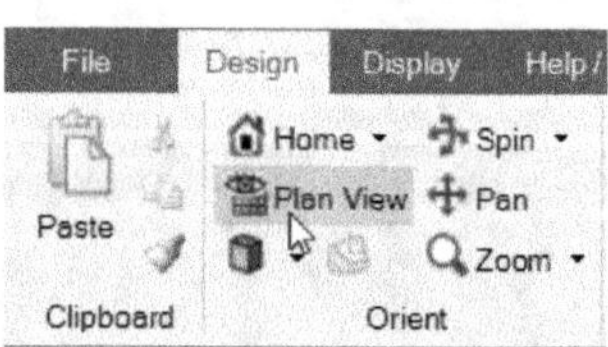

You begin by sketching the circle.

5.   On the ribbon, click **Design > Sketch > Circle**.

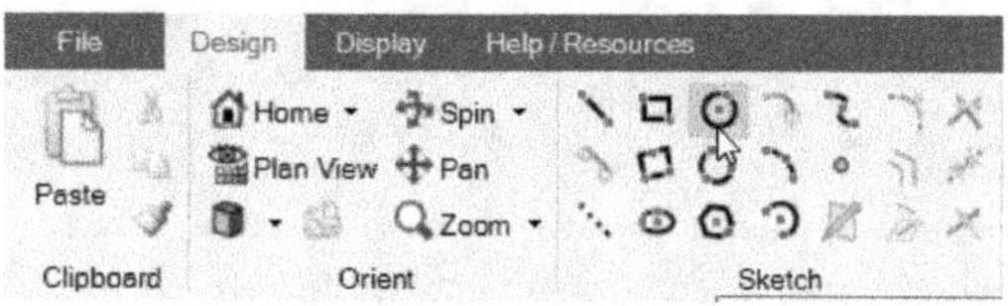

6. Select the sketch origin located at the center of the sketch window.
7. Move the cursor outward and type 4 in the diameter.
8. Press ENTER.

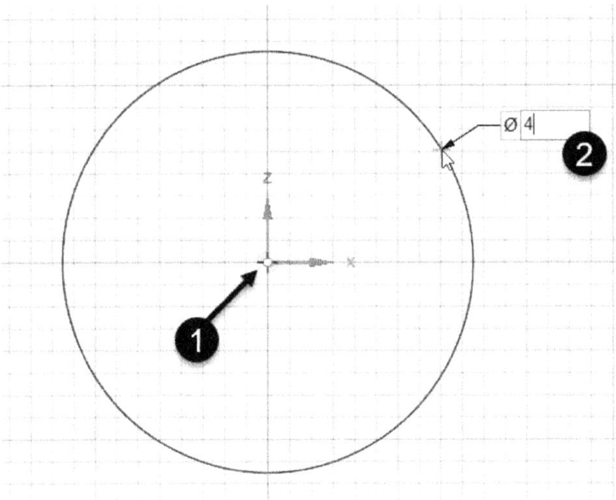

9. Press **Esc** to deactivate the tool.

Converting the Circle into a Solid

You can convert the circle into a solid by extruding it.

1. Click **Design > Mode > 3D Mode** on the ribbon to change the mode to 3D mode.

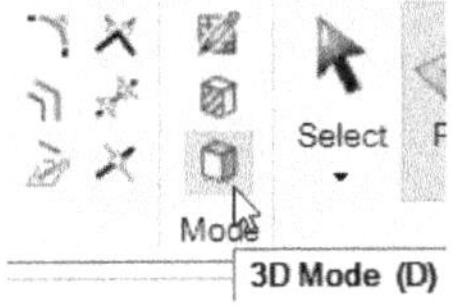

2. Click **Design > Orient > Home** on the ribbon; the view orientation is changed.
3. Activate the **Pull** tool (click **Design > Edit > Pull** on the ribbon).

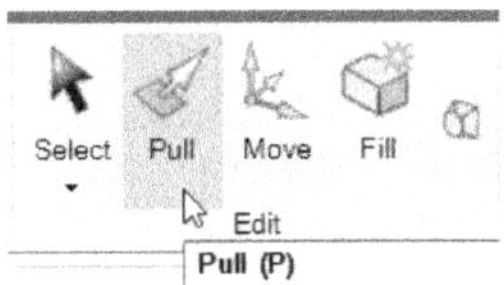

4. Click in the region enclosed by the sketch.
5. Drag the pointer.
6. Type-in **0.4** in the Distance box and press Enter to create the extrusion.

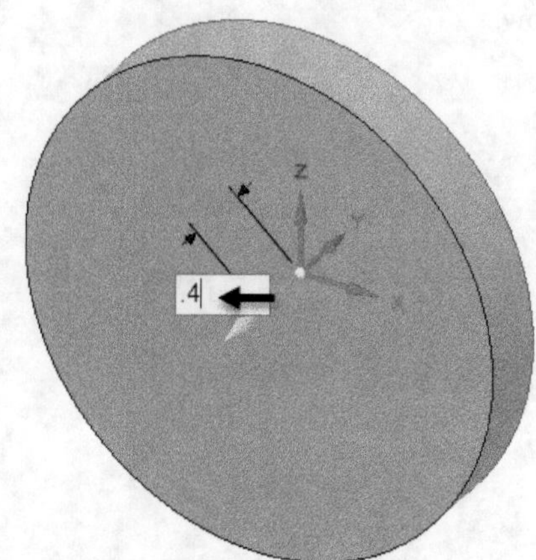

7. Press **Esc**.

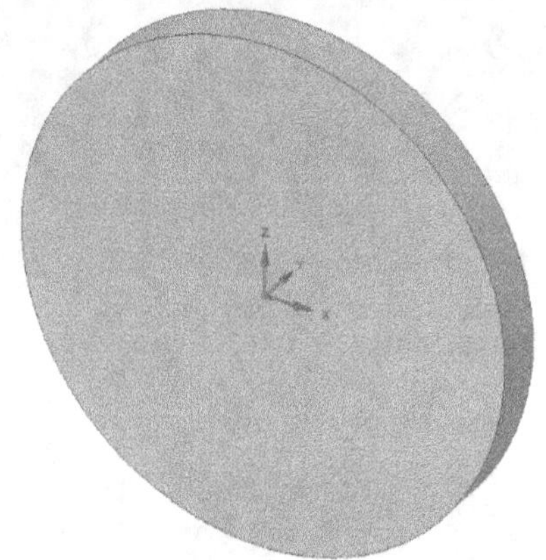

To magnify a model in the graphics area, you can use the zoom tools available on the **Zoom** drop-down on the **Orient** panel.

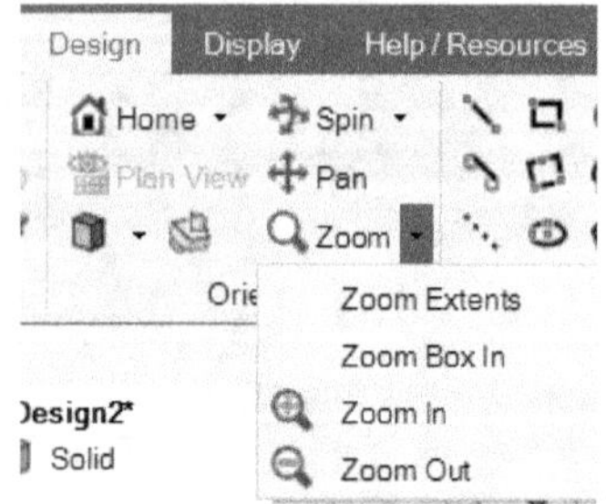

Click **Zoom Extents** to display the full part size in the current window.

Click **Zoom Box In**, and then drag the pointer to create a rectangle; the area in the rectangle zooms to fill the window.

Click **Zoom In** to zoom in to the design.

Click **Zoom Out** to zoom out of the model.

To display the part in different display modes, select the options in the **Graphics** drop-down available on the Style panel of the **Display** ribbon tab.

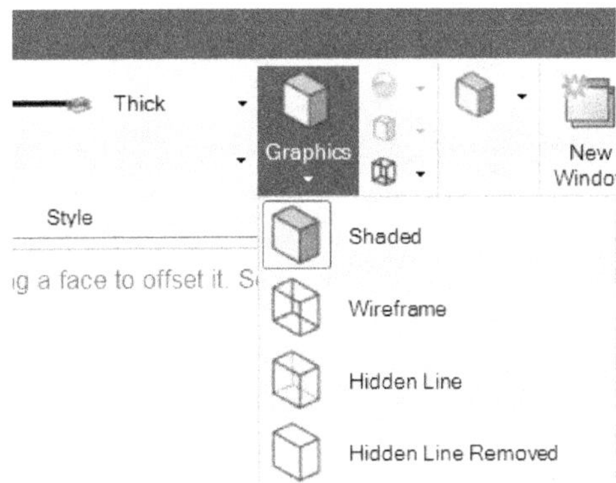

Shaded

Wireframe

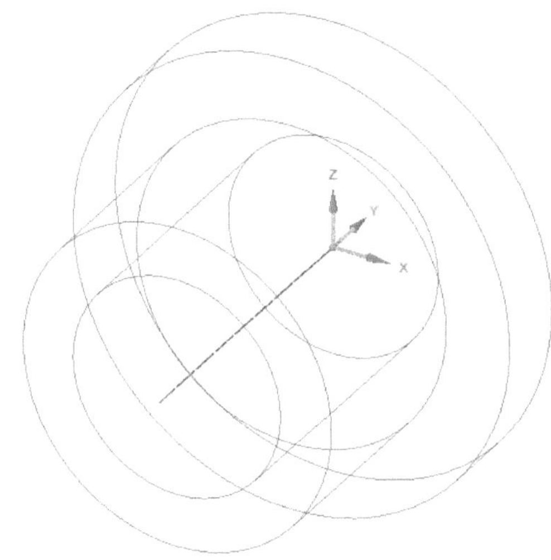

Hidden Line

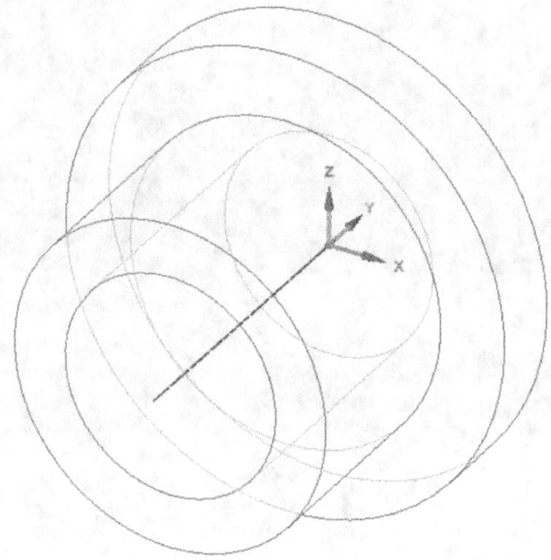

Hidden Line Removed

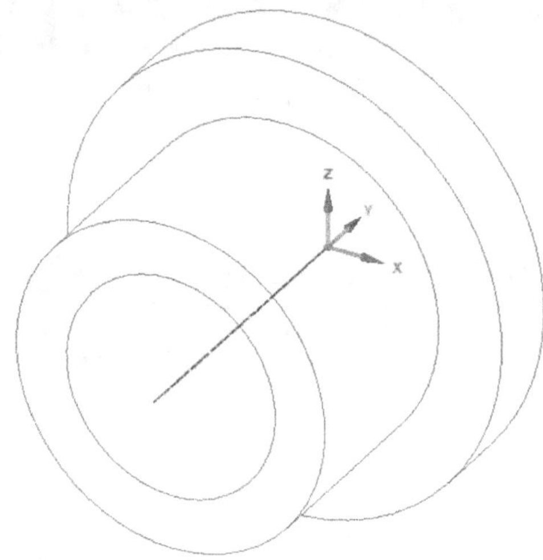

The default display mode for models is **Shaded**. You may change the display mode whenever you want.

Adding an Extrusion

Now, you need to draw a sketch on the model face or plane, and then extrude it

1. Click **Design > Mode > Sketch Mode** on the ribbon (or) press **K** on the Keyboard.
2. Click on the front face of the design model.

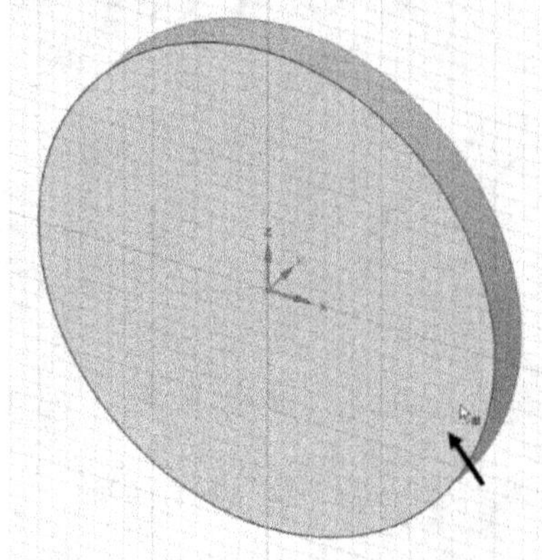

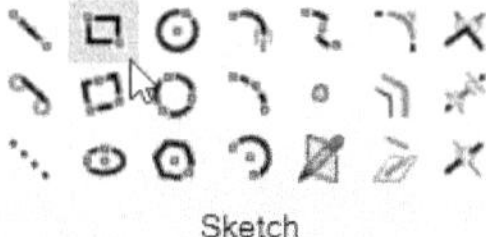

5. On the **Options – Sketch** panel, check the **Define rectangle from center** option.

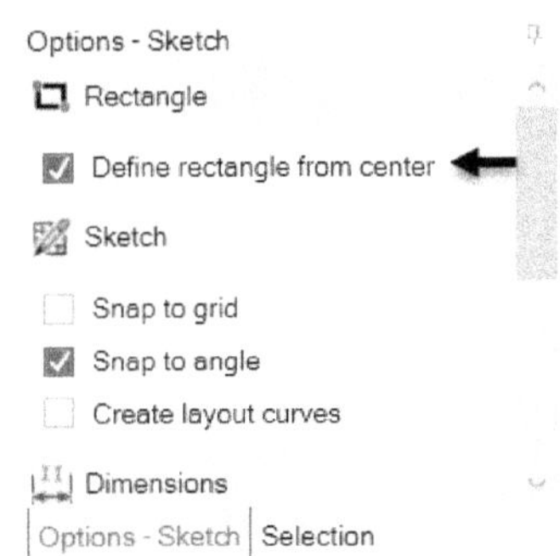

6. Select the origin point of the sketch.
7. Move the pointer outward.
8. Type 6 in the height box.
9. Press the TAB key and type 0.472 in the width box.
10. Press ENTER to create a rectangle.

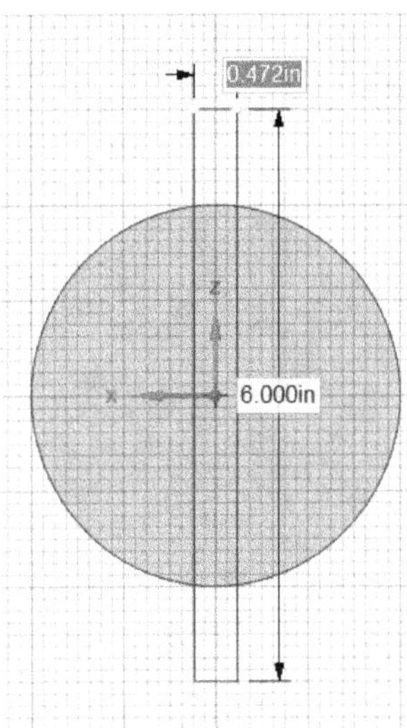

11. Click **Design > Sketch > Trim Away** on the ribbon.
12. Click on the unwanted portions of the sketch, as shown.

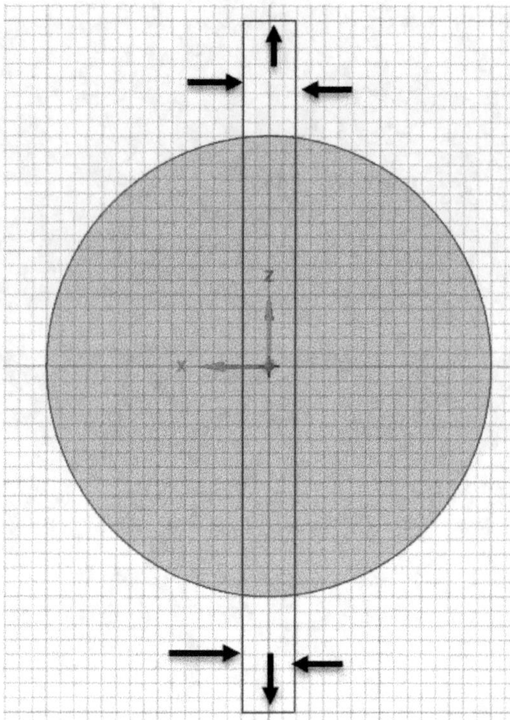

13. Activate the **3D Mode** (click **Design > Mode > 3D Mode** on the ribbon).
14. Click **Design > Orient > Spin** on the ribbon.
15. Click and hold the left mouse button and drag the pointer towards the right, as shown.

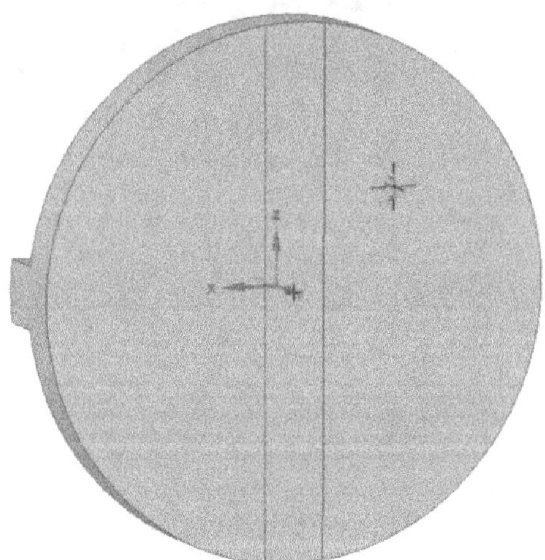

16. Press **Esc** to deactivate the tool.

17. Activate the **Pull** tool and click in the region bounded by the two vertical lines.

18. Click on the yellow arrow and move outward and enter **0.4** in the box. Press Enter to create the extrusion.

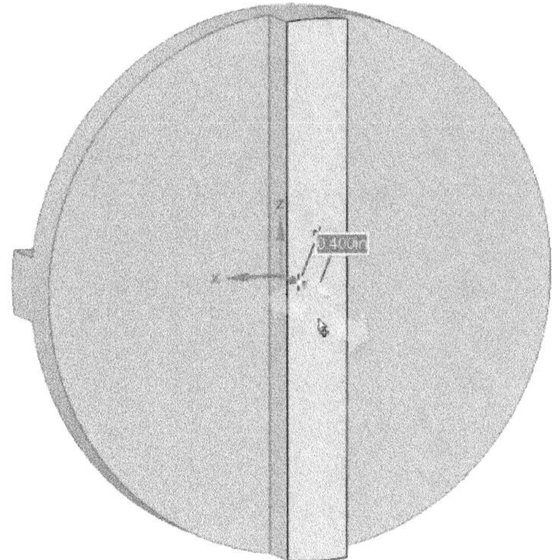

19. Press **Esc** to deactivate the pull tool.
20. Click **Design > Orient > View** drop-down > **Isometric** on the ribbon.

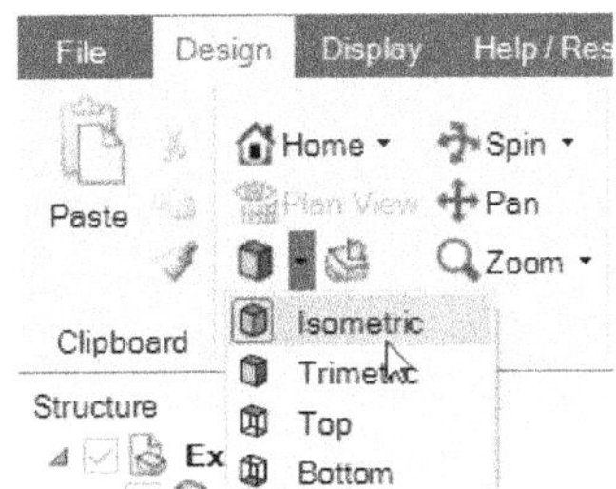

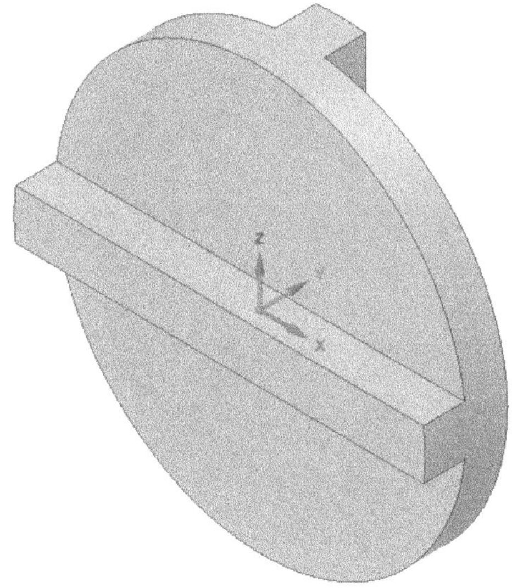

Saving the Part

1. Click **File > Save** on the ribbon or click the **Save** icon on the **Quick Access Toolbar**.
2. On the **Save As** dialog, click the **New Folder** button and type Oldham Coupling. Press Enter.
3. Double-click on the **Oldham Coupling** folder.
4. Type-in **Disc** in the **File Name** box.
5. Click **Save** to save the file.
6. Click **File** menu > **Close** to close the file.

TUTORIAL 2

In this tutorial, you create a flange by performing the following operations:

- Creating a revolved solid
- Creating cutout
- Adding fillets

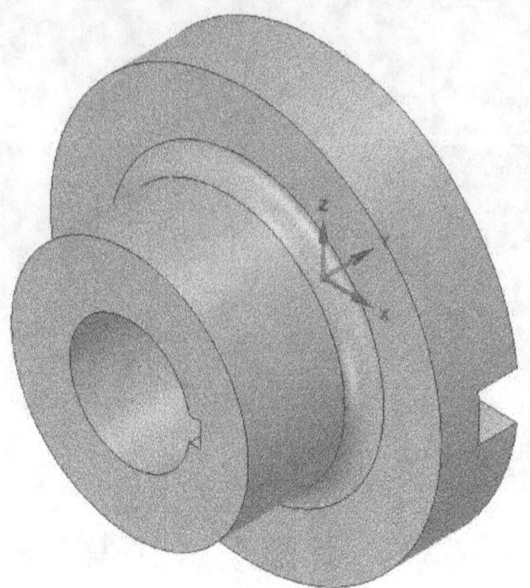

Sketching a Revolve Profile

1. Click **File > New > Design**.
2. Click **Select New Sketch Plane** on the Mini Toolbar.
3. Click in the second quadrant of the coordinate system to select the **YZ** plane.

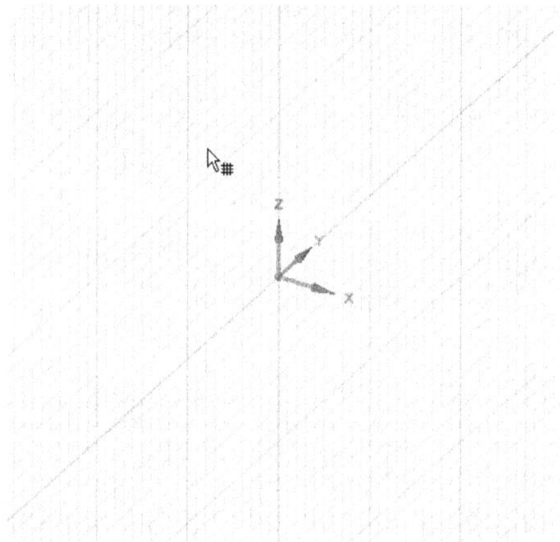

4. Click **Design > Orient > Plan View** on the ribbon.
5. Click **Design > Sketch > Line** on the ribbon.

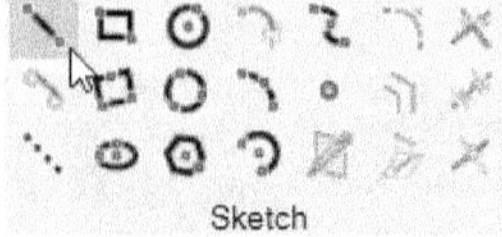

6. On the **Options – Sketch** panel, click the **Cartesian dimensions** icon.

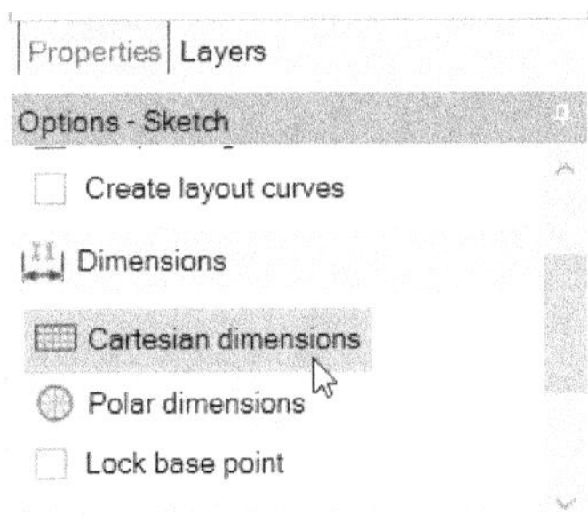

7. Select the sketch origin to define the base point.

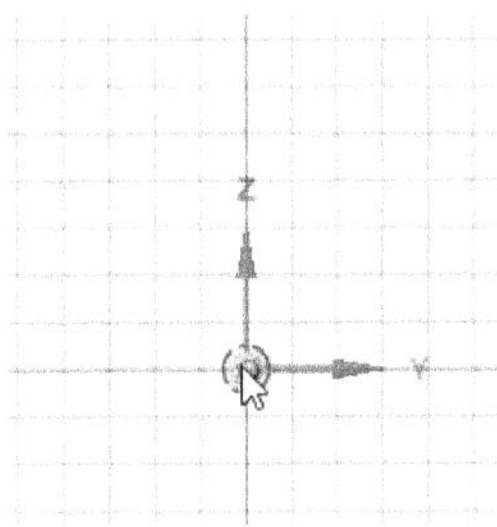

8. Move the pointer upward.
9. Type 0 in the horizontal and press the TAB key.
10. Type 0.6 in the vertical box and press ENTER; the start point of the line is defined.

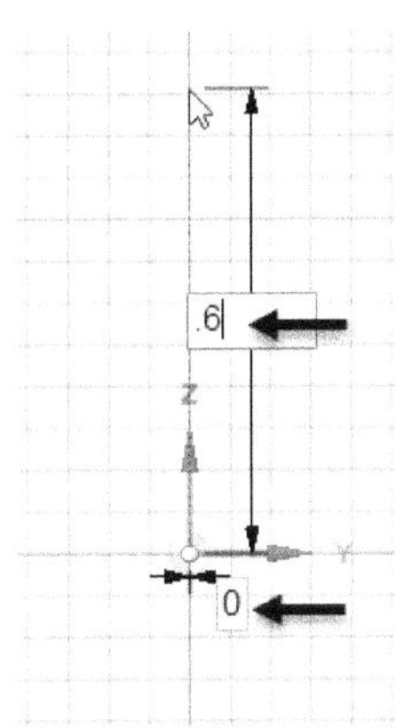

11. Move the pointer horizontally toward left and enter -2 in the box.
12. Press ENTER to create a horizontal line of 2 inches.

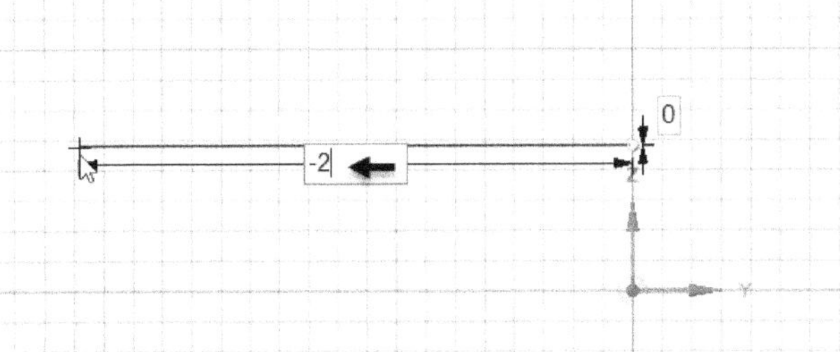

13. Move the pointer vertically upward.
14. Enter 0.6 in the box and click to create the line.

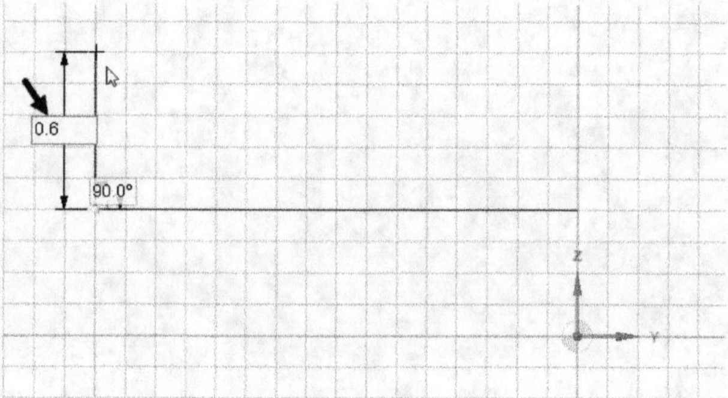

15. Likewise, create the other lines in the sequence, as shown.

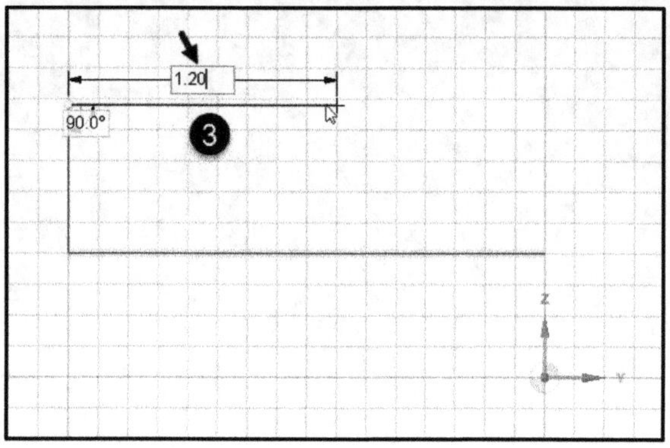

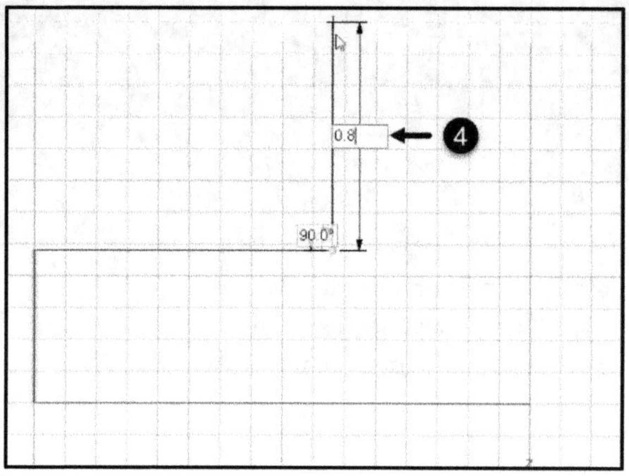

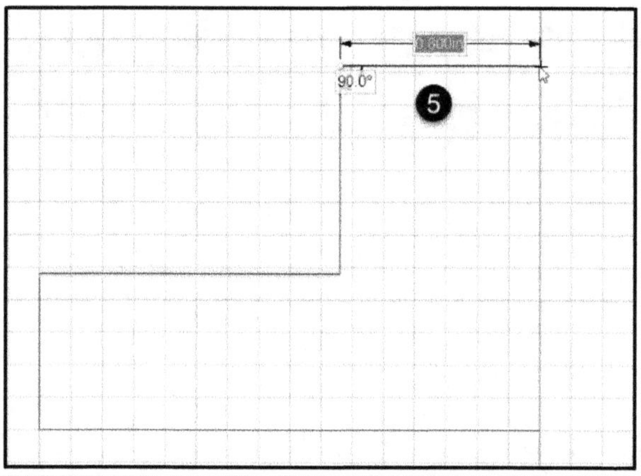

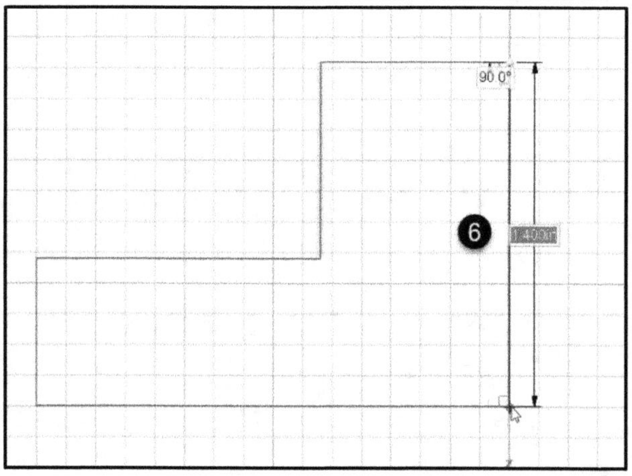

16. Click **Design > Sketch > Construction Line** on the ribbon.

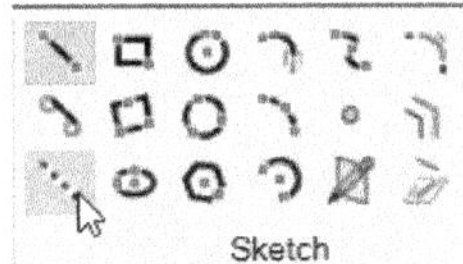

17. Create a construction line by specifying the start and endpoints, as shown below.

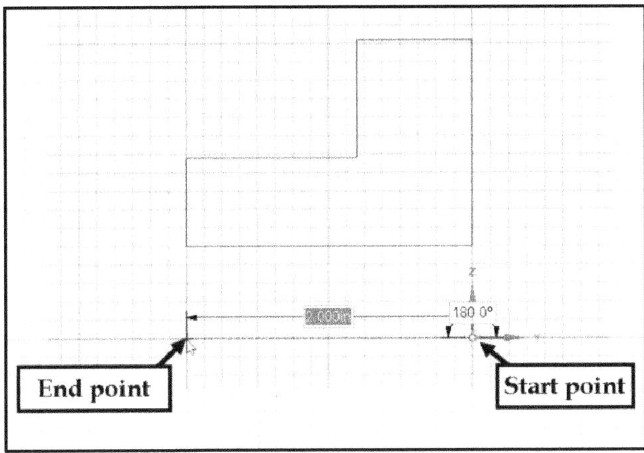

18. Press **Esc**.
19. Click **Design > Mode > 3D Mode** on the ribbon.
20. Click **Design > Orient > Home** on the ribbon.

Creating the Revolved Solid

1. On the ribbon, click **Design > Edit > Pull** and select the sketch surface.
2. Click the **Revolve** icon on the tool guide in the Design window.

3. Click on the construction line to define the axis of revolution.

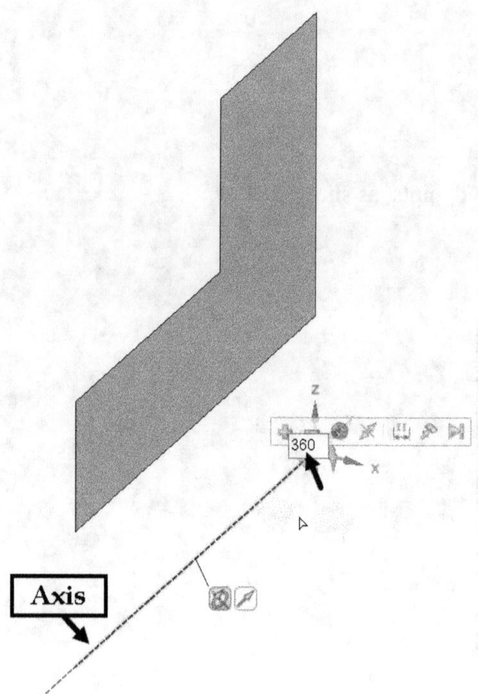

4. Click the **Full Pull** icon.

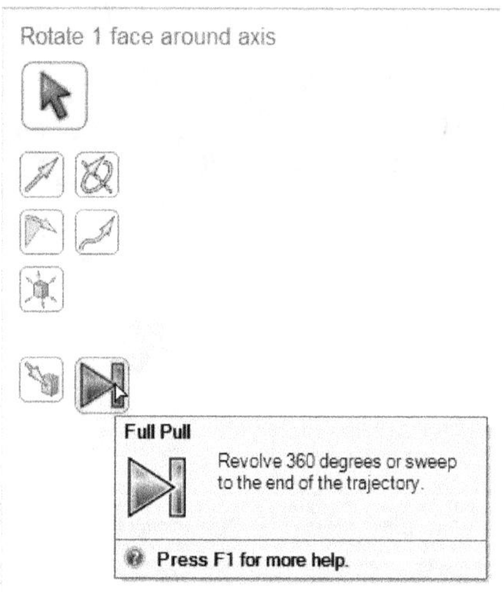

5. Press Esc.

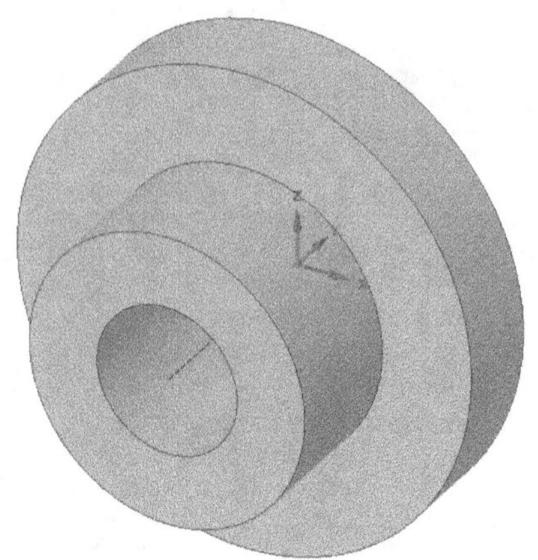

Creating the Cutout

1. On the ribbon, click **Design > Orient > View** tool drop-down > **Back.**

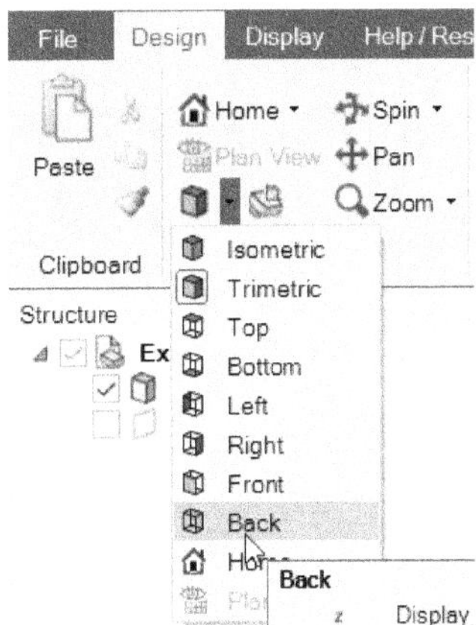

2. Click **Design > Mode > Sketch Mode** and select the back face of the design model, as shown.

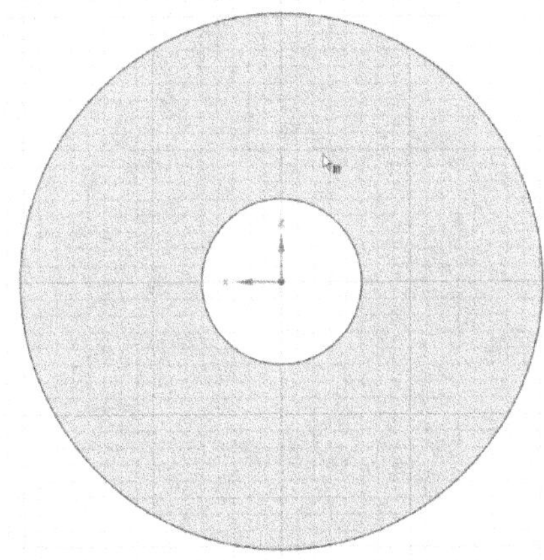

3. On the ribbon, click **Design > Sketch > Rectangle**.

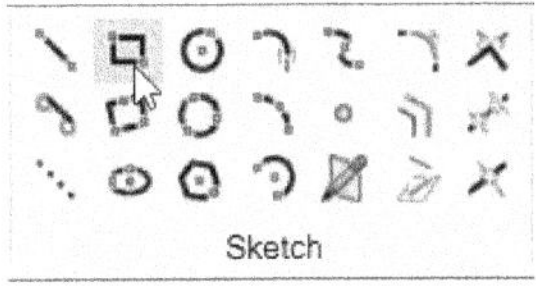

4. Check the **Define rectangle from center** option on the **Options – Sketch** panel on the bottom-left corner.

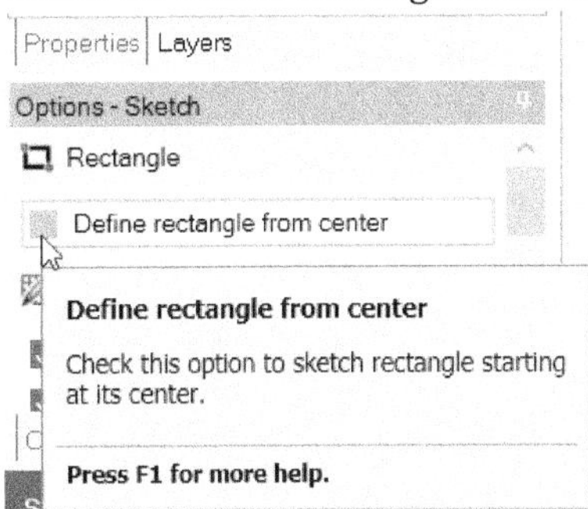

5. Select the origin to define the center point.
6. Move the cursor diagonally toward the right.
7. Enter .472 in the vertical dimension box.
8. Press the Tab key and enter 4.1 in the horizontal dimension box. Press Enter twice.

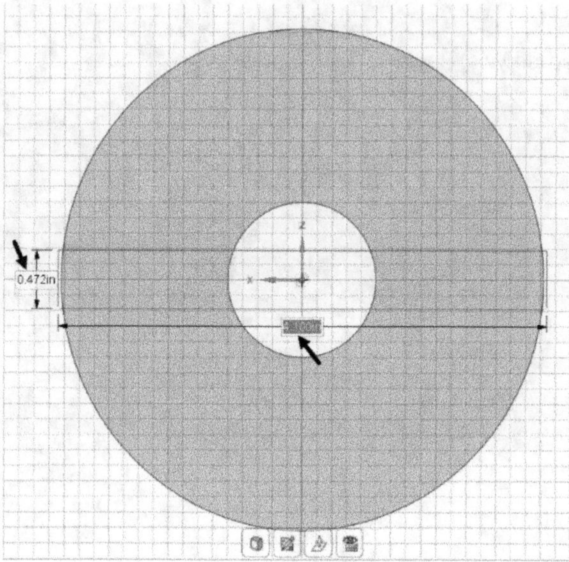

9. Press Esc to deactivate the tool.
10. Click **Design > Mode > 3D Mode** on the ribbon.
11. Activate the **Pull** tool.
12. Press the Ctrl key and click inside the sketch regions, as shown.

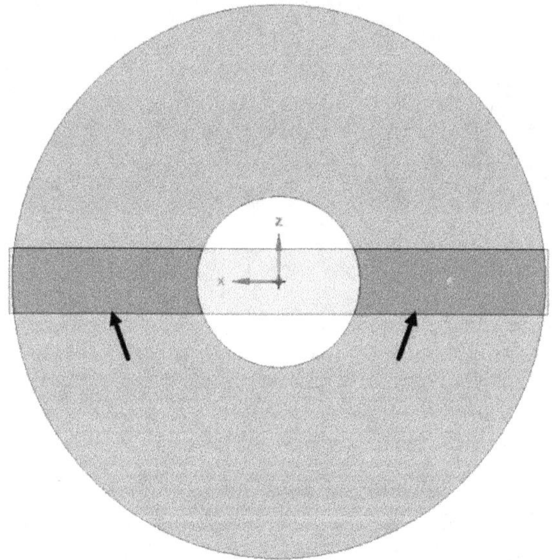

13. Click the **Cut** option under the **Options – Pull** panel on the bottom left corner.

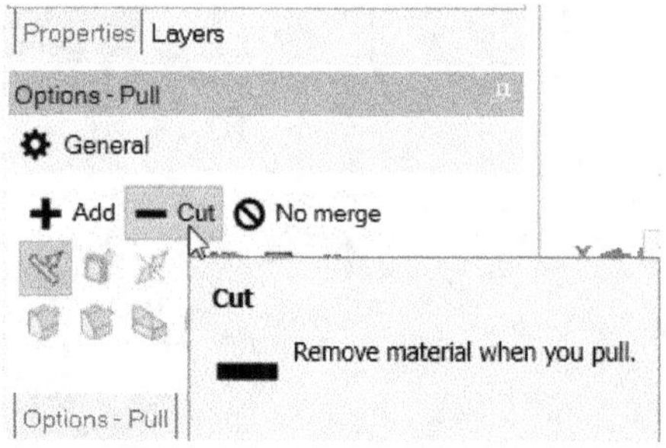

14. Press **Spacebar** and type-in **-0.4** in the box.
15. Press **Enter** twice to create the cutout.
16. Uncheck the **Surface** option in the **Structure** panel.

17. Activate the **Spin** tool and rotate the model to see the result.

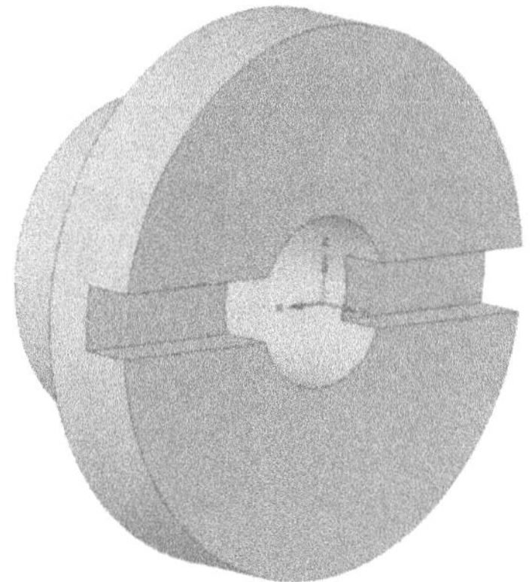

Creating another Cutout

1. Click **Design > Orient > Home** on the ribbon.

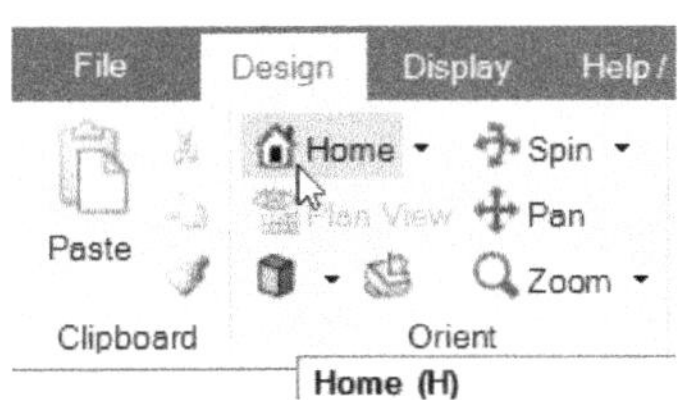

2. Create a sketch on the front face of the base.

   - On the ribbon, click **Design > Mode > Sketch Mode.**
   - Select the front face of the model.

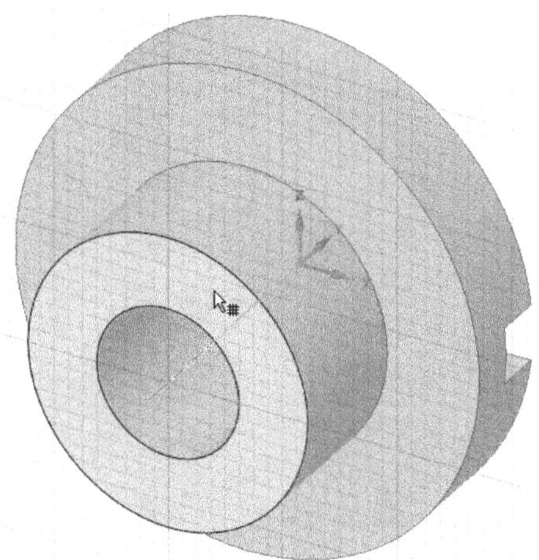

   - Click **Design > Orient > Plan View** on the ribbon.
   - On the ribbon, click **Design > Sketch > Rectangle**.
   - Check the **Define rectangle from center** option on the **Options – Sketch** panel on the bottom-left corner.

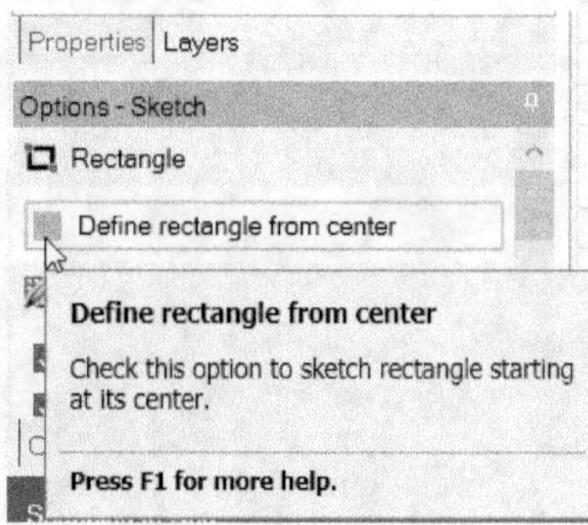

- Click on the quadrant point of the inner circular edge, as shown.

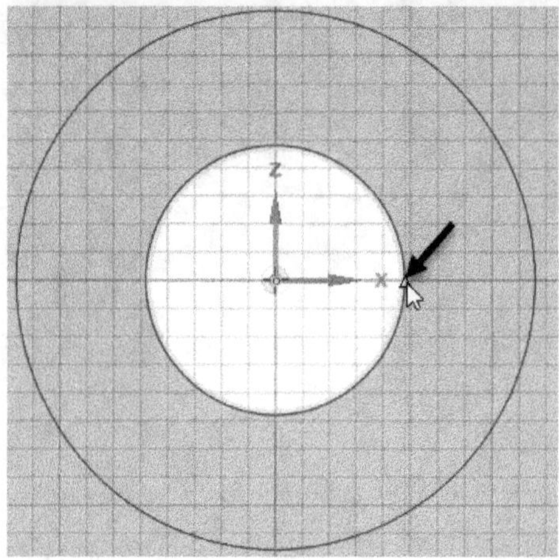

- Move the pointer horizontally toward the right.
- Type 0.236 and press the TAB key.
- Type 0.236, and press ENTER.

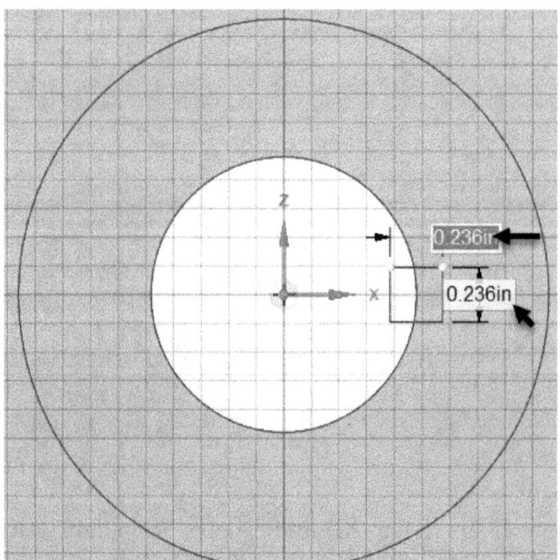

- Press **Esc**.

3. Click **Design > Mode > 3D Mode** on the ribbon.
4. Click **Design > Orient > Home** on the ribbon.
5. Activate the **Pull** tool on the ribbon.
6. Click in the region enclosed by the three lines and circular edge.

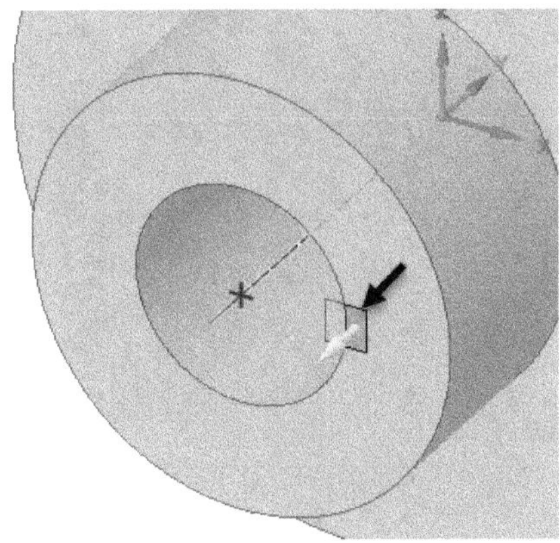

7. Under the **Options – Pull** panel, click the **Cut** icon on the left.

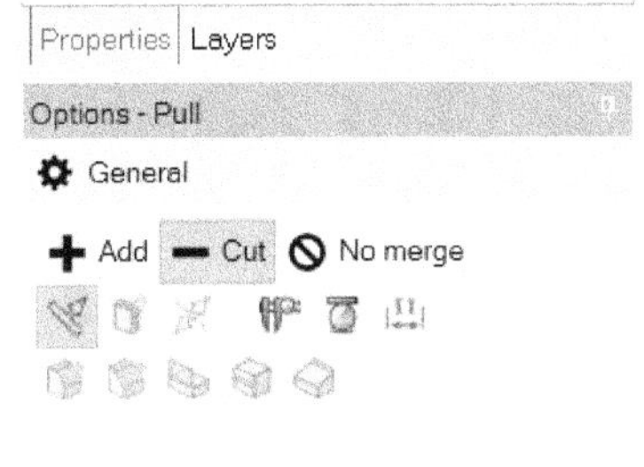

8. Drag the pointer into the model, as shown. Next, release it.

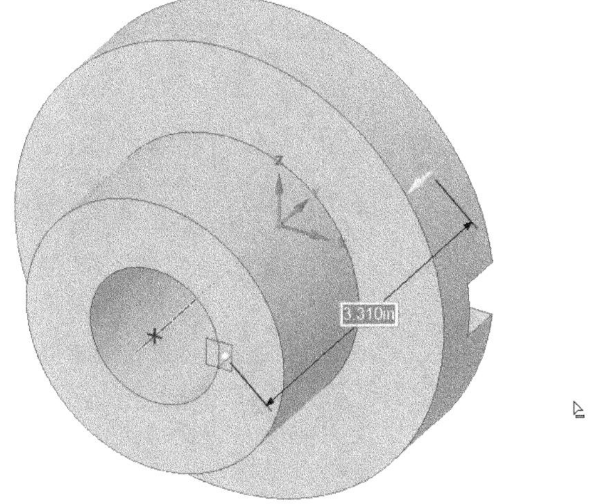

9. Press Esc.
10. Uncheck the **Surface** option in the Structure panel.

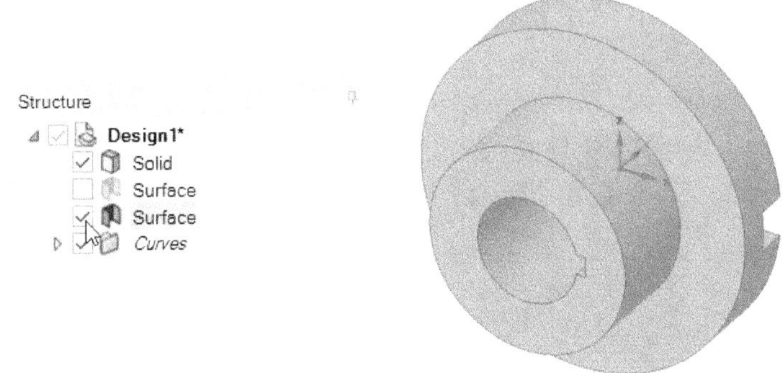

Adding a Round

1. On the Toolbar, click **Design > Edit > Pull** (or) press **P** on the Keyboard.

2. Click on the inner circular edge.

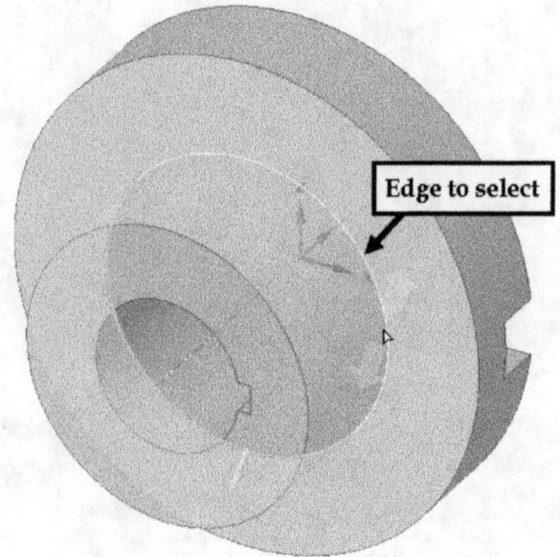

3. Click the **Round** icon on the **Options-Pull** panel on the bottom-left corner.

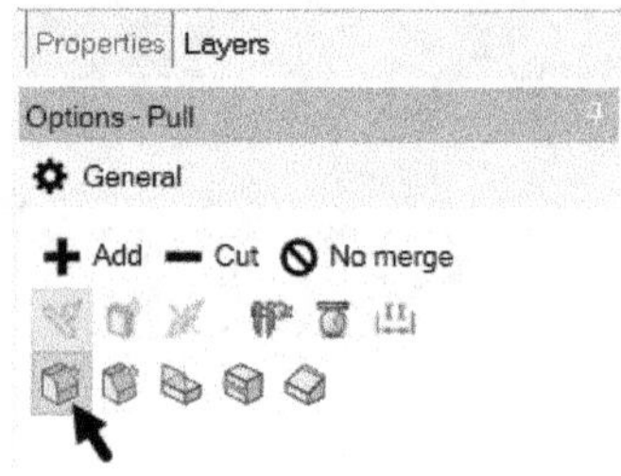

4. Press Spacebar and enter **0.2** in the box.
5. Press Enter to add the round.

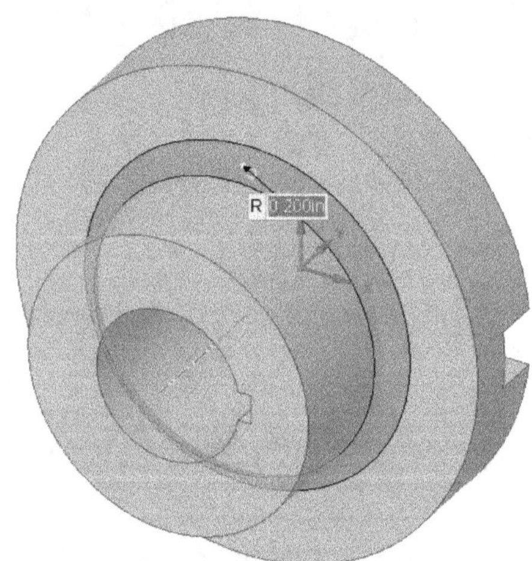

6. Press Esc.

Saving the Part

1. Click **Save** on the **Quick Access Toolbar**.
2. On the **Save As** window, type-in **Flange** in the **File Name** box.
3. Browse to the **Oldham Coupling** folder.
4. Click **Save** to save the file.
5. Click **File > Close**.

TUTORIAL 3

In this tutorial, you create the Shaft by performing the following operations:

- Creating a cylinder

- Creating a cutout

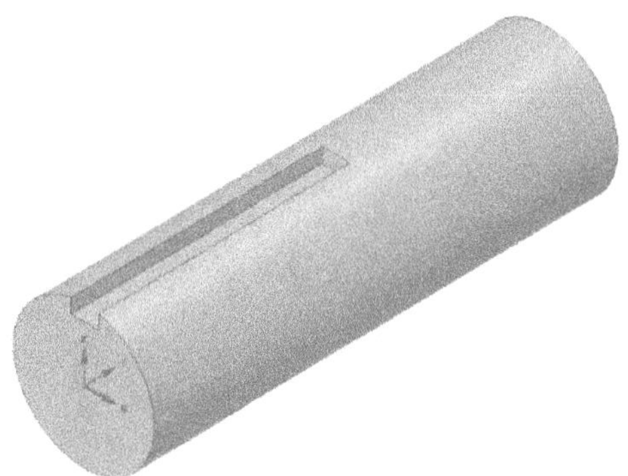

Creating the Cylinder

1. Click the **Design** tab > **Insert** group > **Cylinder** tool on the ribbon.

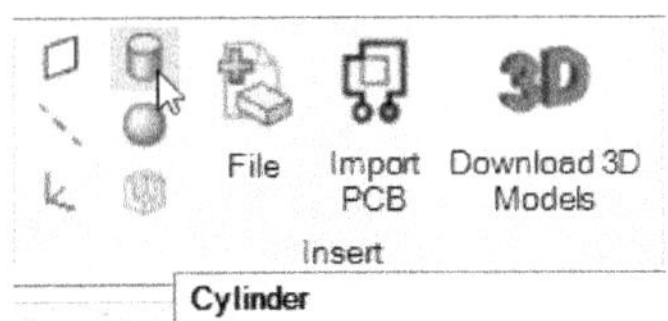

2. Click on the origin and move the cursor along the Y-axis.
3. Enter **4** in the box and press Enter on the keyboard.

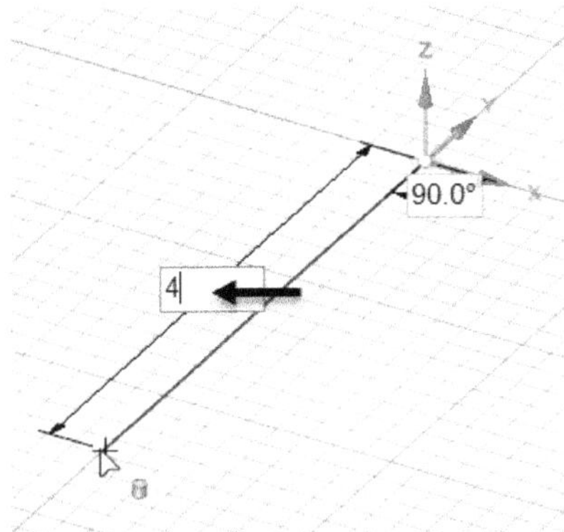

4. Next, move the cursor outward and type-in **1.2** in the box to specify the diameter of the cylinder.

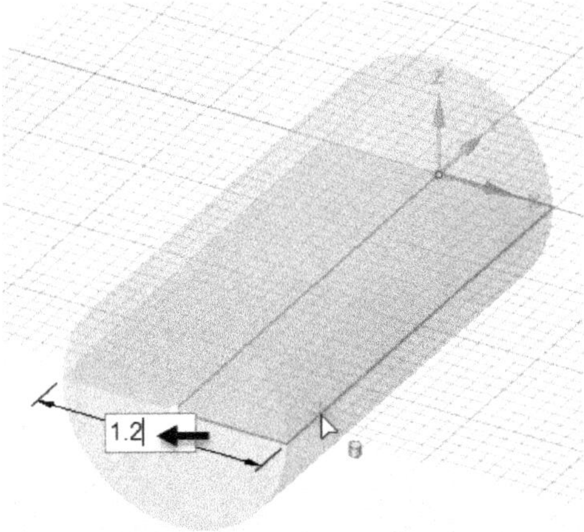

5. Press Enter on the keyboard to create the cylinder.

6. Press Esc to deactivate the tool.
7. Click **Design > Mode > 3D Mode** on the ribbon (or) click the **3D Mode** icon on the Mini Toolbar.

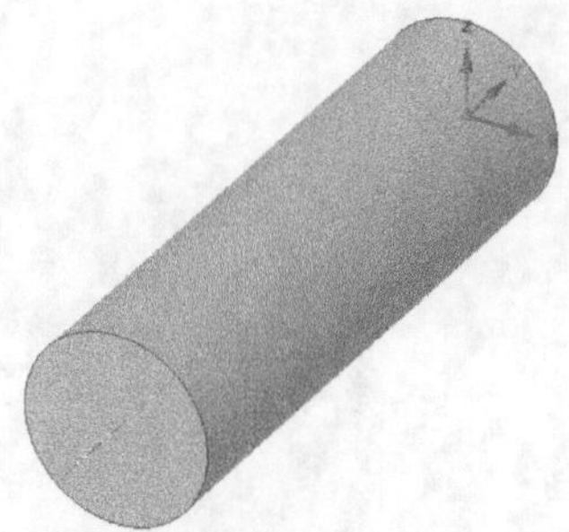

Creating the Cutout

1. Create a sketch on the front face of the base.

   - On the ribbon, click **Design > Mode > Sketch Mode**.
   - Select the front face of the cylinder.
   - Click **Design > Orient > Plan View** on the ribbon.
   - On the ribbon, click **Design > Sketch > Rectangle**.
   - Check the **Define rectangle from center** option on the **Options – Sketch** panel on the bottom-left corner.

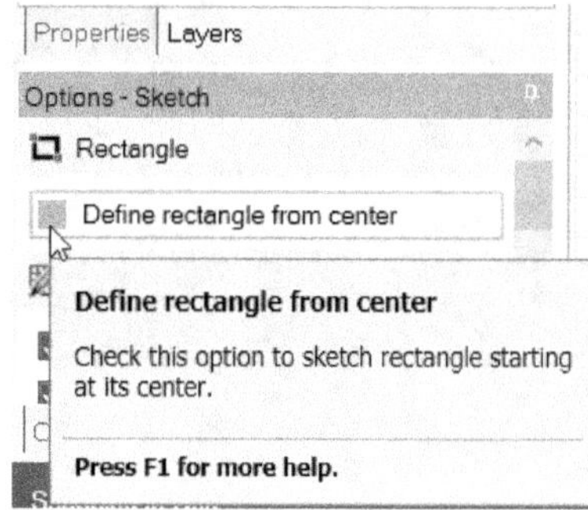

   - Click on the quadrant point of the circular edge of the model.

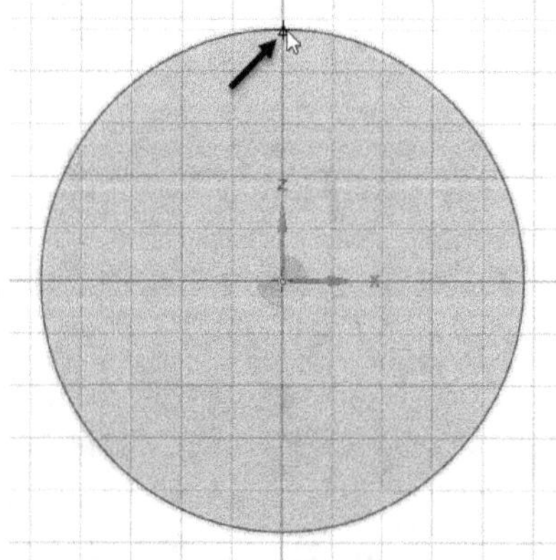

   - Move the cursor outward.
   - Type-in **0.236** and press TAB.
   - Type-in **0.236** and press ENTER.

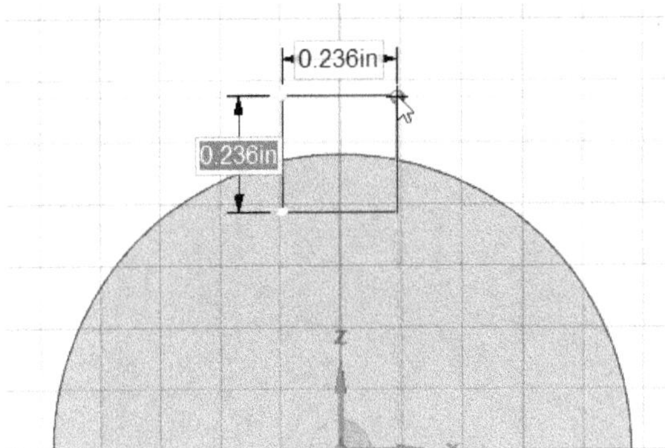

- Press **Esc** to deactivate the tool.
2. Click **Design > Orient > Home** on the ribbon.
3. Click **Design > Mode > 3D Mode** on the ribbon.
4. Click the **Pull** tool on the **Edit** group.
5. Click in the region enclosed by the sketch.

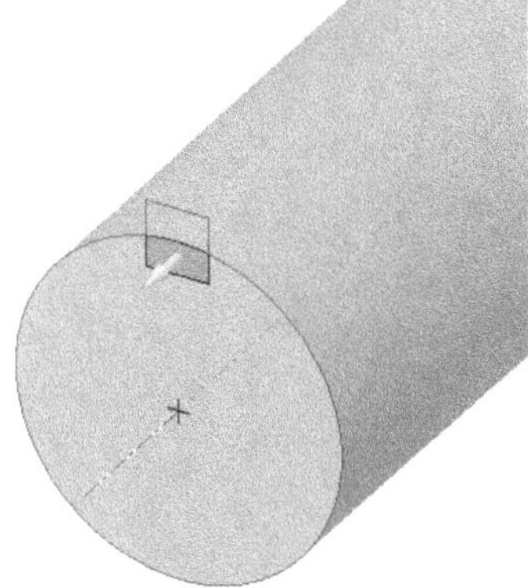

6. Click the **Cut** icon in the **Options – Pull** panel on the bottom left corner.
7. Drag the cursor towards the right, as shown.
8. Type-in **2.165** in the box and press Enter to create the cutout.

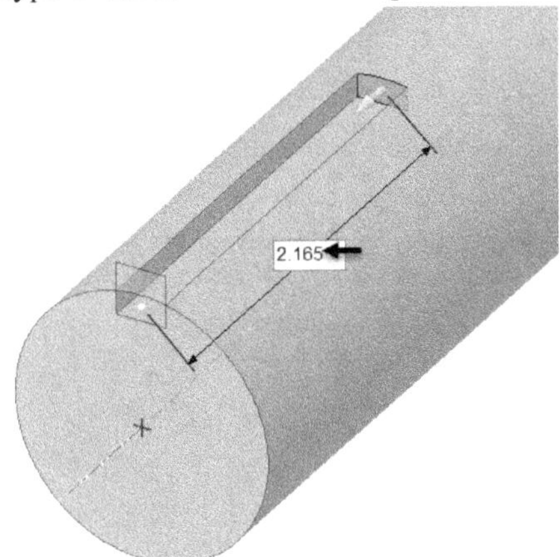

9. Uncheck the **Surface** option in the **Structure** panel.

Saving the Part
1. Click **Save** 🖫 on the **Quick Access Toolbar**.
2. On the **Save As** dialog, type-in **Shaft** in the **File Name** box.
3. Click **Save** to save the file. Make sure that you save the file in the **Oldham Coupling** folder.
4. Click **File > Close**.

TUTORIAL 4

In this tutorial, you create a Key by performing the following:

- Creating an Extrusion
- Applying draft

Creating a Box

1. Click the **Select New Sketch Plane** icon on the Mini Toolbar in the design window.
2. Click in the first quadrant of the Coordinate system to select the XZ plane.

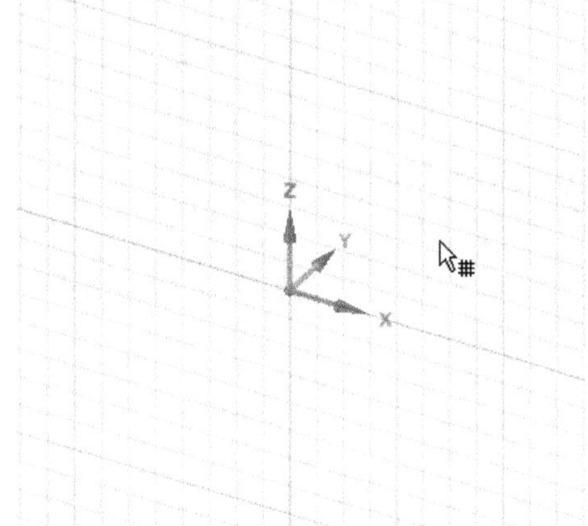

3. Click **Design > Orient > Plan View** on the ribbon to change the orientation to the sketch plane.
4. Click **Design > Sketch > Rectangle** on the ribbon.
5. Click on the origin point to define the first corner of the rectangle and enter **0.236** in the box — press TAB.
6. Move the pointer diagonally upward and enter **0.236** in the box. Press Enter.

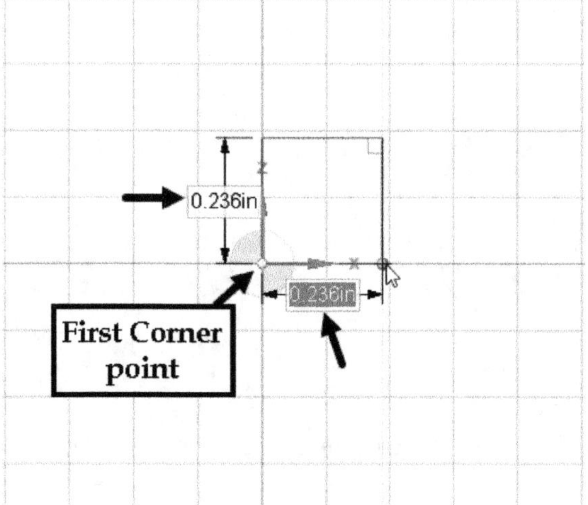

7. Press **Esc** to deactivate the sketch tool.

8. Click **3D Mode** on the Mini Toolbar in the design window.
9. Click the **Home** view on the **Orient** group of the ribbon.
10. Click **Design > Edit > Pull** on the ribbon and select the sketch region.
11. Click and drag the pointer towards the right.
12. Type-in **2** in the box.
13. Press Enter to create the extrusion.
14. Press Esc to deactivate the tool.

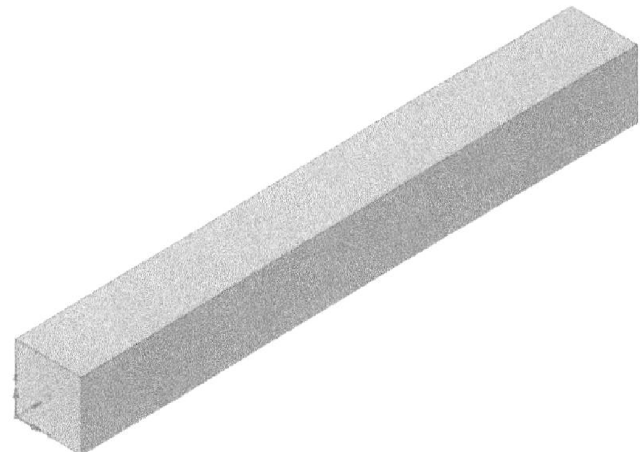

Applying Draft

1. Click **Design > Edit > Pull** on the ribbon.
2. Click the **Draft** icon on the active **Tool guide** in the design window, as shown.

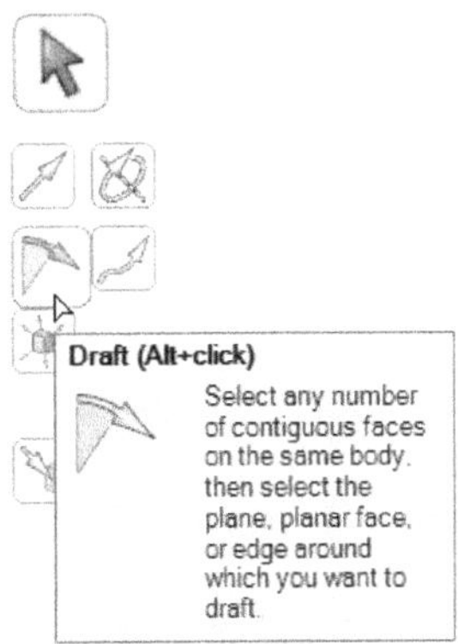

3. Select the front face as the parting plane.

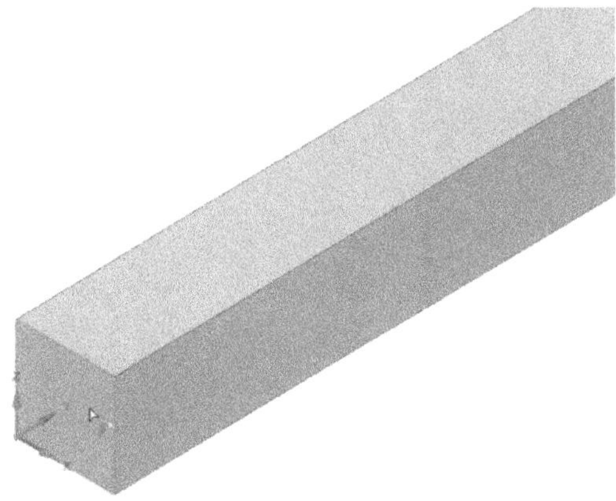

4. Select the top face as the face to be drafted.

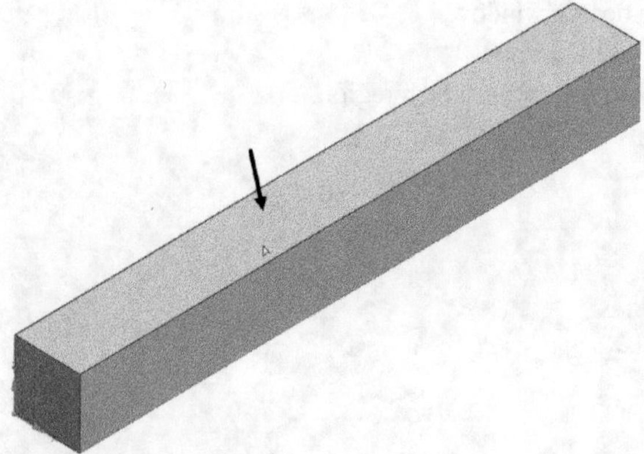

5. Type-in **-1** in the angle box provided.
6. Press Enter to create the draft.

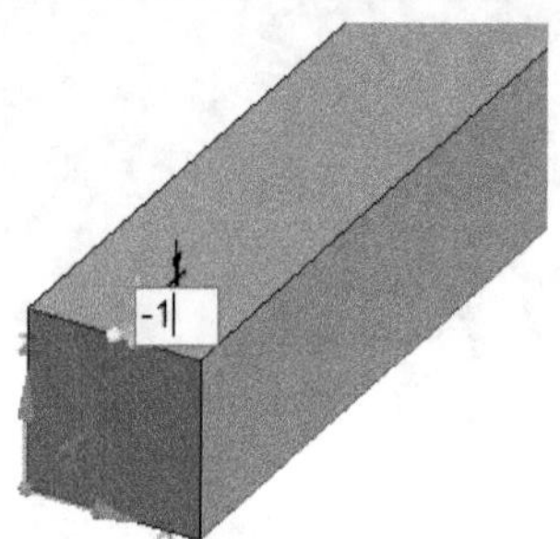

7. Press Esc.

Saving the Part

1. Click **Save** on the **Quick Access Toolbar**.
2. On the **Save As** dialog, type-in **Key** in the **File Name** box.
3. Click **Save** to save the file.
4. Click the **Close** icon on the file tab.

Chapter 3: Assembly Basics

In this chapter, you will:

- Add Components to the assembly
- Fix the components together

TUTORIAL 1

This tutorial takes you through the creation of your first assembly. You create the Oldham coupling assembly:

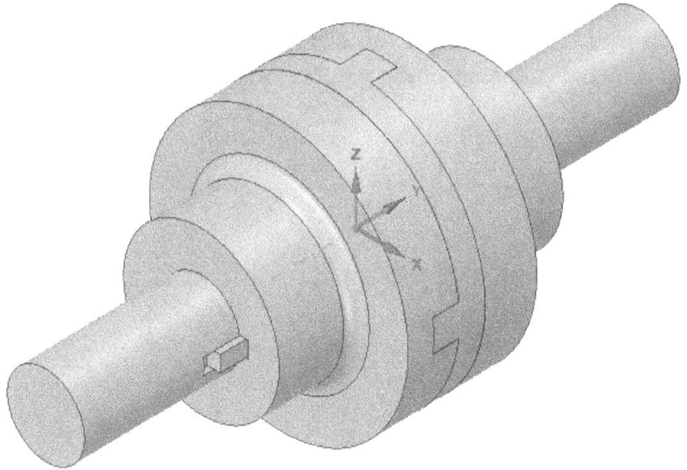

There are two ways of creating an assembly model.

- Top-Down Approach
- Bottom-Up Approach

Top-Down Approach

The assembly file is created first, and components are created in that file.

Bottom-Up Approach

The components are created first and then added to the assembly file. In this tutorial, you create the assembly using this approach.

Inserting the Base Component

You need to save the design before inserting a component into it.

1. Click **File > New > Design**; a new design file is opened.
2. On the ribbon, click **Design > Insert > File**.

3. On the **Open** dialog, go to the **Oldham Coupling** folder and double-click on the Flange.rsdoc file.

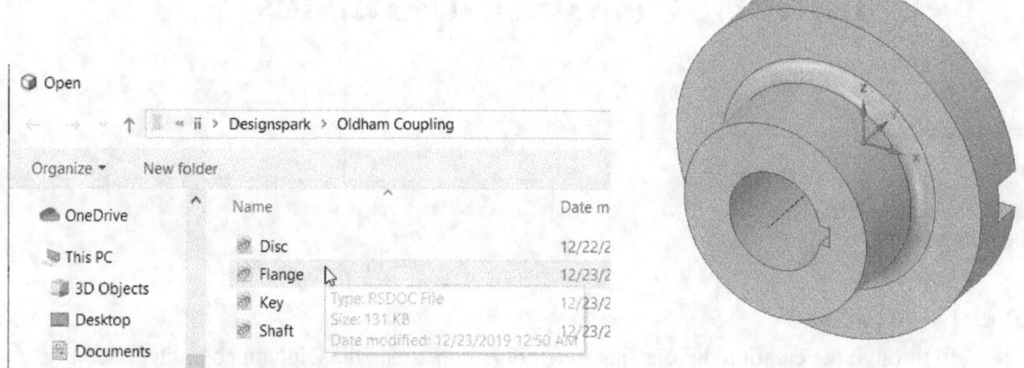

Adding the second component

1. To insert the second component, click **Design > Insert > File** on the ribbon.
2. On the **Open** dialog, go to the **Oldham Coupling** folder and double-click on the Shaft.rsdoc file.

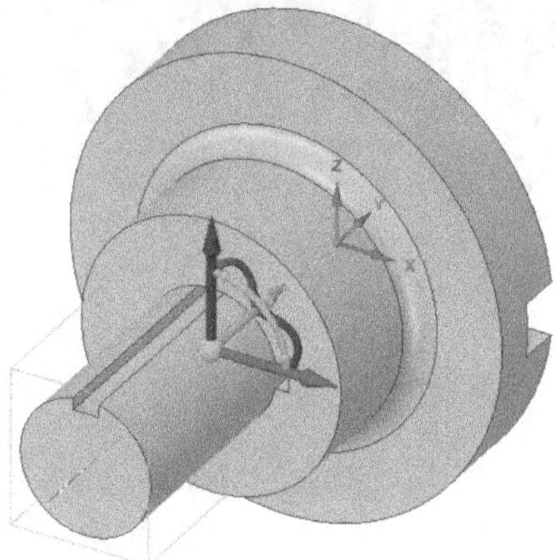

3. Click and drag the X-axis of the Move triad toward left.

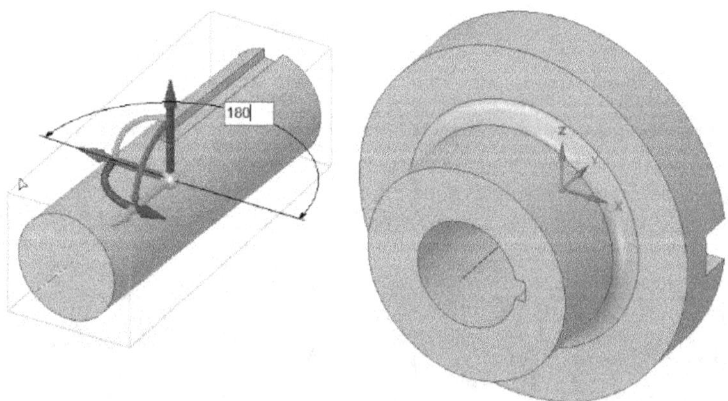

Assembling the Components

After inserting the components into the design, you need to assemble them. Designspark Mechanical provides you with the **Move** tool to assemble the components.

1. On the ribbon, click **Design > Edit > Move**.
2. Select the **Shaft** from the **Structure** panel.

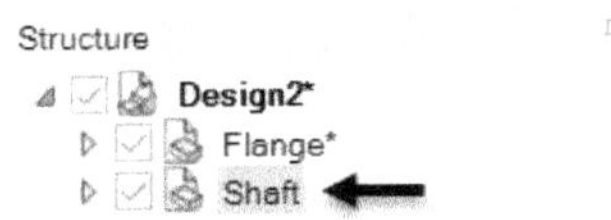

3. Click and drag the blue angular handle of the move triad.
4. Type 180 in the angle box and press ENTER.

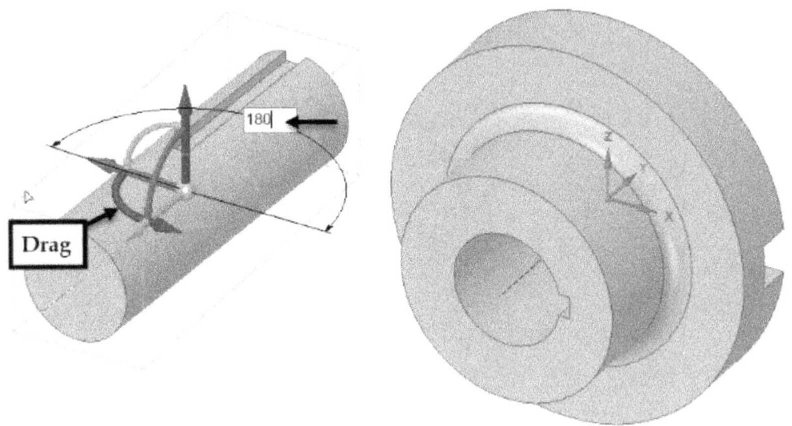

5. Click and drag the green rotate handle of the triad.
6. Type 270 in the angle box and press ENTER.

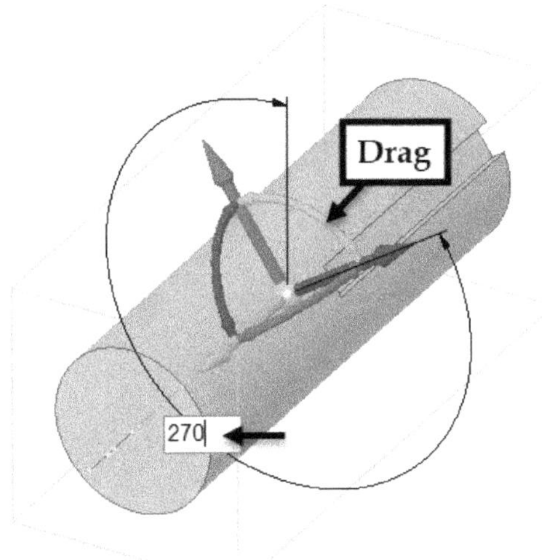

7. Press and hold the middle mouse button and drag the pointer; the model is rotated.

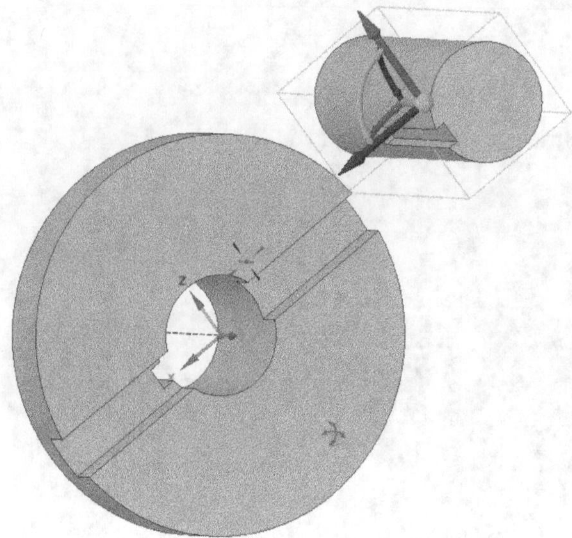

8. Click and drag the origin of the triad.
9. Release it on the end face of the shaft, as shown.

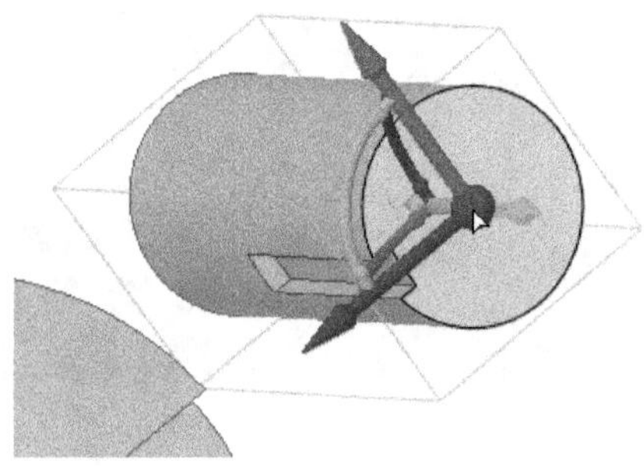

10. Click the **Up To** icon on the top left corner of the graphics area.

11. Select the flat face of the flange, as shown.

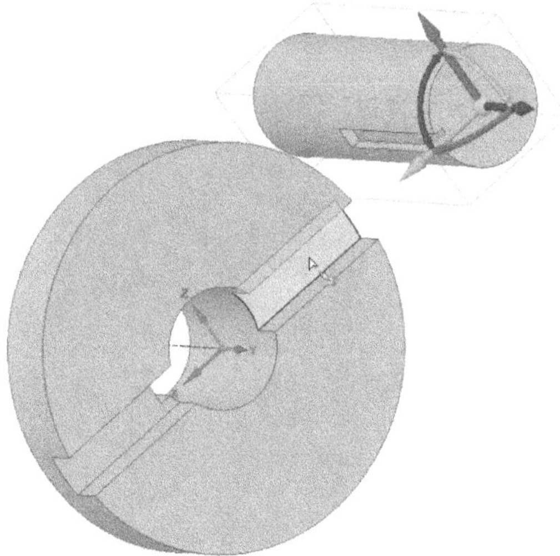

The end face of the shaft is aligned to the selected flat face.

12. Click the **Up To** icon on the top left corner of the graphics area.
13. Select the Y-axis of the coordinate system; the axis of the shaft is made coincident to the Y-axis of the coordinate system.

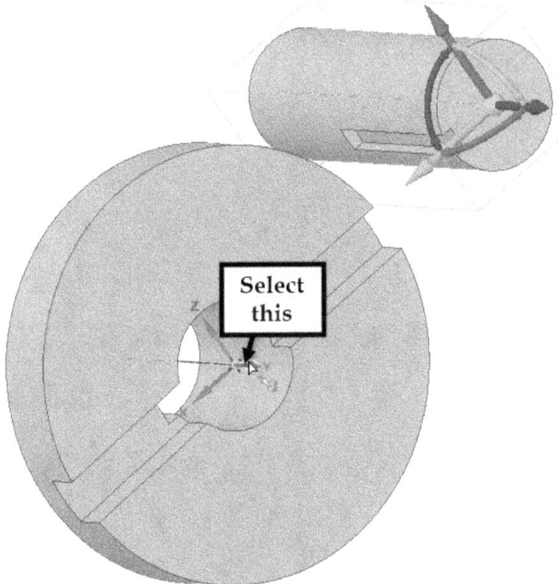

14. On the ribbon, click **Design** > **Orient** > **View** drop-down > **Back**; the back face of the model is displayed.
15. Click on the blue rotate handle of the triad.
16. Press the Space bar on your keyboard.
17. Type 90 and press ENTER.

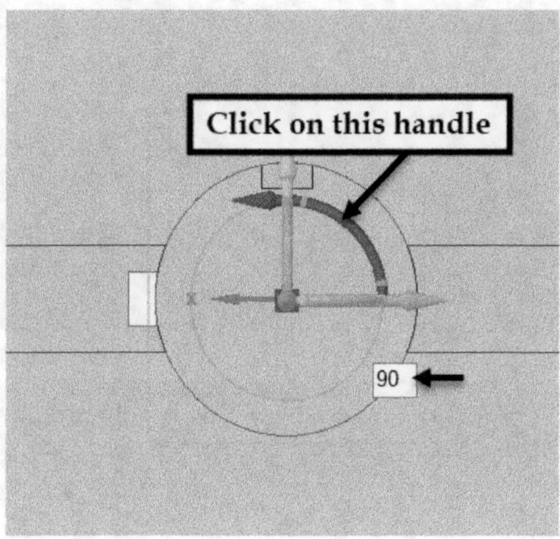

Adding the Third Component

1. Right-click on the Flange, and then select **Hide**.

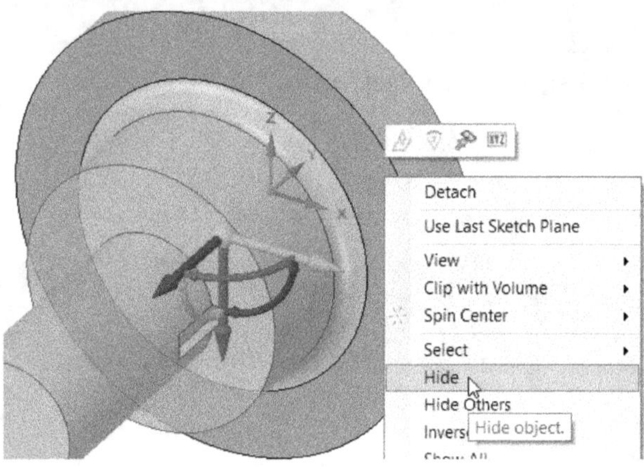

2. To insert the third component, click **Design > Insert > File** on the ribbon.
3. On the **Open** dialog, go to the **Oldham Coupling** folder and double-click on the key.rsdoc file.
4. Click and drag the X-axis of the Move triad toward the right.

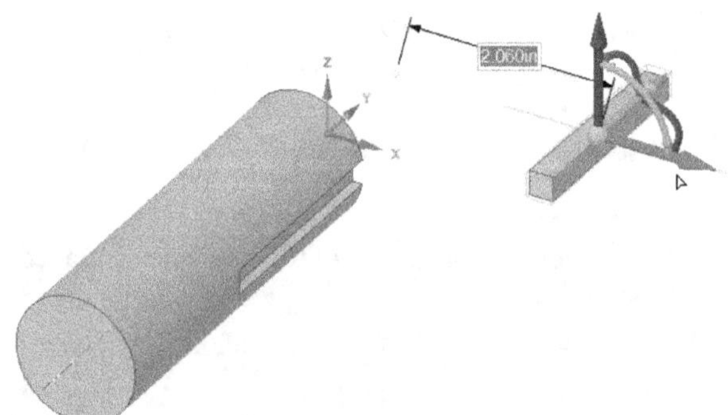

5. Click on the blue rotate handle, and then press the **Space** key on your keyboard.
6. Type **180** in the angle box and press ENTER.

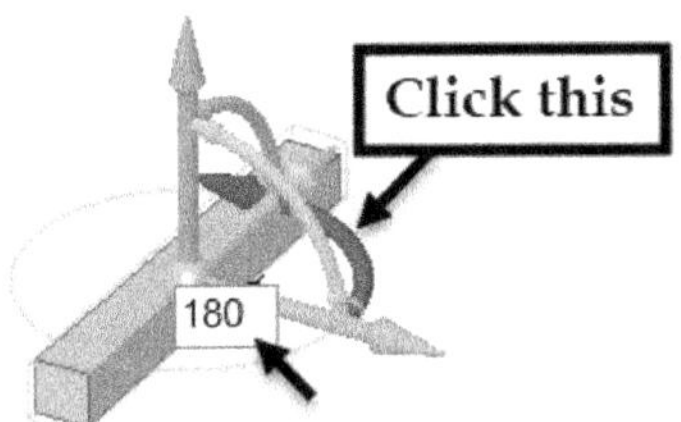

7. Click on the green rotate handle and press the **Space** key on the keyboard.
8. Type **270,** and press ENTER.

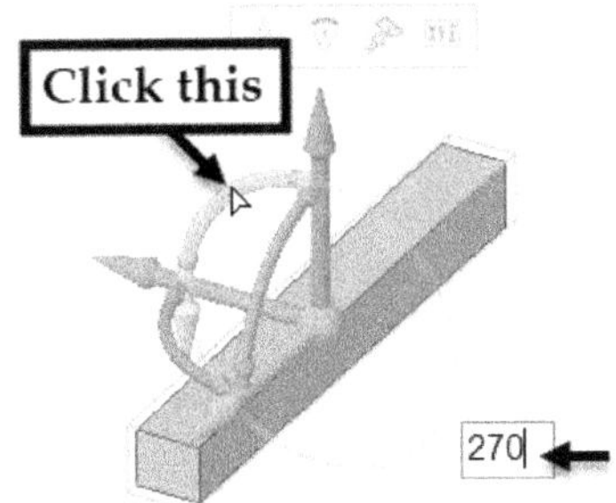

9. Press and hold the middle mouse button and drag the pointer; the model is rotated.

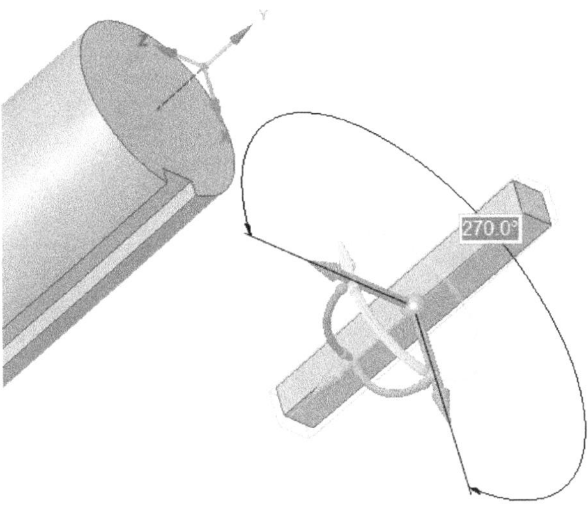

10. Click and drag the origin of the triad.
11. Release it on the end face of the key.

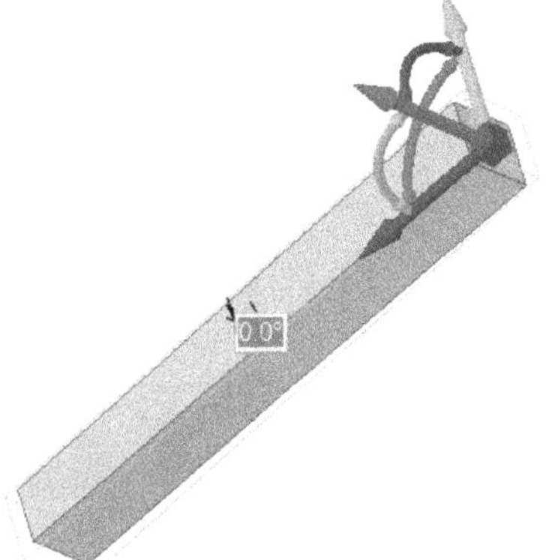

12. Click the **Up To** icon on the top-left corner of the graphics area.
13. Click on the end face of the shaft; the end face of the key is aligned with the end face of the shaft.

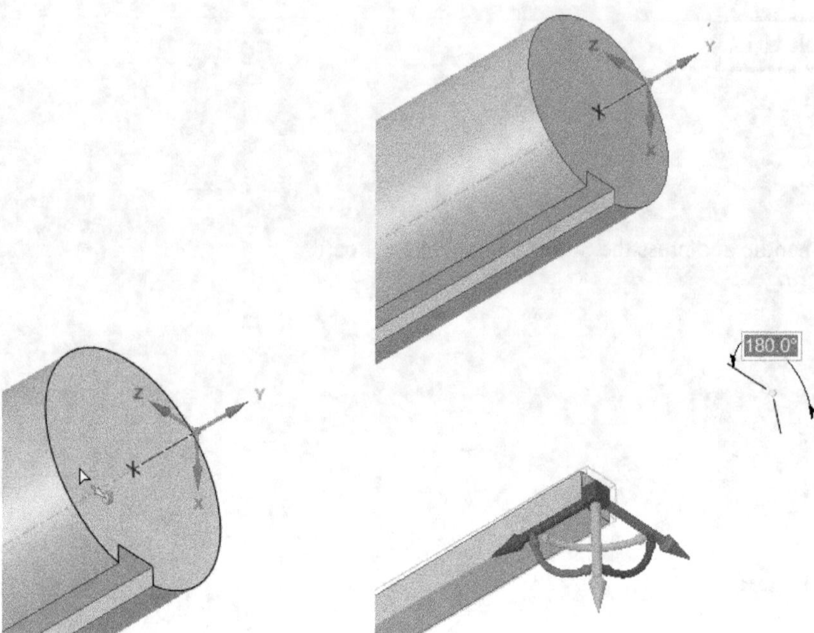

14. Click and drag the origin of the triad.
15. Release it on the top face of the key.

16. Press and hold the middle mouse button and drag the pointer such that the cut-out on the shaft is displayed.

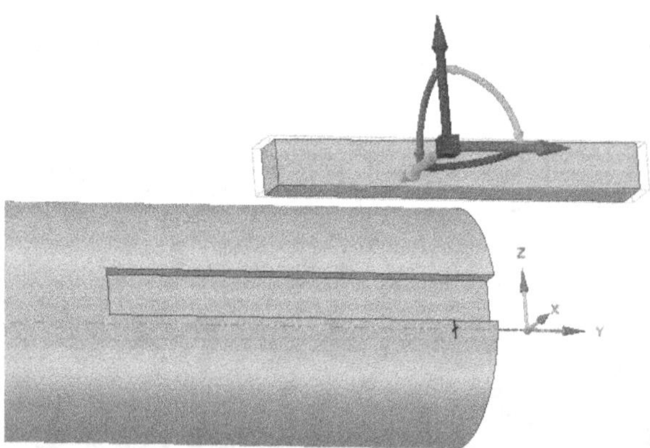

17. Click the **Up To** icon on the top-left corner of the graphics area.
18. Click on the face of the cut-out, as shown.

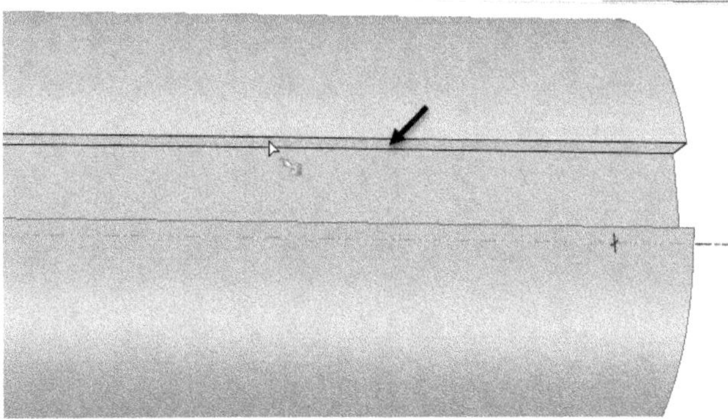

19. Click and drag the origin of the triad.
20. Release it on the face of the key, as shown.

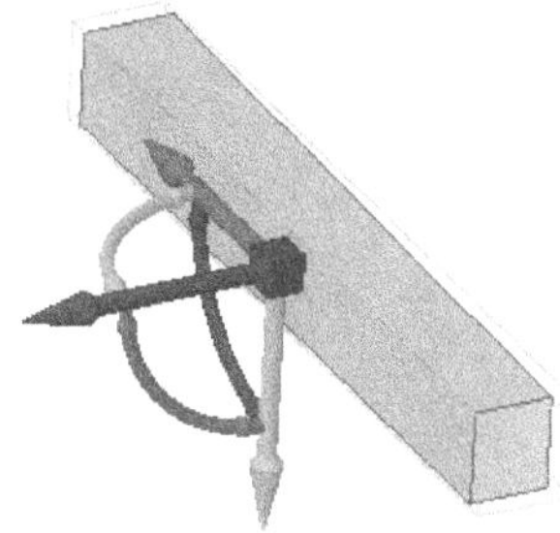

21. Click the **Up To** icon on the top-left corner of the graphics area.
22. Click on the face of the cut-out, as shown.

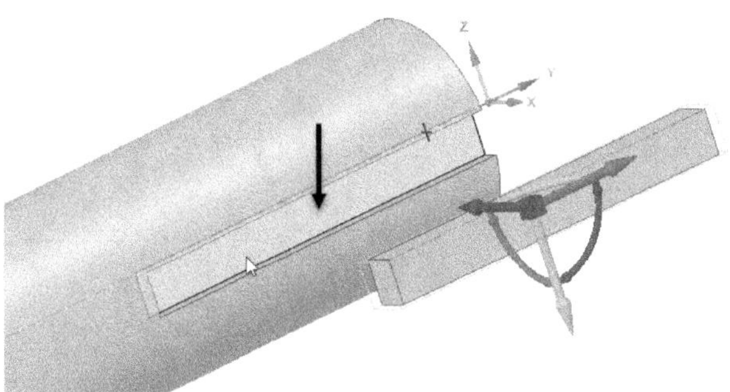

The key is inserted in the cutout of the shaft.

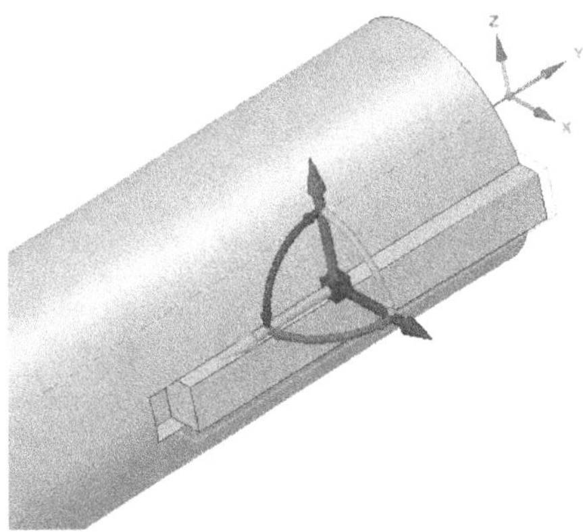

23. Right-click and select **Show All**.

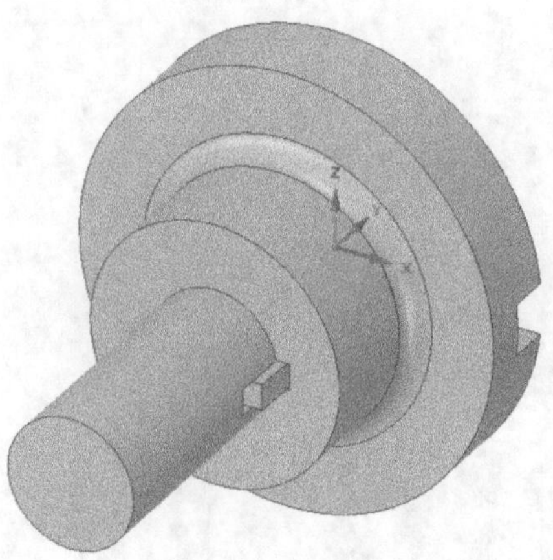

24. Click **Save** on the **Quick Access Toolbar**.
25. Type **Flange_assembly** in the **File name** box.
26. Click **Save**.
27. Click **File > Close**.

Creating the Main Assembly

1. Click **File > New > Design**.
2. Click **Design > Insert > File** on the ribbon.
3. On the **Open** dialog, go to the **Oldham Coupling** folder and double-click on the Disc.rsdoc file.

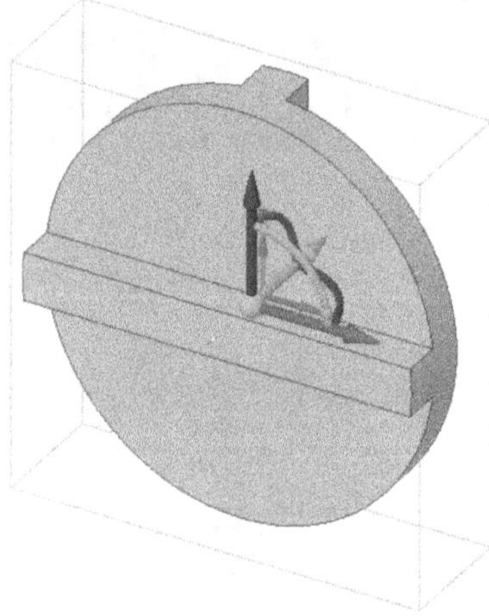

4. Click **Design > Insert > File** on the ribbon.
5. On the **Open** dialog, go to the **Oldham Coupling** folder and double-click on the Flange_assembly.rsdoc file.
6. Click and drag the X-axis of the Move triad toward left.

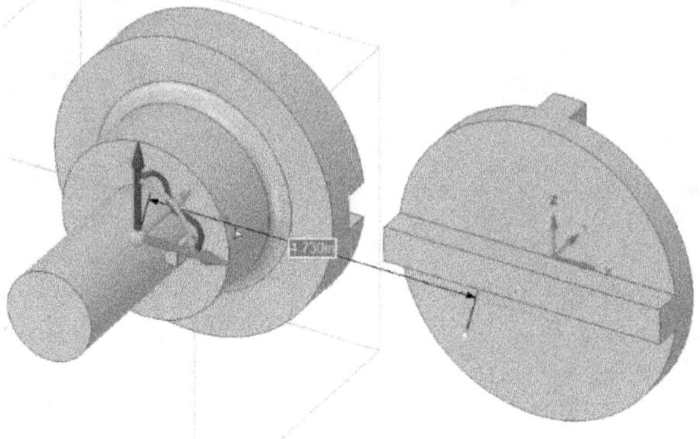

7. Press and hold the middle mouse button and drag the pointer such that the back face of the assembly is displayed.
8. Click and drag the origin of the triad.
9. Release it on the flat face of the shaft, as shown.

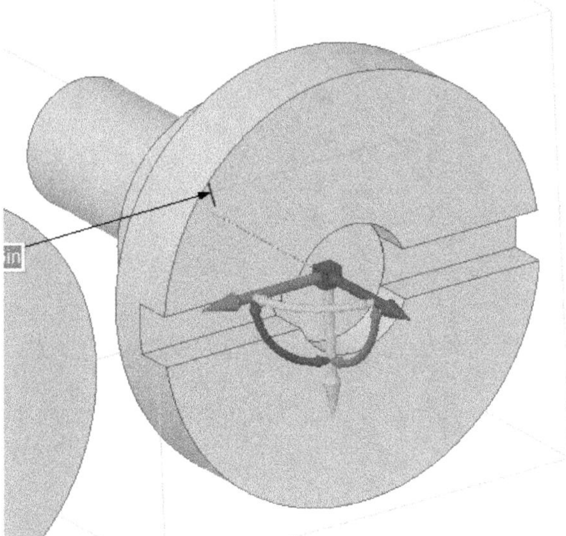

10. Click the **Up To** icon on the top-left corner of the graphics area.
11. Select the flat face of the Disc, as shown.

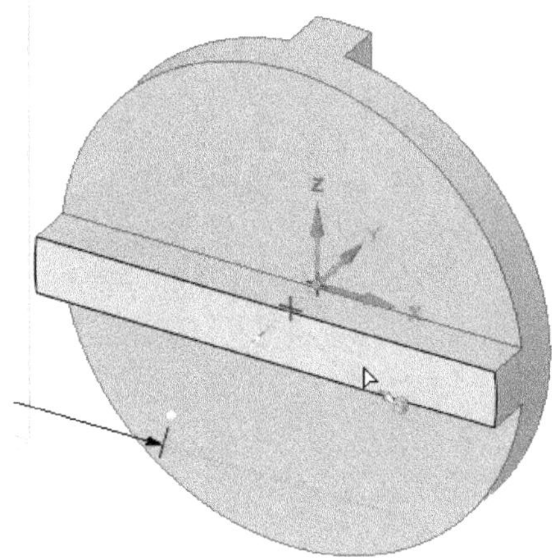

The flat face of the shaft is aligned with the flat face of the Disc.

12. Click the **Up To** icon on the top left corner of the graphics area.
13. Select the Y-axis of the coordinate system.

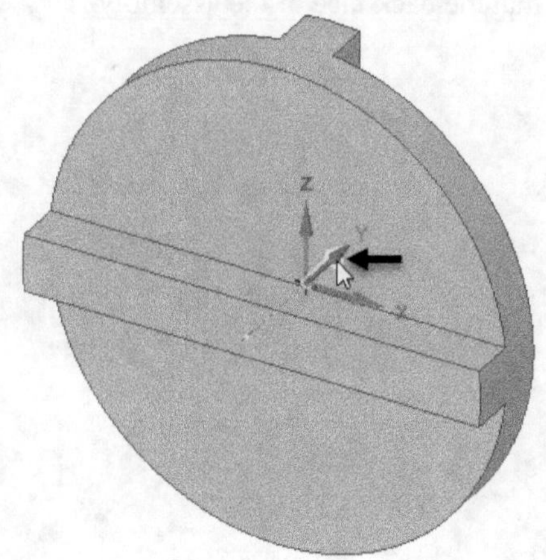

The flange assembly is made coaxial to the disc.

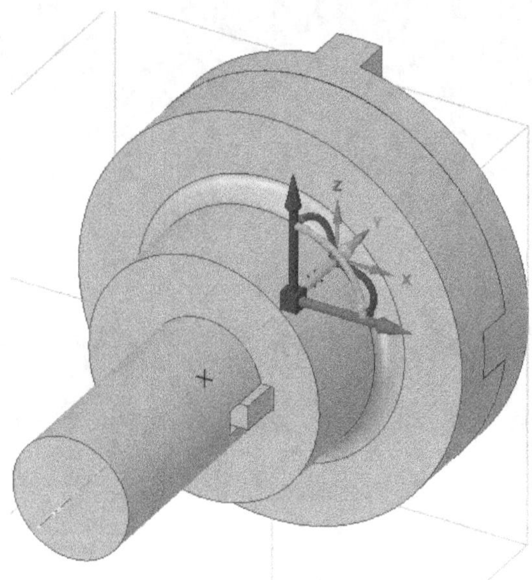

Placing the second instance of the Sub-assembly

1. Click **Design > Edit > Move** on the ribbon.
2. On the **Options – Move** panel, check the **Create patterns** option.
3. Select the **Flange_assembly** component from the Structure panel.

4. Click on the X-axis and drag it toward the right.
5. Click in the graphics area.

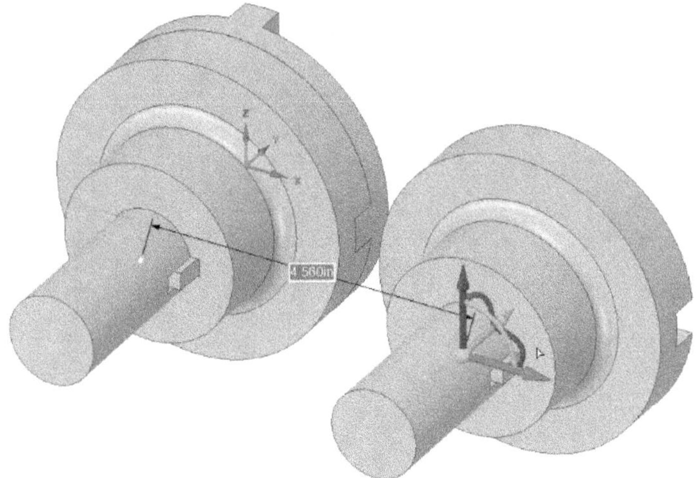

6. In the **Structure** panel, right-click on the **Pattern**.
7. Select **Unpattern** from the menu; the patterned is exploded.

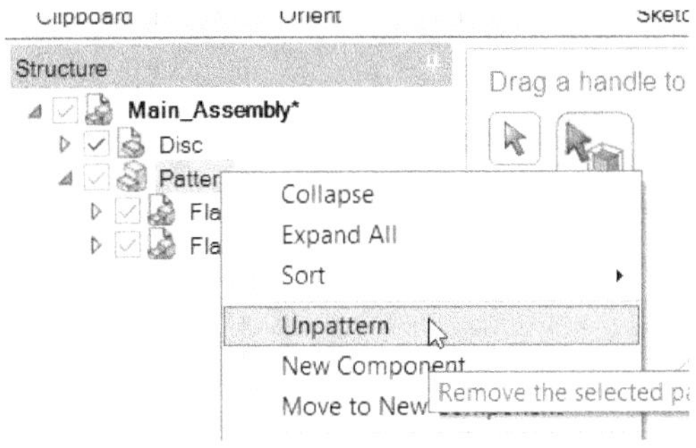

8. Expand the **Pattern** node on the **Structure** panel, and then select the second Flange assembly.

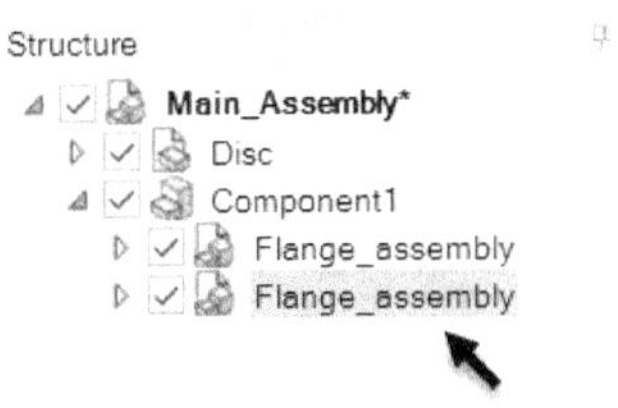

9. Click on the blue Rotate handle, as shown.
10. Press the Space key on your keyboard.
11. Type 180 in the **Angle** box displayed in the graphics window, and then press Enter.

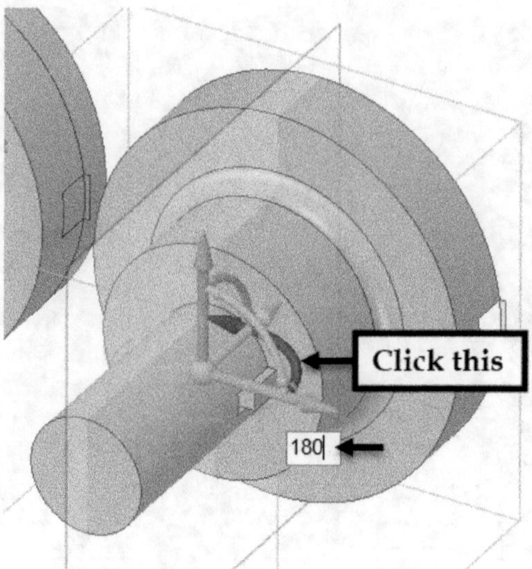

12. Click on the green Rotate handle, and then press the SPACEBAR.
13. Type 90 in the **Angle** box displayed in the graphics window, and then press Enter.

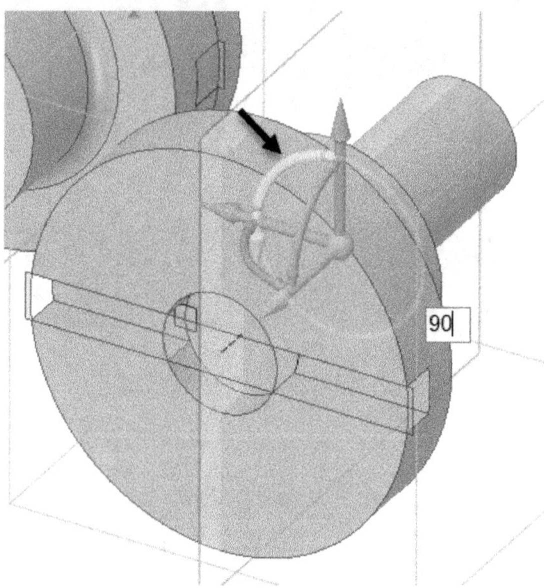

14. On the **Structure** panel, select the second Flange assembly.
15. Click and drag the origin of the triad.
16. Release it on the end face of the shaft, as shown.

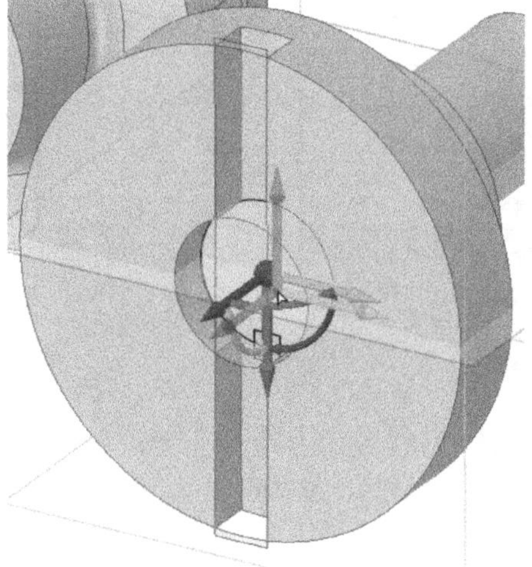

17. Click the **Up To** icon on the top left corner of the graphics area.
18. Select the flat face of the Disc, as shown.

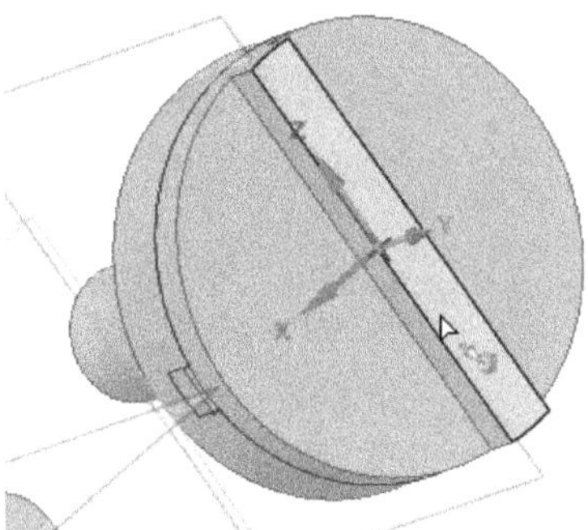

19. Click the **Up To** icon on the top left corner of the graphics area.
20. Select the Y-axis of the coordinate system.

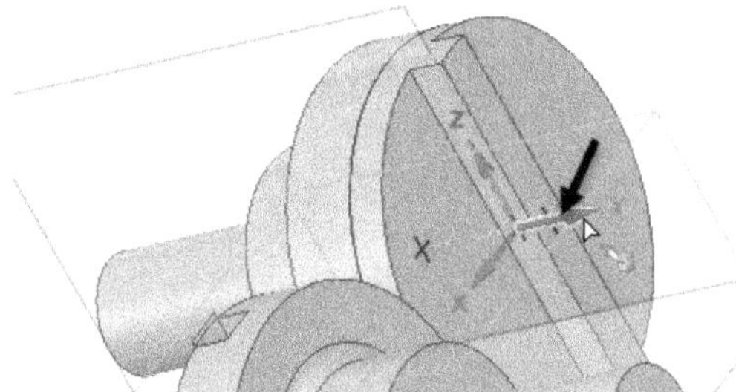

The flange assembly is assembled with the Disc.

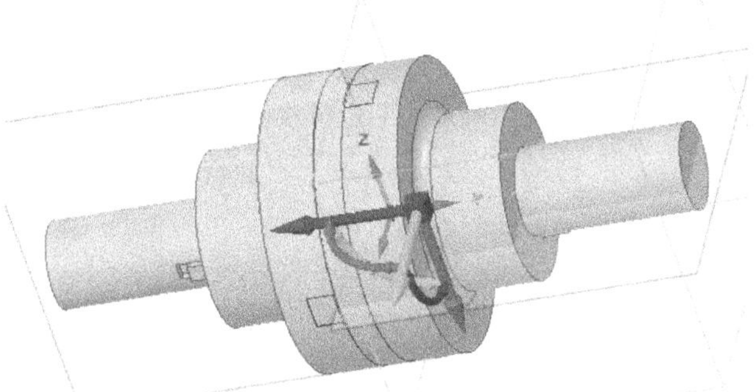

21. Click **Save** on the Quick Access Toolbar.
22. On the **Save As** dialog, type **Oldham Coupling** in the **File name** box.
23. Click **Save**.

Chapter 4: Sketching

In this chapter, you will learn the sketching tools. You will learn to create:

- Rectangles
- Polygons
- Splines
- Ellipses
- Circles
- Arcs
- Circular pattern
- Trim Entities
- Fillets and Chamfers

Creating Rectangles

A rectangle is a four-sided object. You can create a rectangle by just specifying its two diagonal corners. However, there are various tools to create a rectangle. You can access these tools from the **Sketch** panel of the ribbon. These tools are explained next.

1. Click the **Select New Sketch Plane** icon on the Toolbar.
2. Place the pointer on the fourth quadrant and click to select the XY plane.
3. Click **Design > Orient > Plan View** on the ribbon.
4. On the ribbon, click **Design > Sketch > Rectangle** .
5. Select the origin point to define the first corner.
6. Move the pointer diagonally and click to define the second corner.

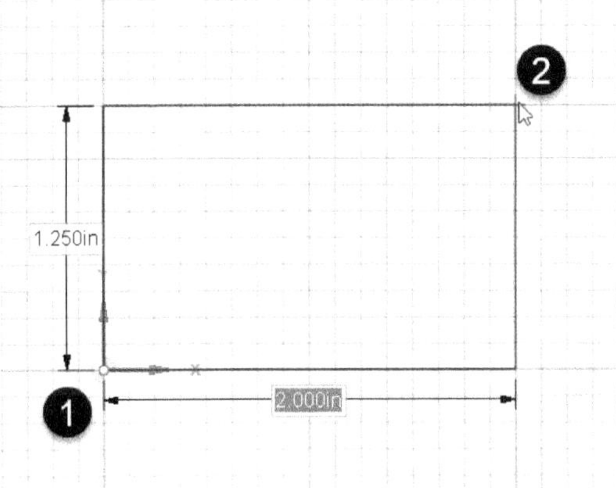

7. If you want to create the Center Rectangle, then activate the **Rectangle** tool from the **Sketch** panel.
8. On the **Options - Sketch** panel, check the **Define rectangle from center** option to create a center rectangle.
9. Click on the origin point to define the center point of the rectangle.
10. Move the pointer diagonally and click to define the corner point.

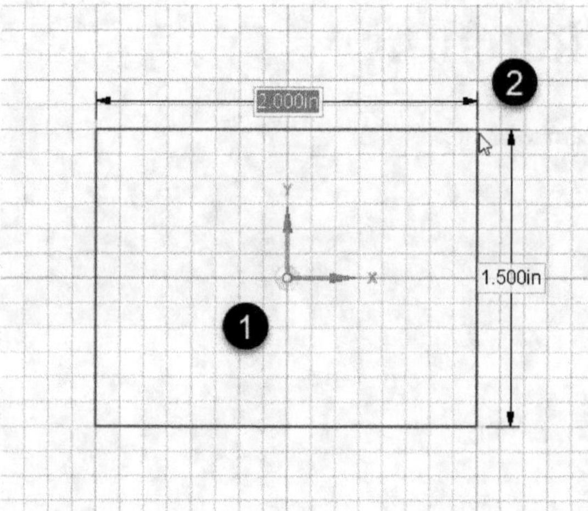

11. On the ribbon, click **Sketch > Three-Point Rectangle** . This option creates a slanted rectangle.
12. Specify the first corner point of the rectangle.
13. Move the pointer, and then type-in the width of the rectangle.
14. Press the Tab key, and then type-in the inclination angle of the rectangle.

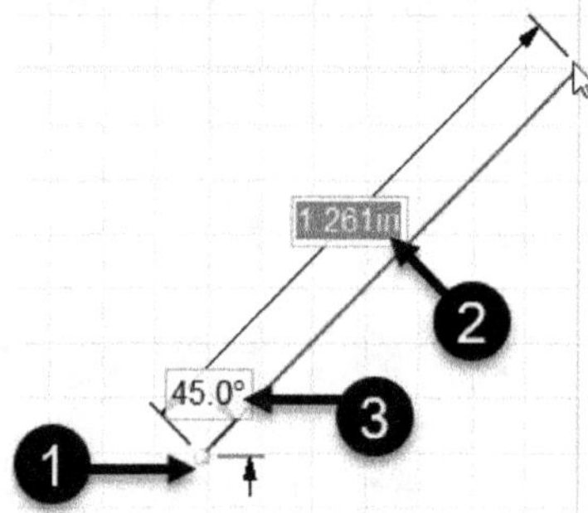

15. Press ENTER and move the pointer.
16. Type-in the height of the rectangle, and then press ENTER.

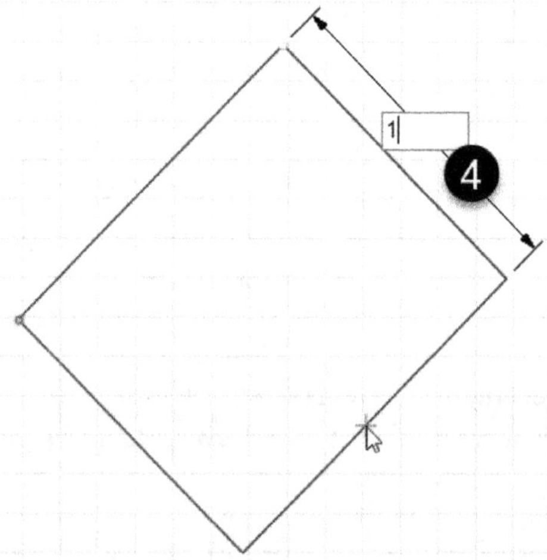

Creating Polygons

A Polygon is a shape having many sides ranging from 3 to 64. In DesignSpark, you can create regular polygons having sides with equal length. You can create a polygon using two methods. These methods are discussed next.

Inscribed Polygon

The inscribed polygon has its sides touching an imaginary circle.

1. Start a sketch.
2. On the ribbon, click **Design > Sketch > Polygon**.

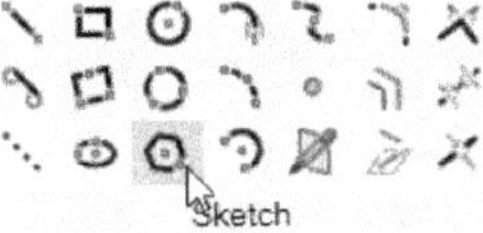

3. Make sure that the **Use internal radius** option is selected on the **Properties** panel.
4. Specify the center point of the polygon.
5. Move the pointer outward. You can now define the diameter, orientation, and the number of sides of the polygon.
6. Type the diameter value and press the TAB key.
7. Type the angle value to specify the orientation.
8. Press the TAB key and type in the number of sides value.
9. Press ENTER to create the polygon.

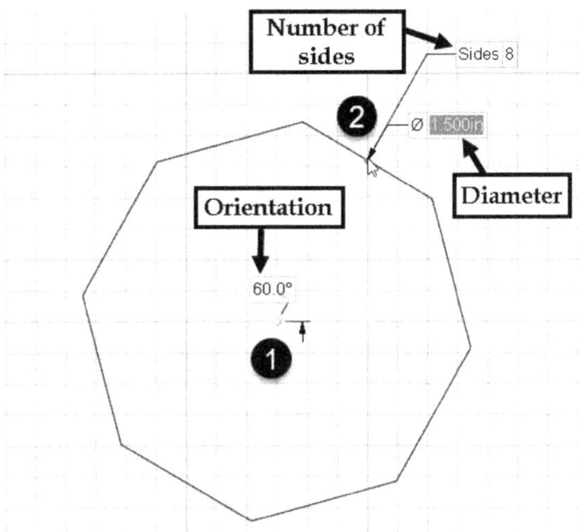

Circumscribed Polygon

The circumscribed polygon has its vertices touching an imaginary circle.

1. On the ribbon, click **Design > Sketch > Polygon.**
2. On the **Properties** panel, uncheck the **Use internal radius** option to draw a circumscribed polygon.

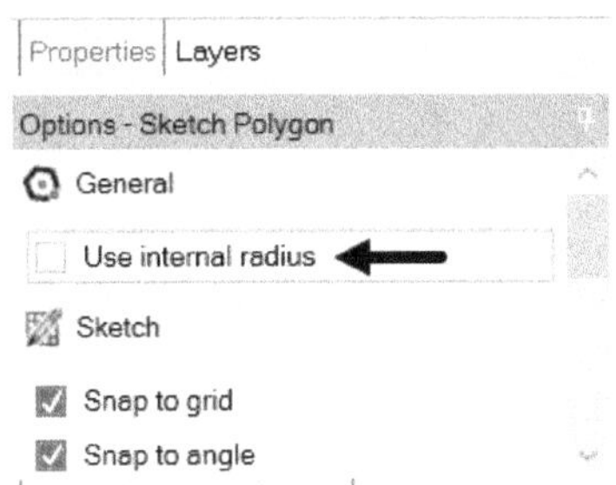

3. Click to define the center of the polygon.
4. Type the diameter value and press the TAB key.
5. Type the angle value to specify the orientation.
6. Press the TAB key and type in the number of sides value.
7. Click to create the polygon.

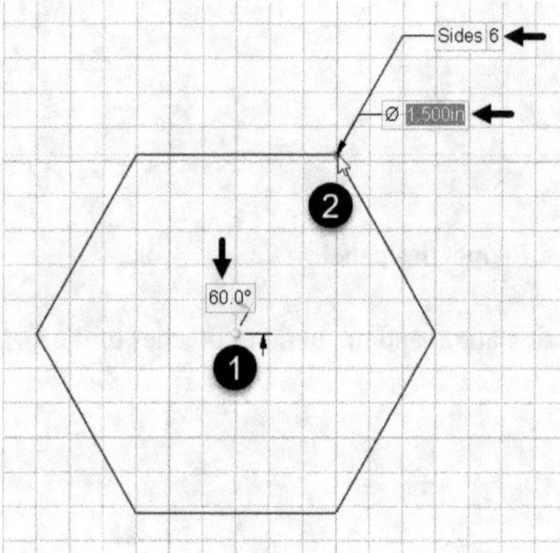

Creating Lines

The **Line** tool is the most commonly used command while creating a sketch. This tool is used to draw lines in **Sketch Mode** (or) to draw lines between points on objects in **3D Mode**.

1. Start a sketch.

2. Click **Design > Sketch > Line**　on the ribbon.
3. Click in the graphics area and move.
4. Type-in the value in the length box attached to the line.
5. Press **Tab** key and type-in the angle value.

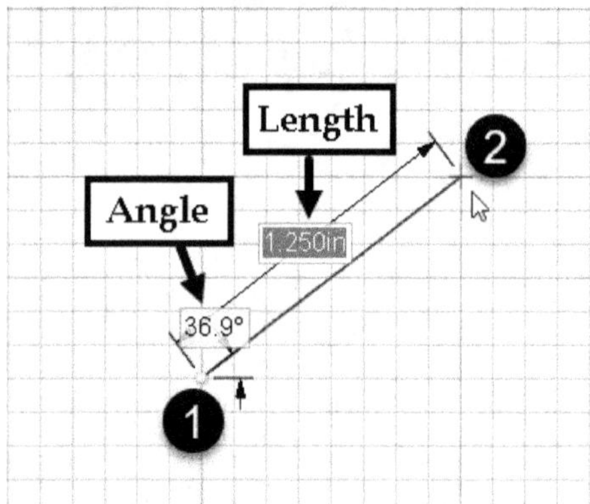

6. Press **Enter** to create a line.

A line is created with precise length and orientation.

Creating a Midpoint line

The **Line** tool can be used to draw a midpoint line.

1. Activate the **Line** tool from the ribbon.
2. On the **Properties** panel, check the **Define line from center** option.

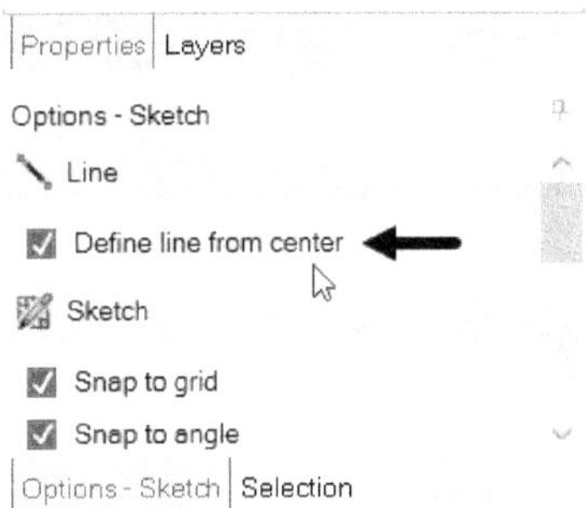

3. Click in the graphics area to specify the midpoint of the line.

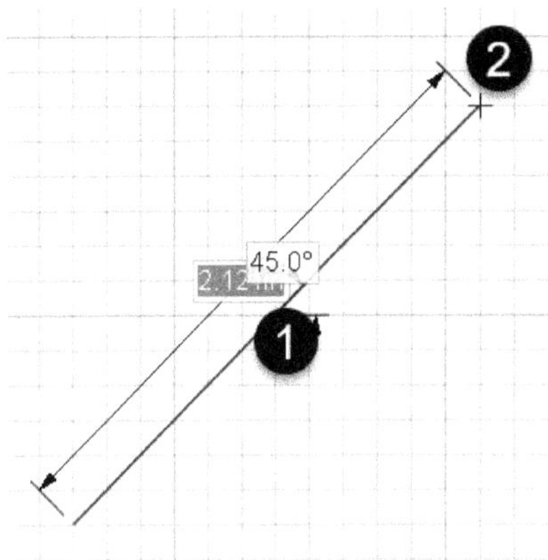

4. Type-in the value in the length box attached to the line.
5. Press the **Tab** key and type-in the angle value.
6. Press Enter to create a midpoint line.

Creating an Arc using the Line tool:

The **Line** tool can also be used to draw arcs continuous with lines.

1. Activate the **Line** tool on the ribbon.
2. Specify the start and endpoints of the line.
3. Right-click and select **Switch to Arc** from the menu.

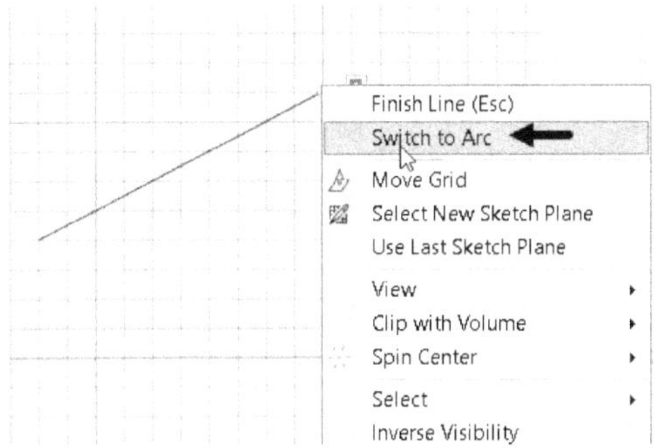

4. Move the cursor and type-in the diameter value.
5. Press the **Tab** key and type-in the angle value.

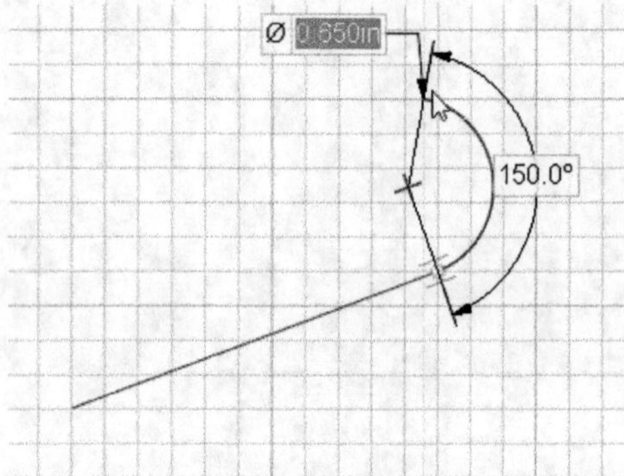

6. Press ENTER to create an arc. You can draw another arc using this tool or switch to the line tool.
7. To switch to the line tool, right-click and select **Switch to Line**.

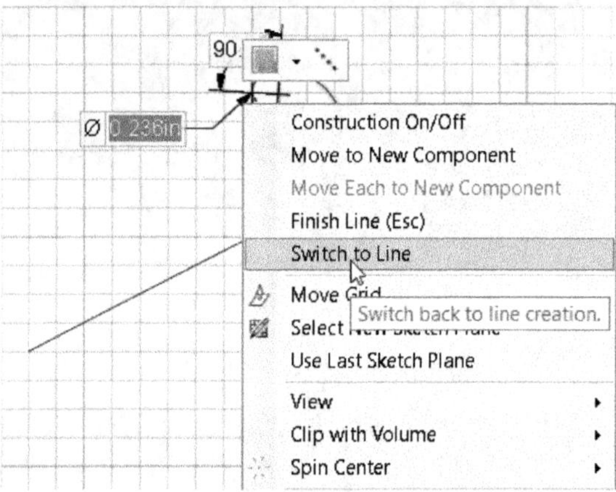

Creating Tangent Lines

This tool is used to draw lines tangent to any curves in your design.

1. Start a sketch.

2. Click **Design > Sketch > Tangent Line** on the ribbon. Note that the tool is disabled if there are no curves or lines in the sketch plane.

3. Select an arc or circle.

4. Move the mouse pointer; you can notice that the line remains tangent to the circle as you move the mouse pointer.

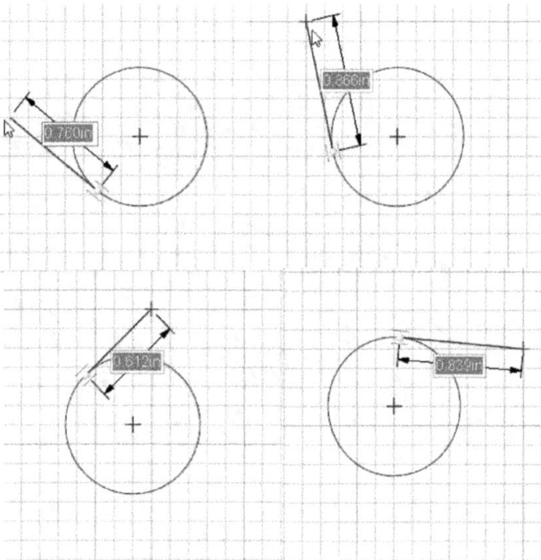

The *Tangency Indicator* shows that the new line is tangent with the circle.

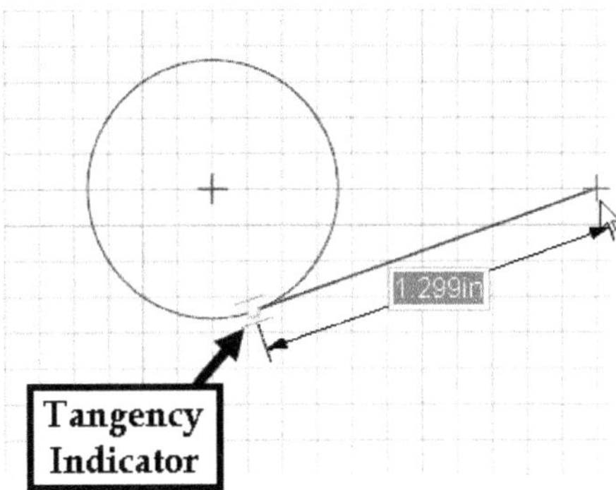

5.   Type –in the length value of the line, and then press ENTER.
6.   Type-in the angle value, and then press ENTER.

Creating a Construction line

The **Construction Line** tool is used to draw lines that help you to create an accurate sketch. The construction line becomes an axis in the 3D mode.

1.   Start a sketch.

2.   Click **Design > Sketch > Construction line** on the ribbon.
3.   Click to define the first point of the line.
4.   Move the pointer and click to define the endpoint of the line. You can also enter a value in length and angle boxes.

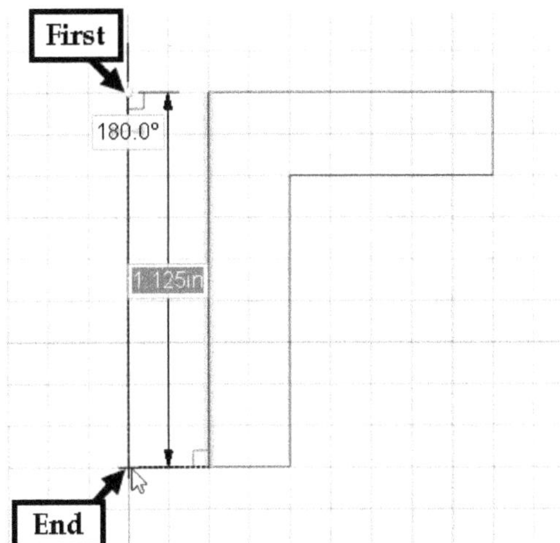

5.   Click **Design > Mode > 3D Mode** on the ribbon to switch to the 3D mode.

Creating Three-Point Arcs

The **Three-Point Arc** tool allows you to create an arc by defining its start, end, and radius.

1. Start a sketch.
2. Click **Design > Sketch > Three-Point Arc** on the ribbon.

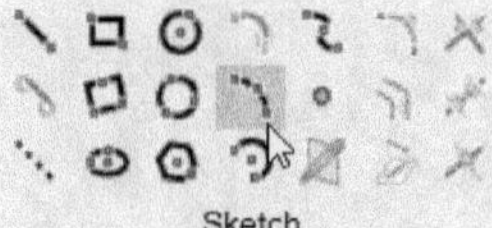

3. Click to define the start point of the arc.
4. Move the pointer and type-in the distance between the start and endpoints of the arc.
5. Press the TAB key and type-in the angle value.
6. Press ENTER.

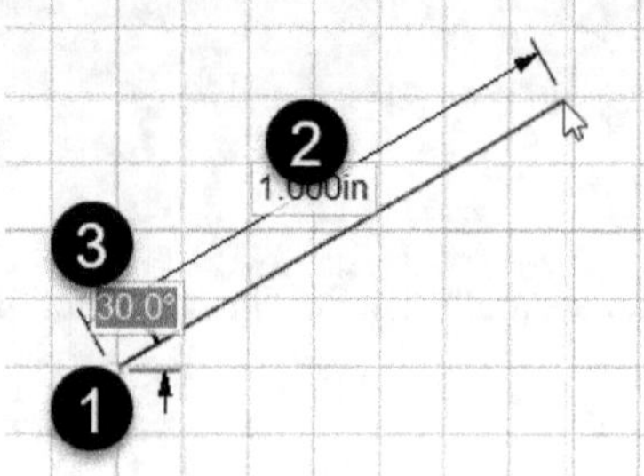

7. Type-in the radius value and press the TAB key.
8. Type-in the arc angle and press ENTER.

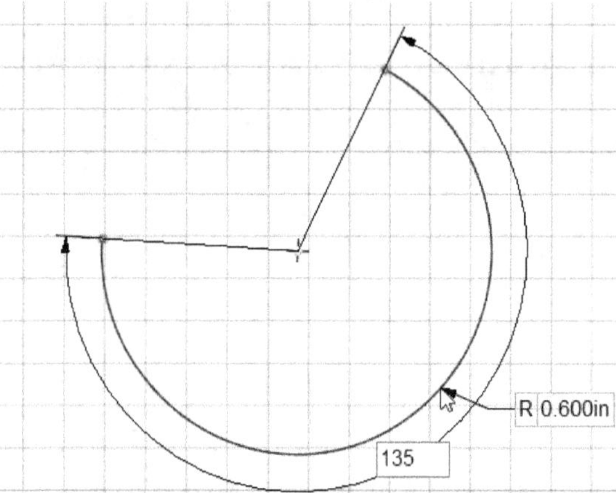

9. Click in the graphics area to create the arc.

Creating a Swept Arc

The **Sweep Arc** tool is used to create an arc by defining the center, start, and endpoints.

1. Start a sketch.
2. Click **Design > Sketch > Sweep Arc** on the ribbon.

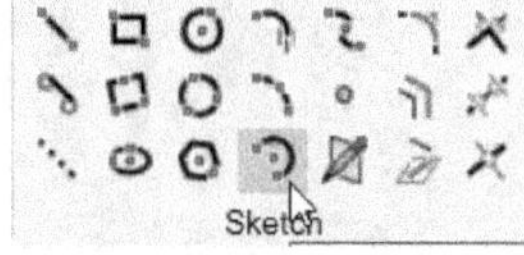

3. Click to define the center point of the arc.
4. Move the pointer and click to define the start point and radius of the swept circle (or) Type-in values of diameter and angle, and press Enter.

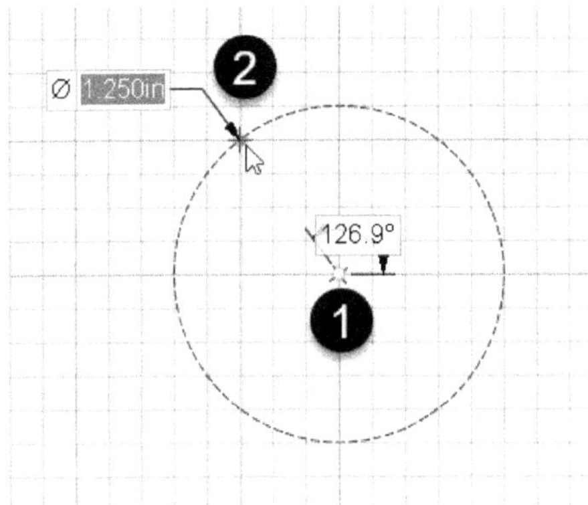

5. Move the pointer and click to define the endpoint of the arc (or) type-in angle value in the angle box and press Enter.

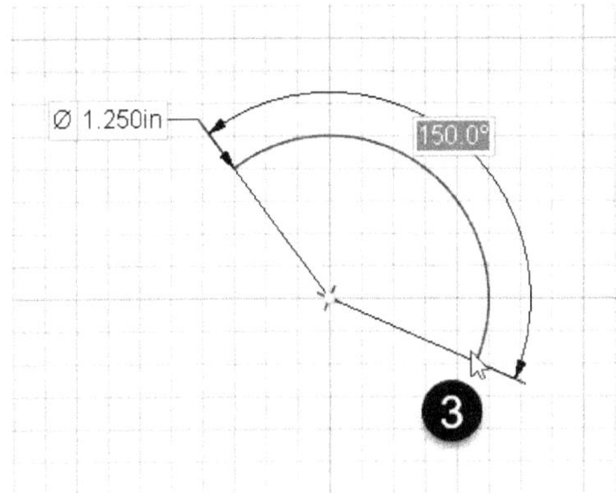

Creating a Tangent Arc

The **Tangent Arc** tool is used to draw an arc that is tangent to an existing curve or existing line.

1. Start a sketch.
2. Click **Design > Sketch > Tangent Arc** on the ribbon.

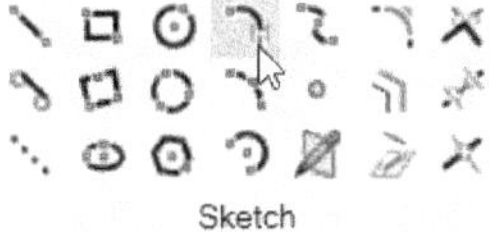

3. Click on the endpoint of the line or arc or circle.
4. Move the pointer and click to define the endpoint of the arc. You can also specify the diameter and angle in the value boxes attached to the arc.

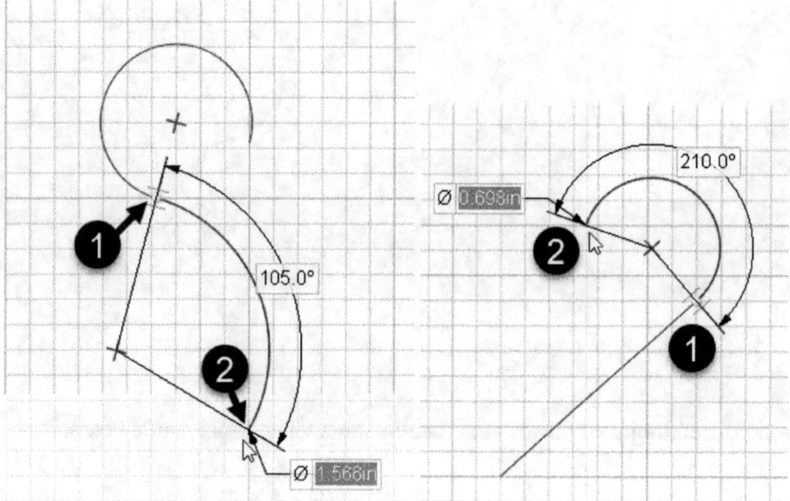

5.   Press **Esc** to deactivate the tool.

Creating a Circle

The **Circle** tool is used to draw a circle in a sketch mode.

1.   Start a sketch.
2.   Click **Design > Sketch > Circle** on the ribbon.

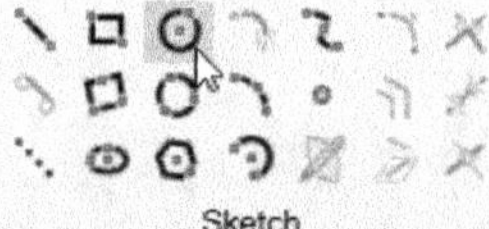

3.   Click to define the center of the circle.
4.   Move the pointer, and then click to define the diameter of the circle. You can also enter the diameter value in the attached box.

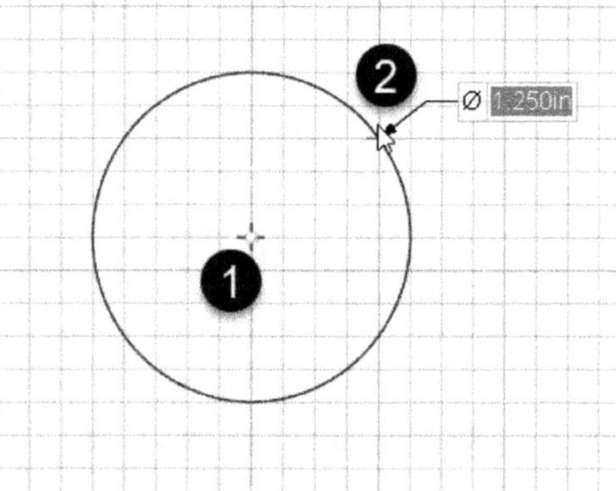

5.   Press **Esc** to deactivate the tool.

Creating a Three-Point Circle

The **Three-Point Circle** tool is used to draw a circle by using three points.

1.   Start a sketch.
2.   Click **Design > Sketch > Three-Point Circle** on the ribbon.

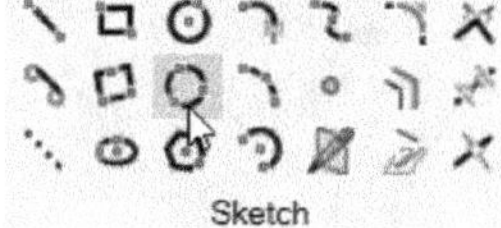

3. Click to define the first point of the circle.
4. Move the pointer, and then click again to define the second point of the circle.
5. Next, move the pointer and click to define the third point of the circle. The third point defines the diameter of the circle.

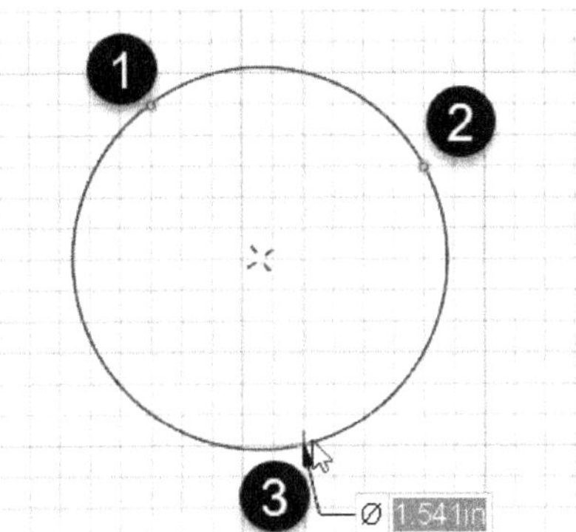

Creating a Spline

A Spline is a continuous curve line without vertices. The **Spline** tool is used to draw splines in a sketch mode.

1. Start a sketch.
2. Click **Design > Sketch > Spline** on the ribbon.

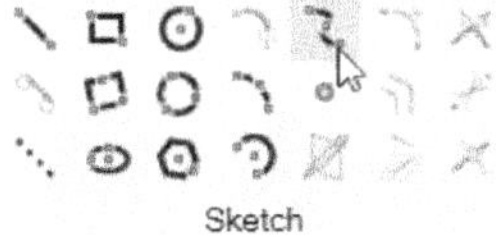

3. Click to define the first point of the spline.
4. Move the pointer and click to define the next point of the spline. You can also type in the values in the length box attached to it.
5. Likewise, move the pointer and define other points of the spline, as shown.

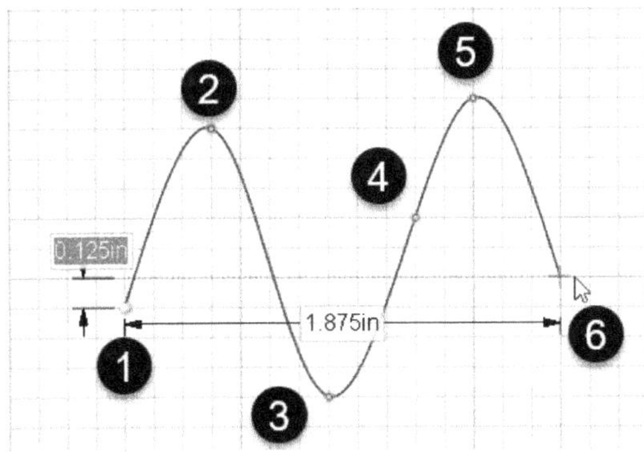

6. Right-click and select **Finish Spline** (or) press **Esc**.

Project to Sketch

The **Project to Sketch** tool helps you to use the edges or vertex of a 3D model to create sketch elements. You can also project an axis onto the sketch grid.

1. Start a sketch.
2. Click **Design > Sketch > Project to Sketch** on the ribbon.
3. Start a sketch on the plane offset to the model face, as shown.

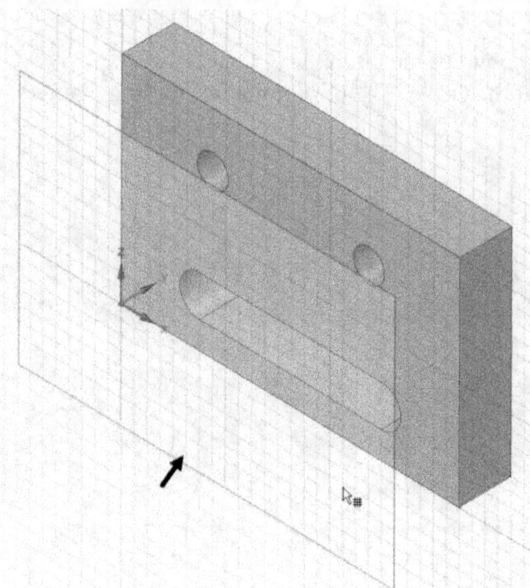

4.   On the ribbon, click **Design > Orient > Plan View** to change the view orientation.

5.   On the ribbon, click **Design > Sketch > Project** .

6.   Click on the edges of the model, as shown.

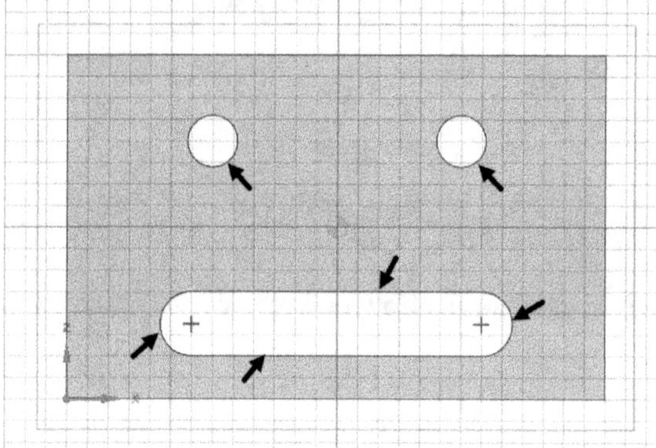

7.   Click **Design > Mode > 3D Mode** on the ribbon.

The selected edges are projected onto the sketch plane.

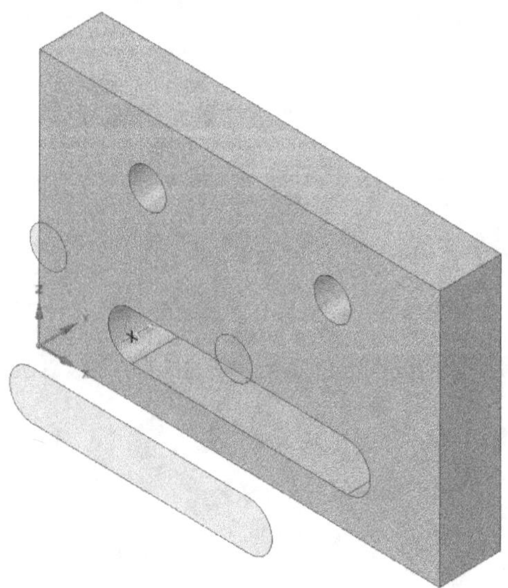

Ellipses

Ellipses are also non-uniform curves, but they have a regular shape. They are splines created in regular closed shapes.

1. Start a sketch.
2. On the ribbon, click **Design > Sketch > Ellipse** ⬭.
3. Pick a point in the design window to define the center of the ellipse.
4. Move the pointer and click to define the radius and orientation of the first axis (or) type-in values in the length and angle boxes, as shown. Press Enter.

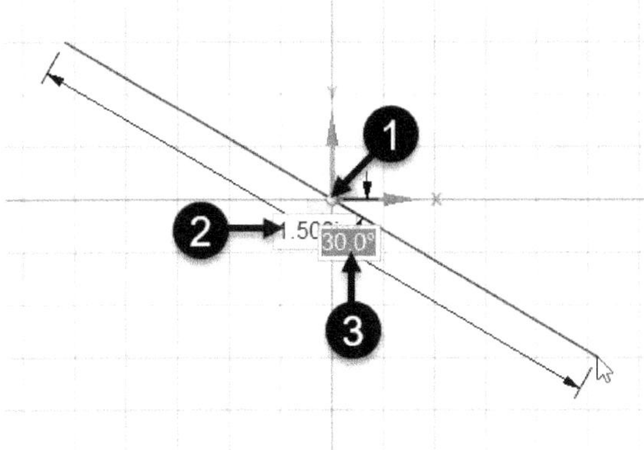

5. Move the pointer and click to define the radius of the second axis (or) type-in a value in the box, as shown. Press Enter.

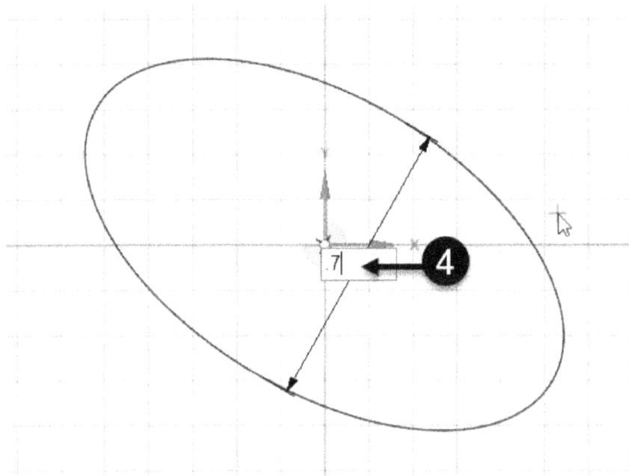

Create Patterns

The **Create Patterns** option is used to creates an arrangement of objects around a point in the specified form.

1. On the ribbon, click **Design > Edit > Move** ⬈.
2. Select the arc and click the origin point of the datum coordinate system, as shown.

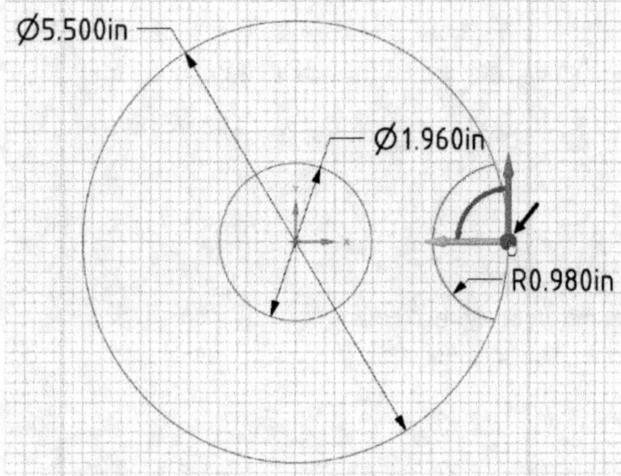

3. Click and drag it towards the left and place it on the origin point of the sketch, as shown.

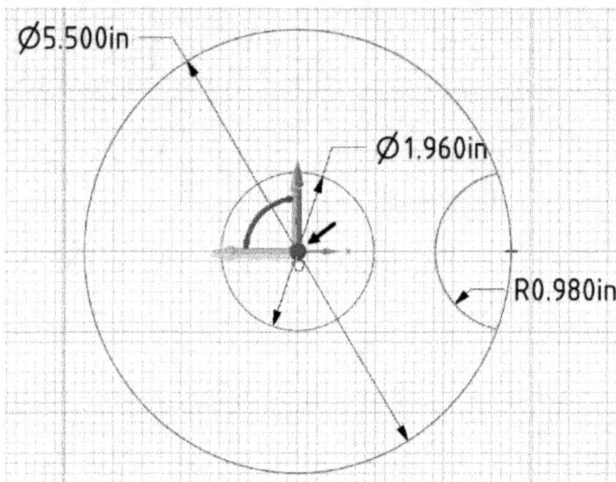

4. On the **Properties** panel, check the **Create patterns** option, as shown.

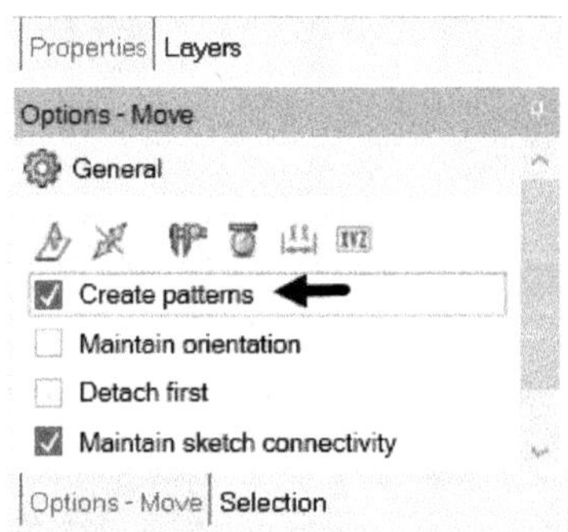

5. Next, click on the rotation handle of the datum coordinate system, as shown.

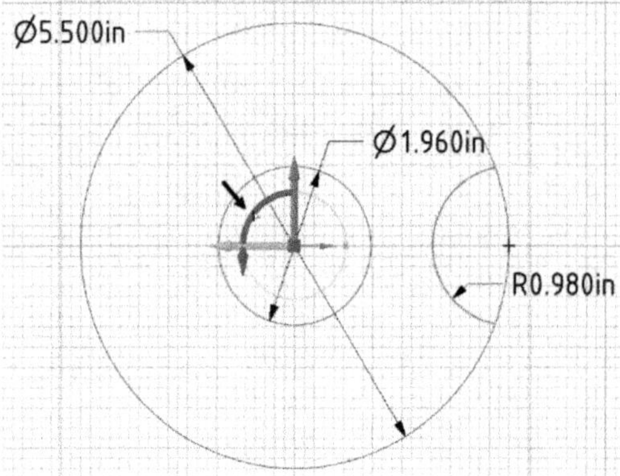

6. Click and rotate the handles in the anti-clockwise direction and type-in **4** and **9** in the **Count** and **Angle** boxes.

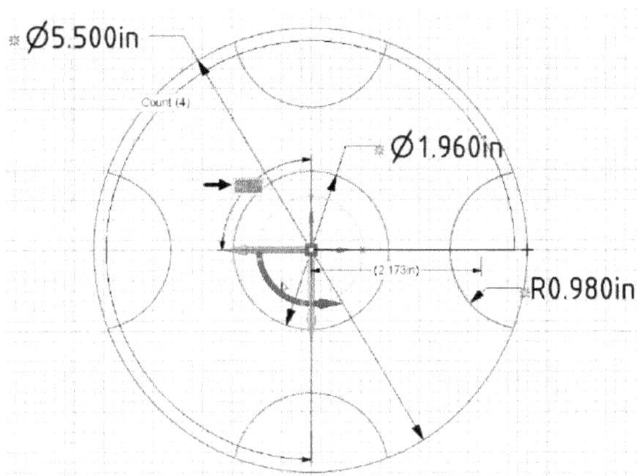

7. Press Enter to create the pattern.

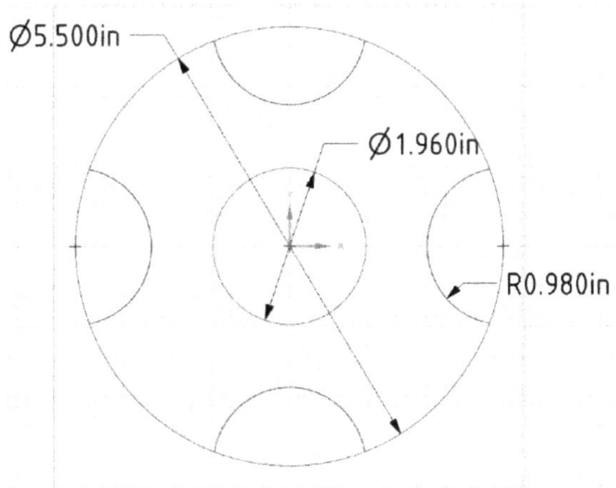

Trim

The **Trim Away** tool removes the unwanted entities of a sketch using a trimming element.

1. On the Ribbon, click **Design > Sketch > Trim Away** .
2. Click on the portions of the sketch, as shown.

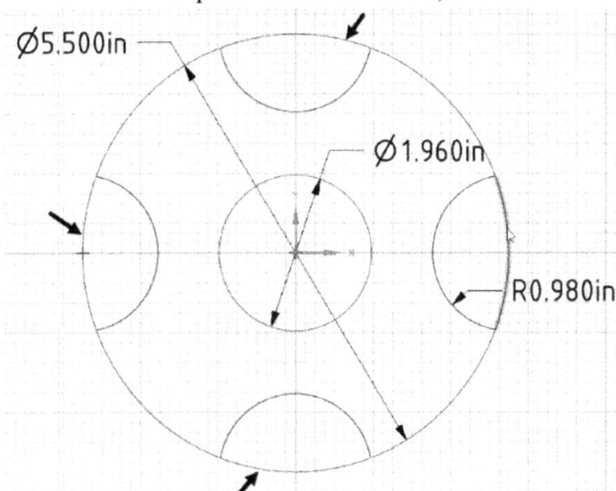

3. Press Esc to deactivate the tool.

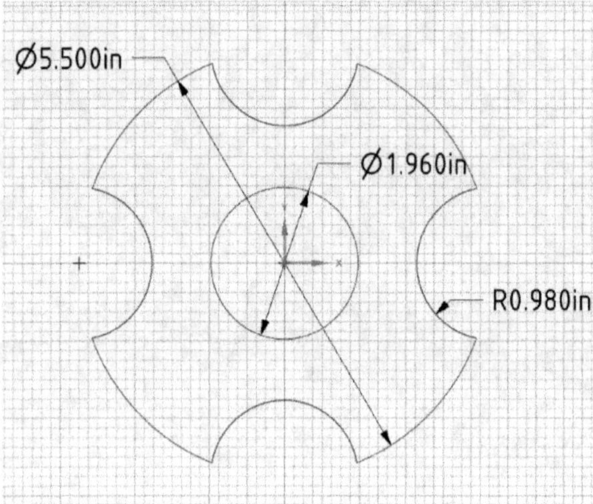

Create Corner

The **Create Corner** tool trims and extends elements to form a corner.

1. Create a sketch, as shown below.

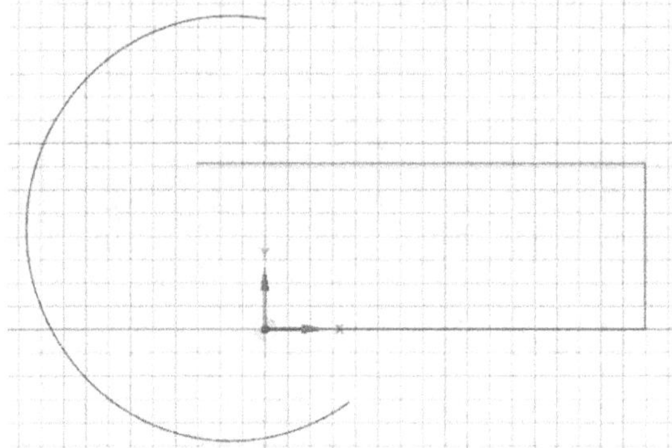

2. Click **Design > Sketch > Create Corner** on the Ribbon.

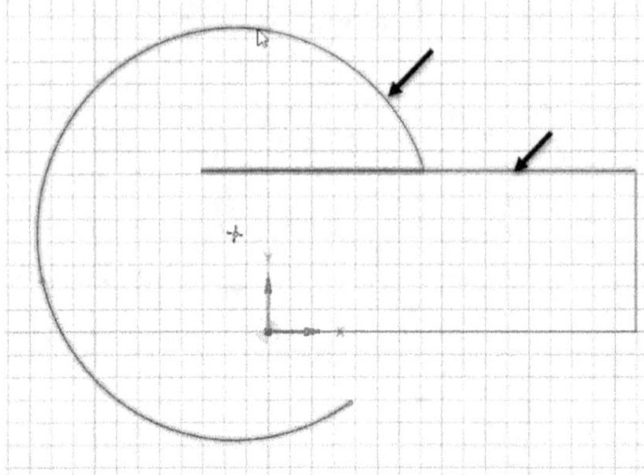

3. Click on the horizontal line at the location, as shown.
4. Click on the arc at the location, as shown.

Likewise, create a corner on the other side, as shown.

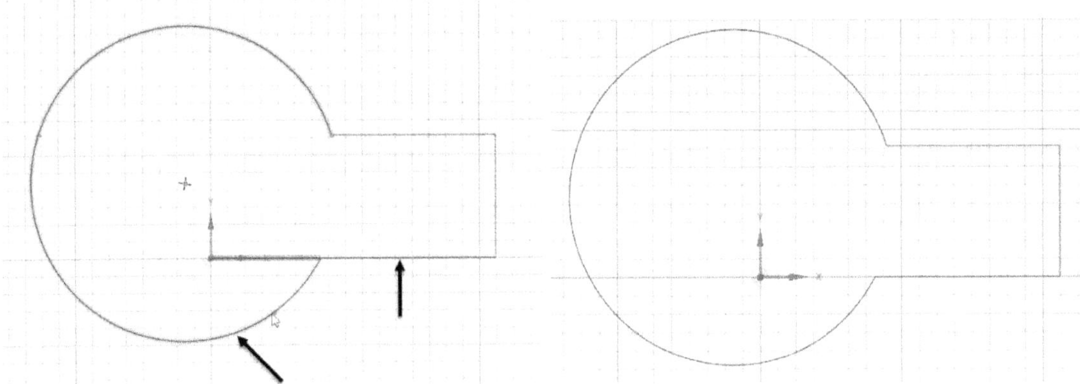

Offset

The **Offset** tool creates parallel copies of lines, circles, and arcs.

1. On the ribbon, click **Design > Sketch > Offset Curve** .
2. Select an entity and notice that only the arc is selected.
3. Type-in the offset value in the box attached to the offset copy.

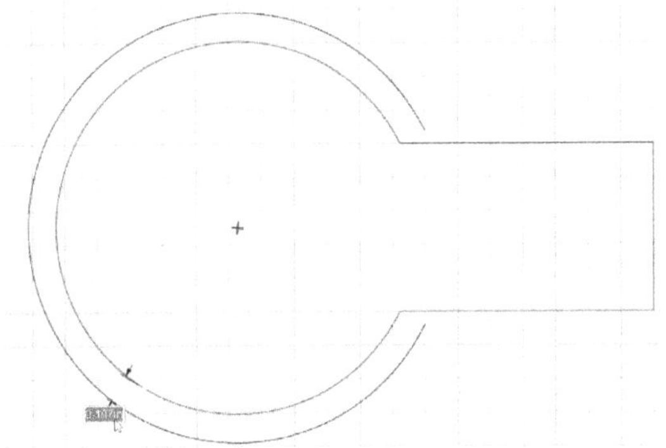

4. On the **Properties** panel, check the **Offset both ways** option to offset on either side of the selected arc.

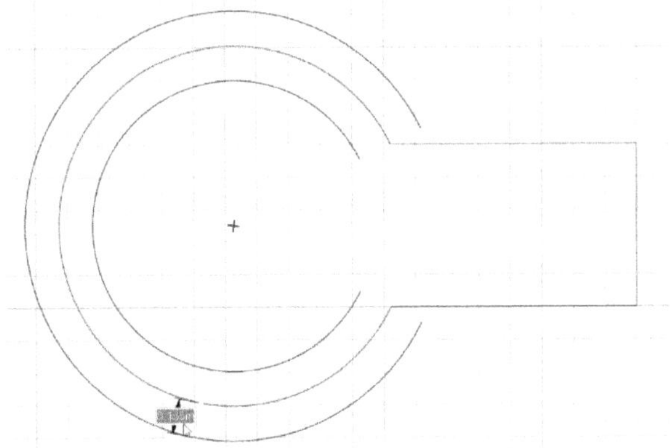

Create Rounded Corner

This tool rounds a sharp corner created by the intersection of two lines, arcs, circles, and rectangle or polygon vertices.

1. Activate this tool (On the ribbon, click **Design > Sketch > Create Rounded Corner**).

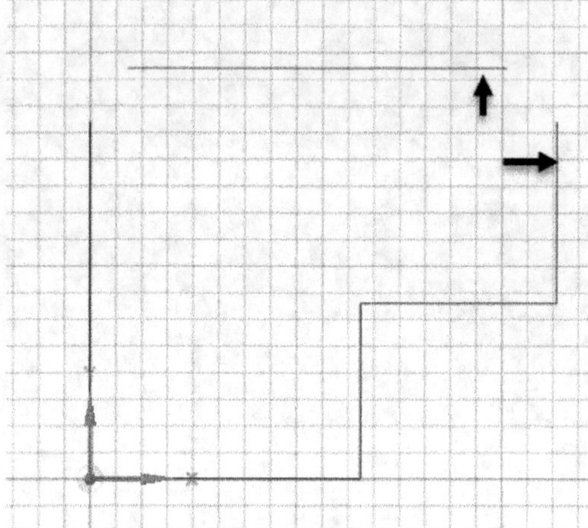

2. Select the elements' ends to be rounded.

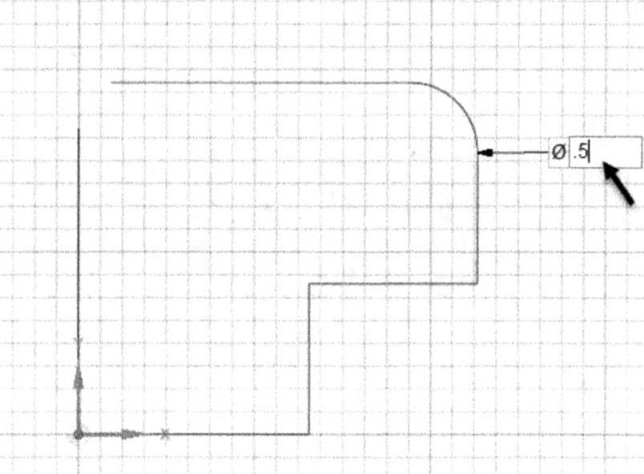

3. Type-in a radius value in the **Radius** box and press Enter. The elements to be rounded are not required to touch each other.

Chapter 5: Additional Modeling Tools

In this chapter, you create models using additional modeling tools. You will learn to:

- Create Slots
- Create circular patterns
- Create holes
- Create chamfers
- Create shells
- Create a loft

TUTORIAL 1

In this tutorial, you create the model shown in the figure:

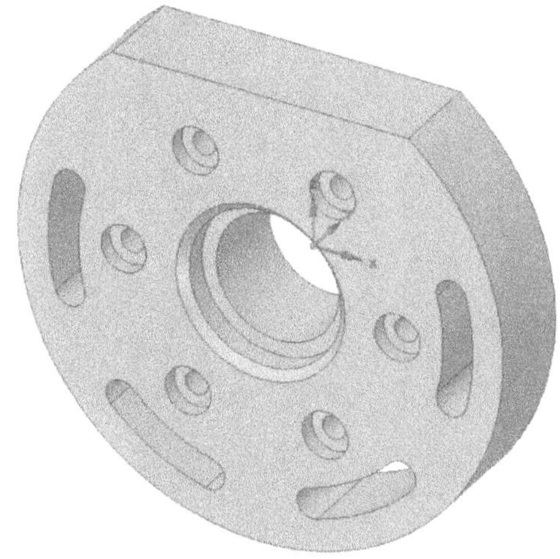

Creating the Base

1. Click **File > New > Design** on the ribbon.

2. Click the **Select New Sketch Plane** icon on the toolbar located on the bottom of the graphics area.

3. Click on the first quadrant to select the XZ Plane.

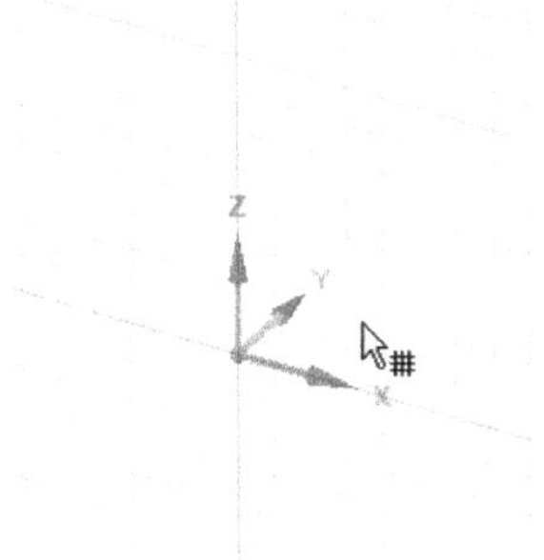

4. On the ribbon, click **Design > Orient > Plan View** to change the view orientation to the sketch plane.
5. Click **Design > Sketch > Circle** on the ribbon.
6. Select the origin point of the sketch.
7. Move the pointer outward and click.
8. Type-in 1.26 in the box and press Enter.

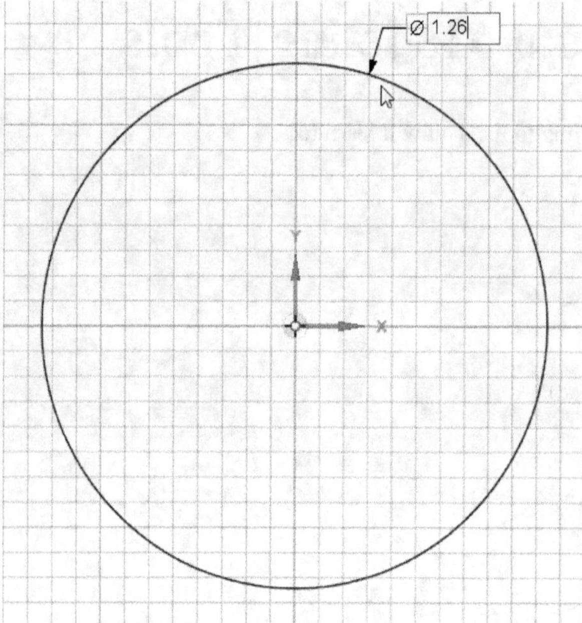

9. Click the **Line** button.
10. Select the left quadrant point of the circle.
11. Move the pointer horizontally toward the right and select the right quadrant point of the circle.

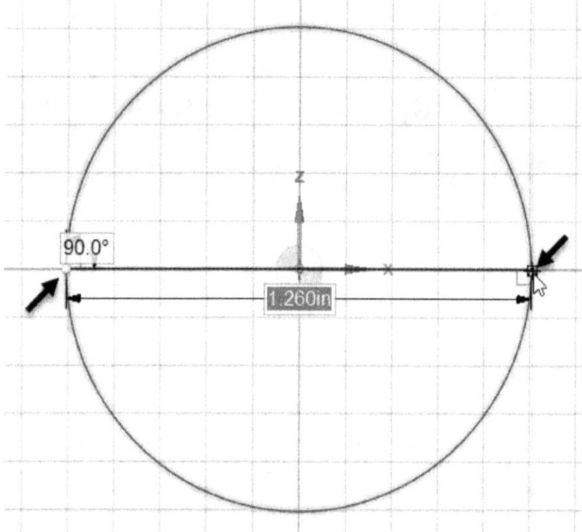

12. Click **Design > Sketch > Offset Curve**.

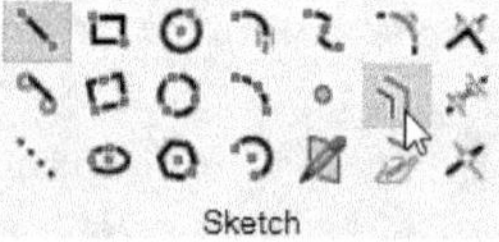

13. Select the horizontal line.
14. Move the pointer upward.
15. Type 0.5 and press ENTER.

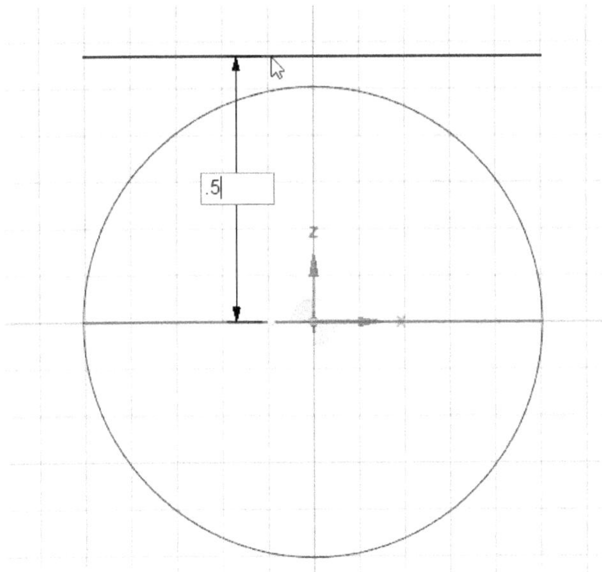

16. On the Ribbon, click **Design > Sketch > Trim** .
17. Click on the portions of the sketch to trim, as shown below.

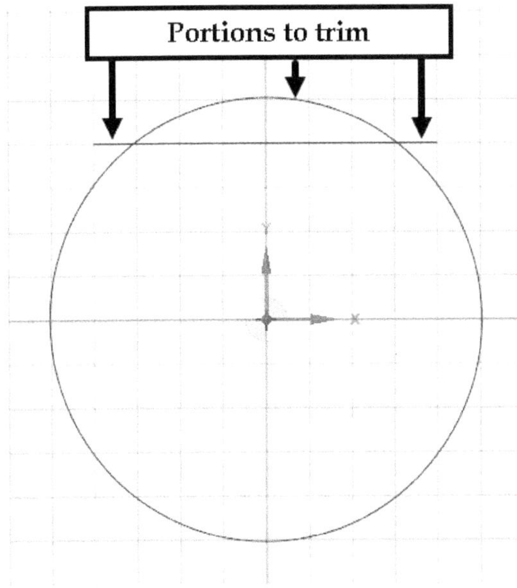

18. Select the horizontal line passing through the center, and then press Delete.

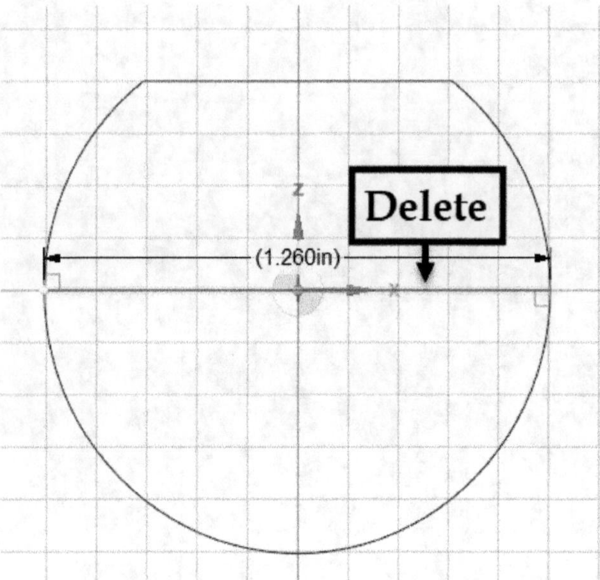

19. Click **Design > Sketch > Sweep Arc** on the ribbon.

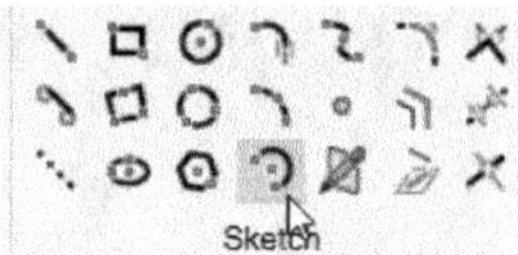

20. Select the origin point of the sketch.
21. Move the pointer toward the top right corner.
22. Type 75 in the angle box and press TAB.
23. Type 1.024 as the diameter and press ENTER.

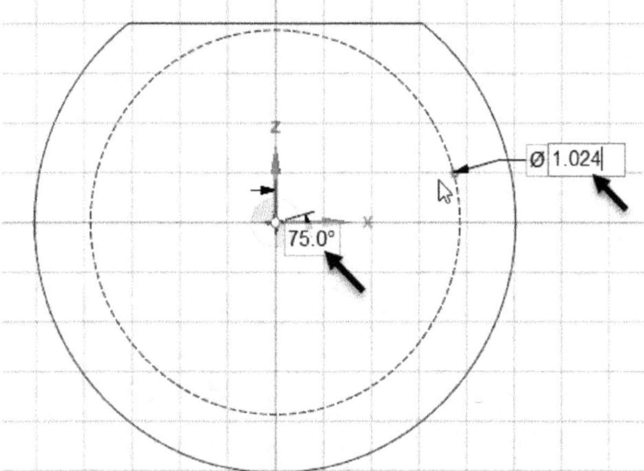

24. Move the pointer downward.
25. Type 30 as the angle, and then press ENTER.

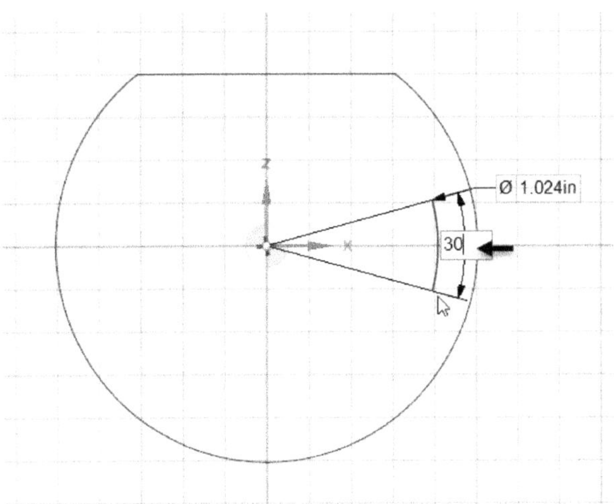

26. Click **Design > Sketch > Offset Curve**.

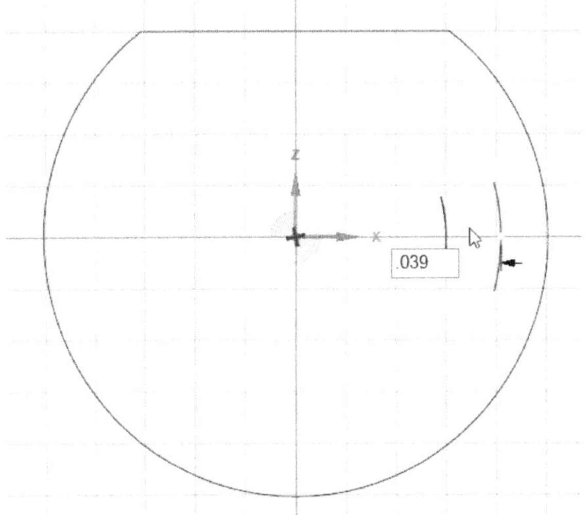

27. Select the arc and move the pointer toward the left.
28. Type 0.039, and press ENTER.

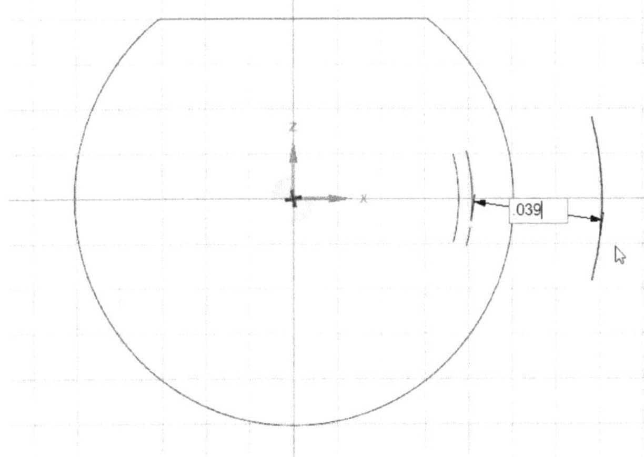

29. Select the original arc and move the pointer toward the right.
30. Type 0.039, and press ENTER.

31. Click **Design > Sketch > Tangent Arc** on the ribbon.

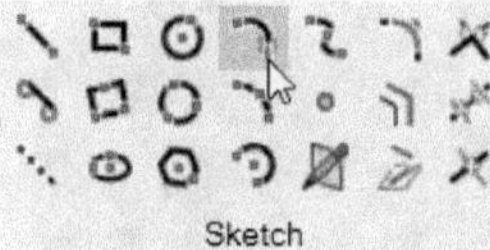

32. Select the upper endpoint of the left arc.

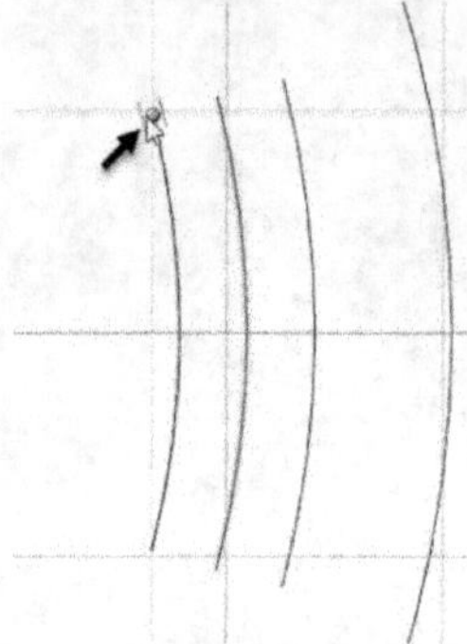

33. Move the pointer toward the right and select the upper-end point of the right arc.

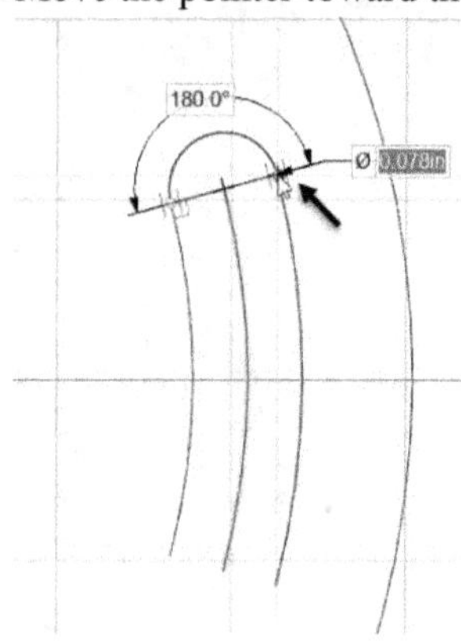

34. Likewise, create a tangent arc by selecting the lower endpoints of the left and right arcs.

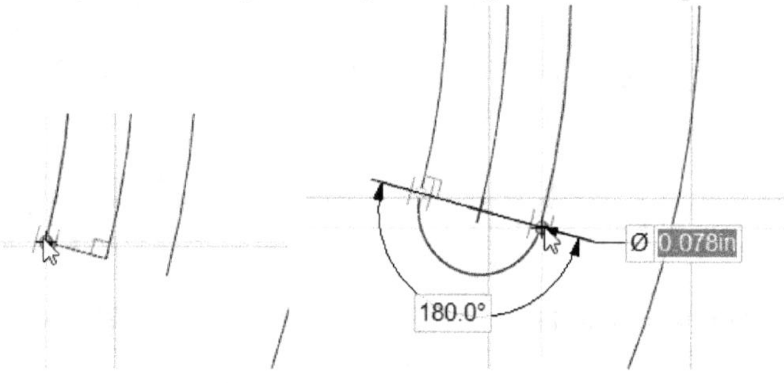

35. Select the center arc and right click.
36. Select **Construction On/Off**.
37. Press Esc.

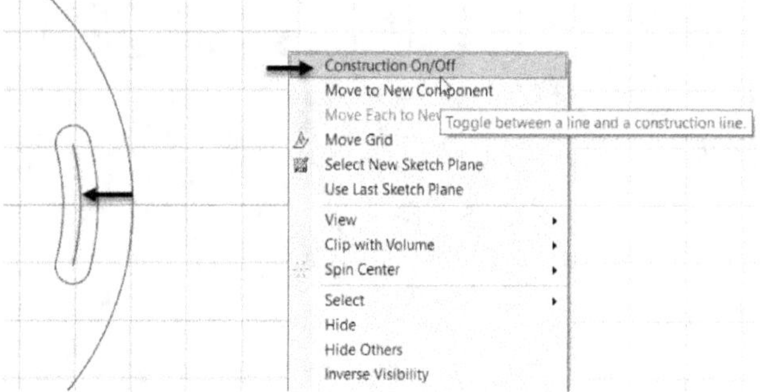

38. Click **Design > Edit > Move** on the ribbon.
39. Click inside the sketch.
40. Press and hold the left mouse button and drag the pointer across the arcs, as shown.

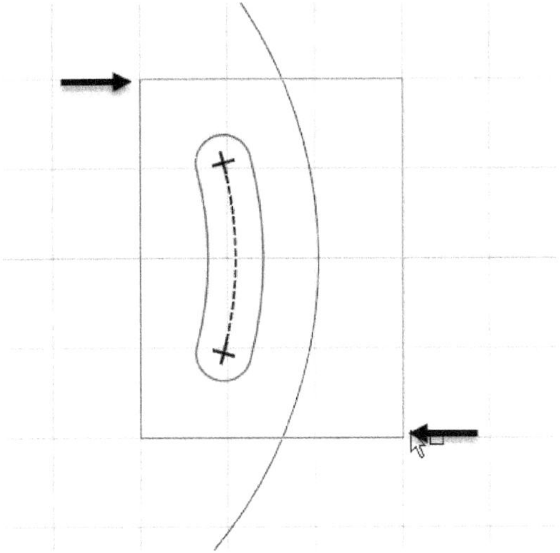

41. Release the left mouse button; the entities inside the selection window are selected.
42. Click the **Anchor** icon on the top-left corner of the graphics area.

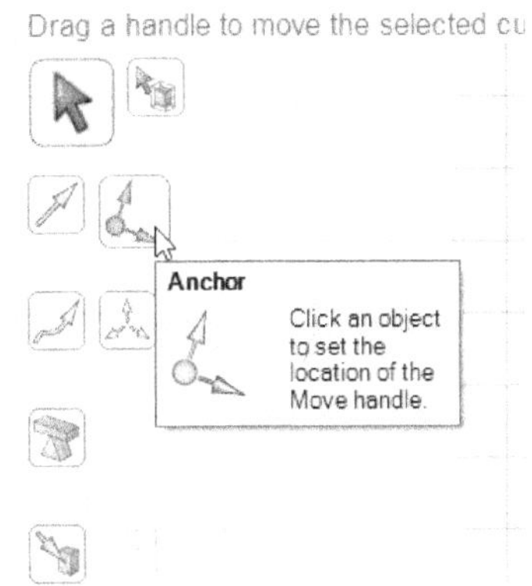

43. Select the origin point of the sketch to define the anchor point.

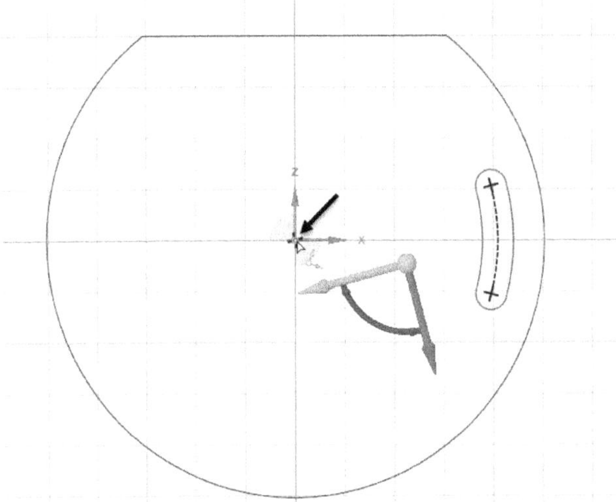

44. Check the **Create patterns** option on the **Options – Move** panel.

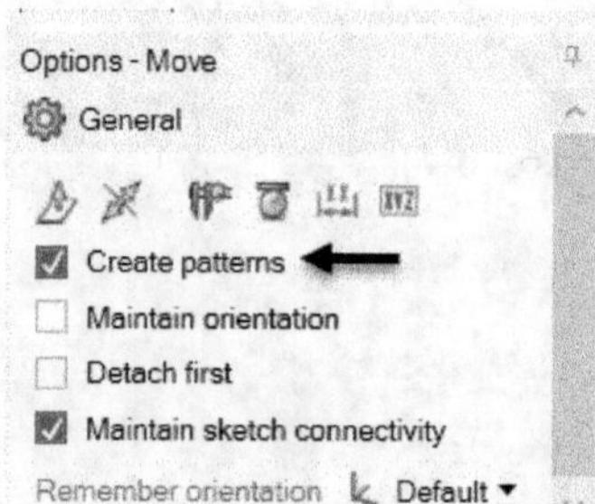

45. Press and hold the left mouse button on the blue rotate handle.
46. Drag the blue rotate handle of the triad toward left.

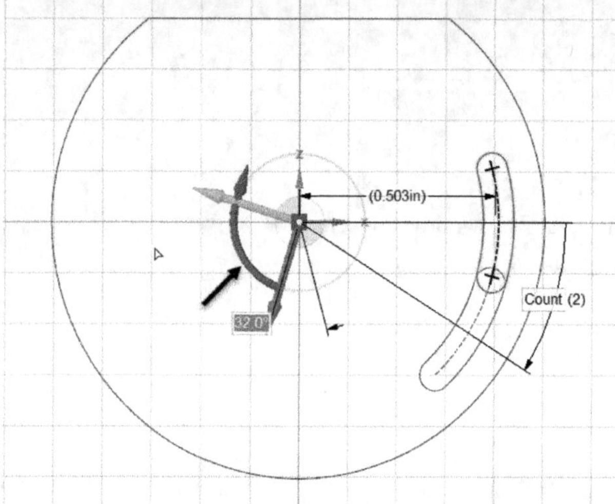

47. Release the pointer.
48. Type 4 in the Count box.
49. Press TAB and type 60 in the angle box.

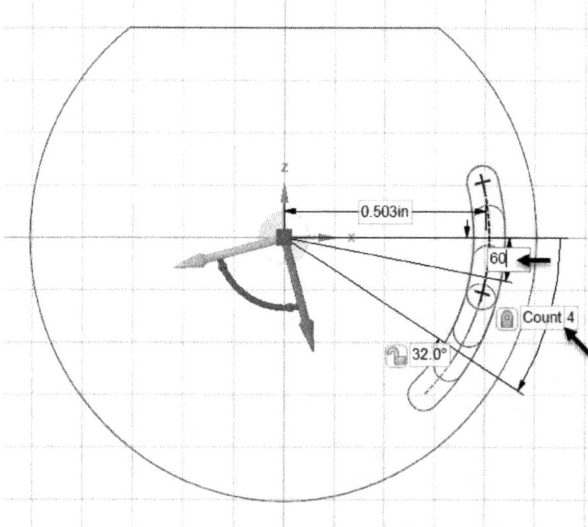

50. Press ENTER.

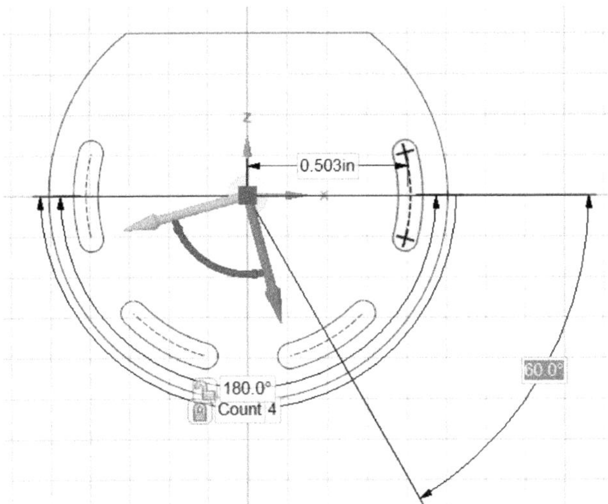

51. Click in the graphics area to deselect the pattern.
52. Click **Design > Mode > 3D Mode** on the ribbon.
53. Click **Design > Orient > Home** on the ribbon.
54. Click **Design > Edit > Pull** on the ribbon.
55. Click in the region enclosed by the sketch.

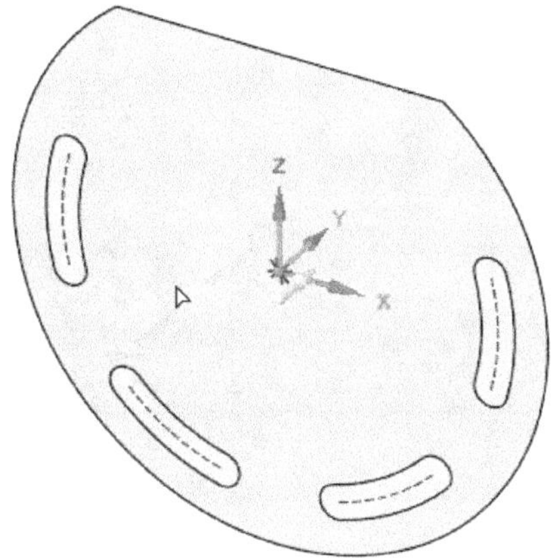

56. Press and hold the left mouse button and drag the pointer toward left.
57. Release the pointer.
58. Type 0.236 in the extrude distance box and then press ENTER.

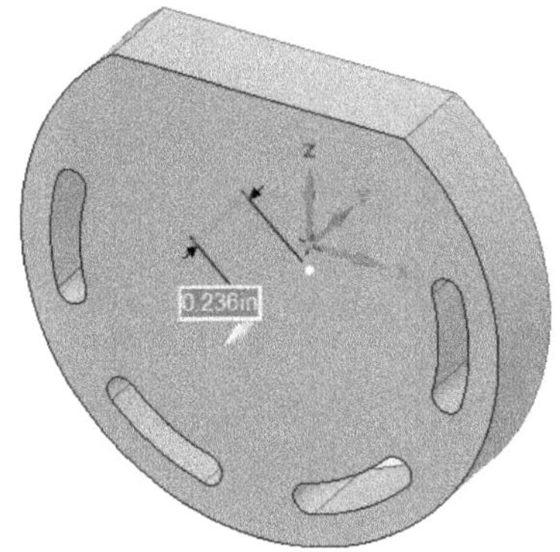

59. Click in the graphics area, and then press ENTER.

Adding an Extrusion to the Base

1. Create a sketch on the back face of the model (use the **Spin** tool available at the bottom right corner of

the window to rotate the model).

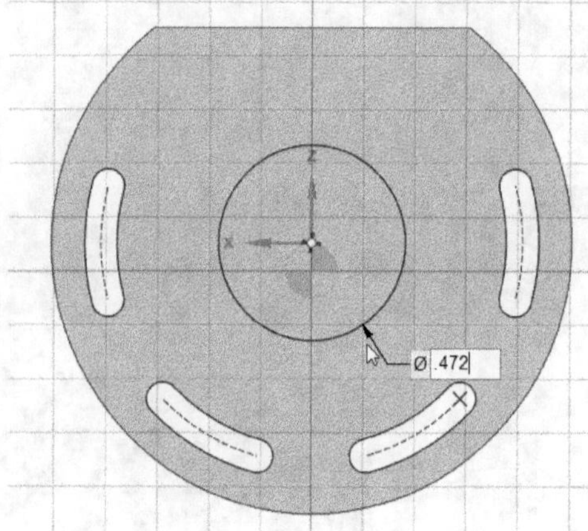

2. Extrude the sketch up to 0.078 distance.

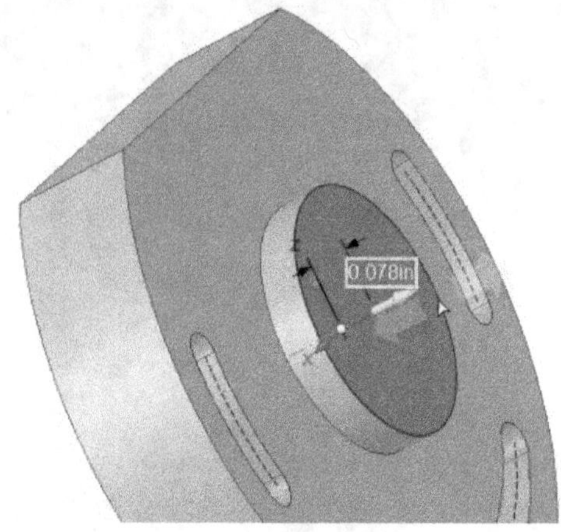

Creating a Counterbore Hole

In this section, you create a counterbore hole concentric to the circular face.

1. Click **Design > Mode > Sketch** on the ribbon.
2. Click on the Y-axis of the coordinate system.

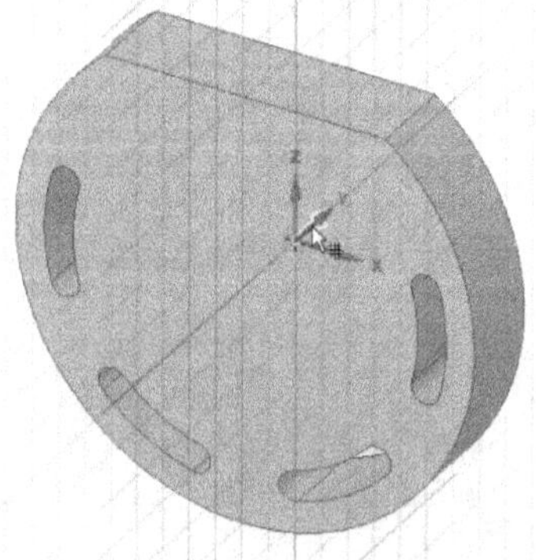

3. Click **Design > Sketch > Line** on the ribbon.
4. Specify the start point of the line, as shown.
5. Move the pointer vertically upward.
6. Type 0.196, and press ENTER.

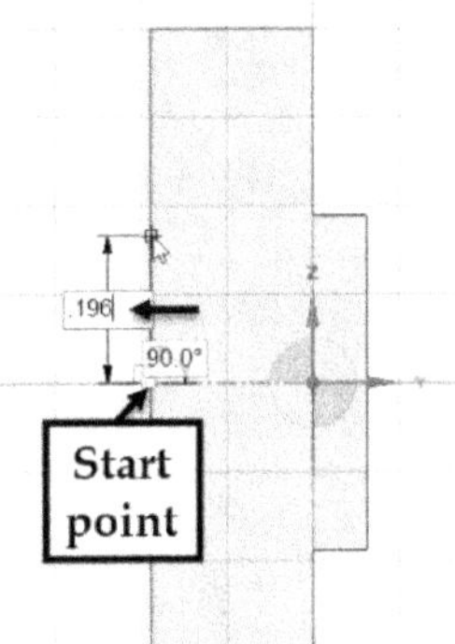

7. Move the pointer horizontally toward the right.
8. Type 0.078, and press ENTER.

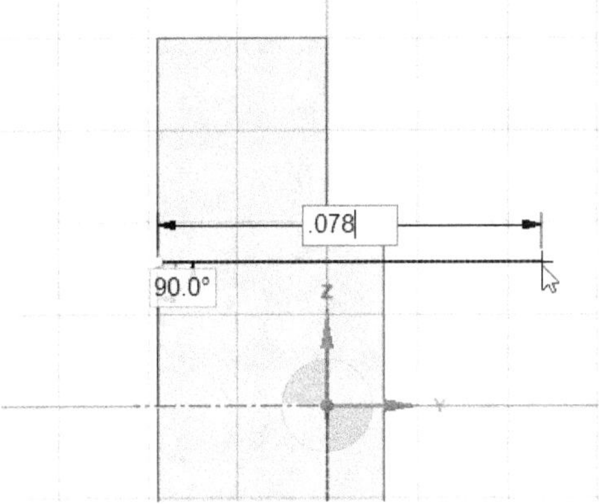

9. Move the pointer vertically downward.
10. Type 0.038, and press ENTER.

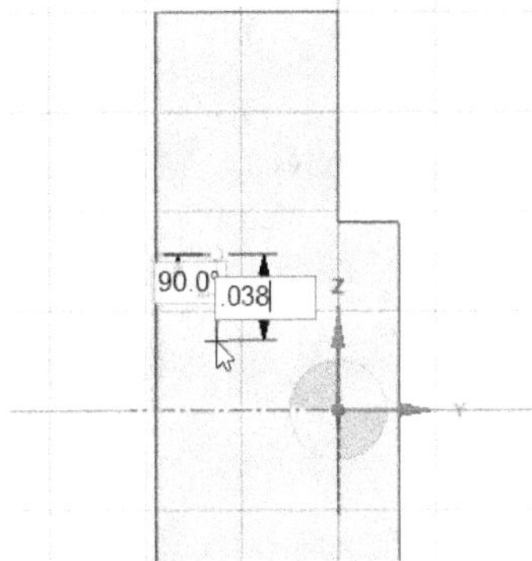

11. Move the pointer horizontally toward the right and click on the edge, as shown.

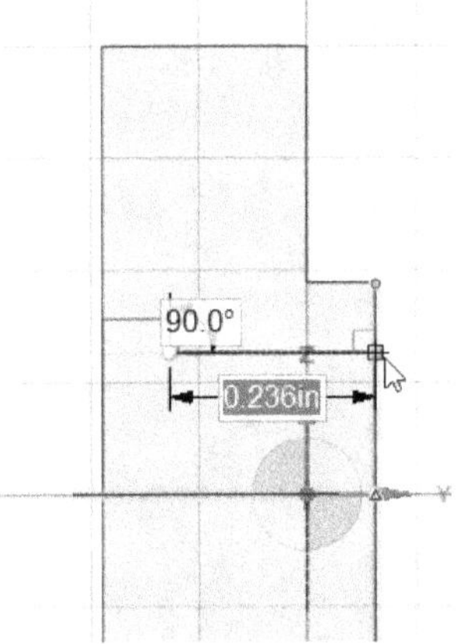

12. Move the pointer vertically downward and select the midpoint of the edge, as shown.

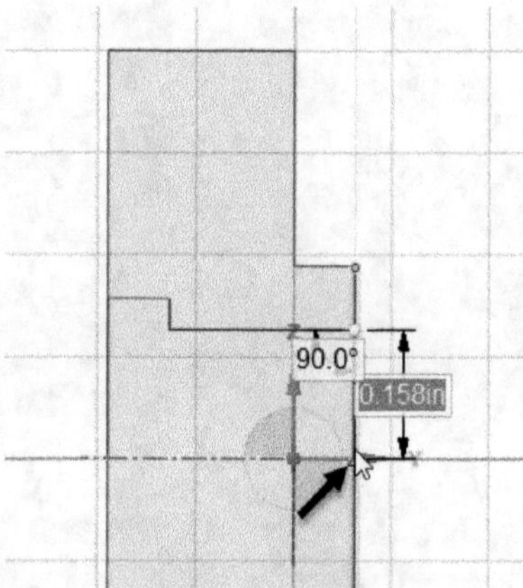

13. Move the pointer horizontally toward the left and select the start point of the sketch.

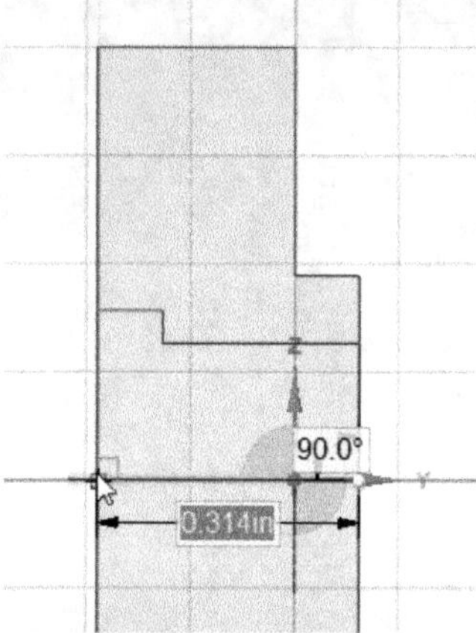

14. Click **Design > Mode > 3D Mode** on the ribbon.

15. Click **Design > Orient > Home** on the ribbon.

16. Click **Design > Edit > Pull** on the ribbon.

17. Select the third surface from the **Structure** panel; the newly created sketch is highlighted.

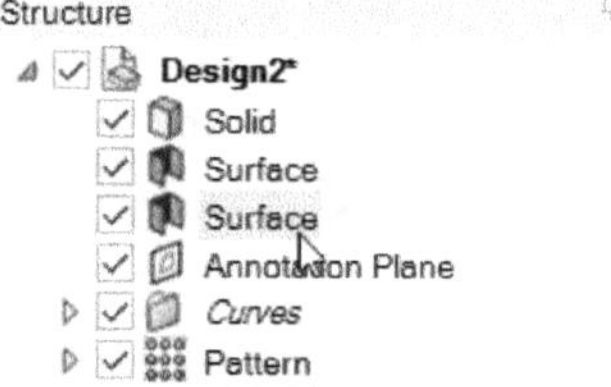

18. Click the **Revolve** icon at the top-left corner of the graphics area.

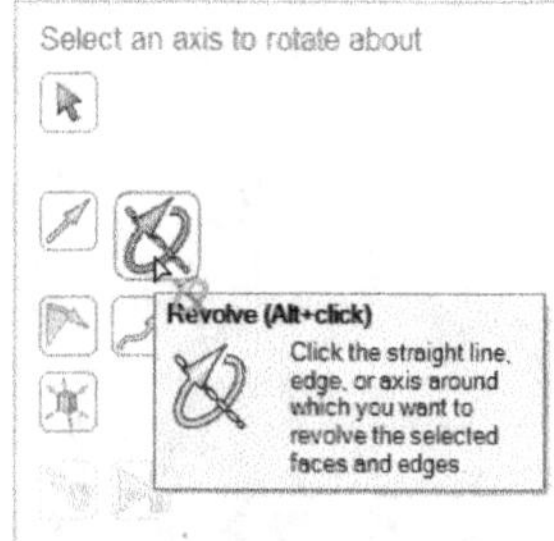

19. Click the **Cut** icon on the **Option – Pull** panel.

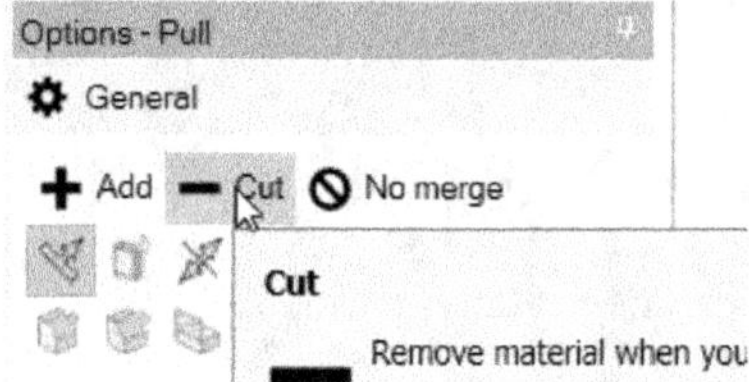

20. Select the centerline, as shown.

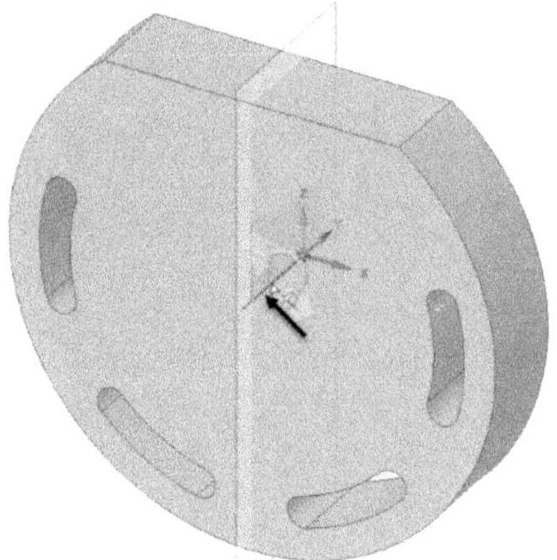

21. Click and drag the pointer toward the left.
22. Release the pointer and type 360.

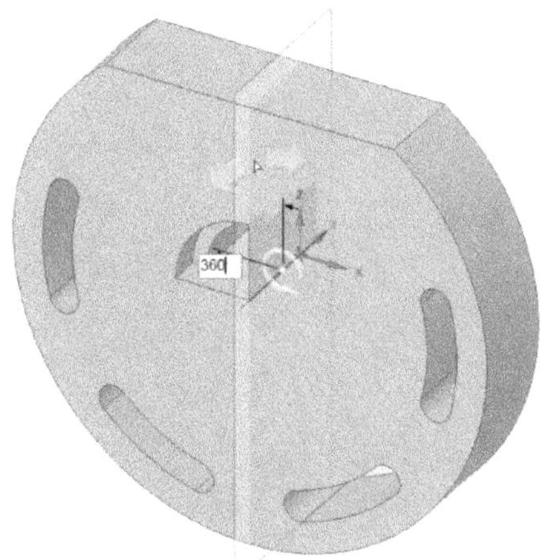

23. Press ENTER to create the revolved cut.

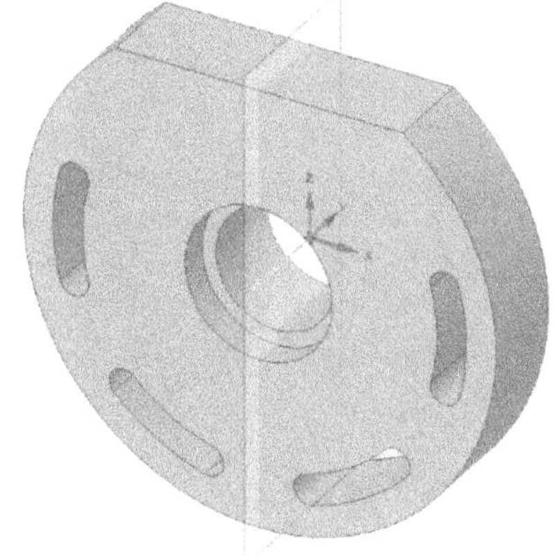

24. Click **Design > Mode > Sketch Mode** on the ribbon.
25. Select the front face of the model.
26. Click **Design > Orient > Plan view** on the ribbon.
27. Click **Design > Sketch > Circle** on the ribbon.
28. Uncheck the **Snap grid** option on the **Options – Sketch** panel located at the bottom left corner.

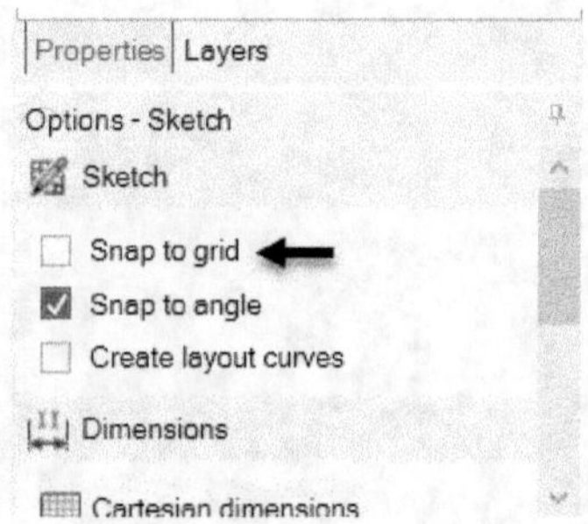

29. On the **Options - Sketch** panel, scroll to the **Dimensions** section and then select the **Cartesian dimension** option.

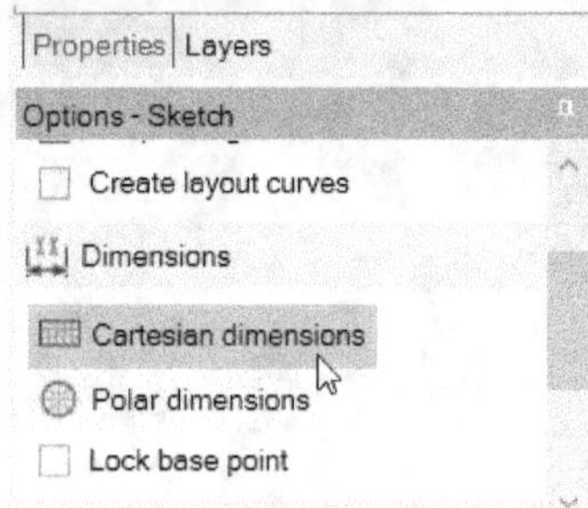

30. Select the origin point of the coordinate system; the base point is defined.
31. Move the pointer horizontally along the X-axis.
32. Press the Tab key and type -0.354 in the dimension box. Next, press ENTER.

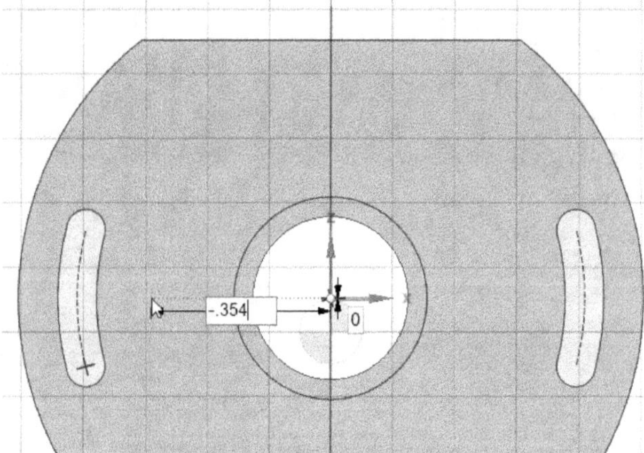

33. Type 0.059 and press ENTER; the circle is created.

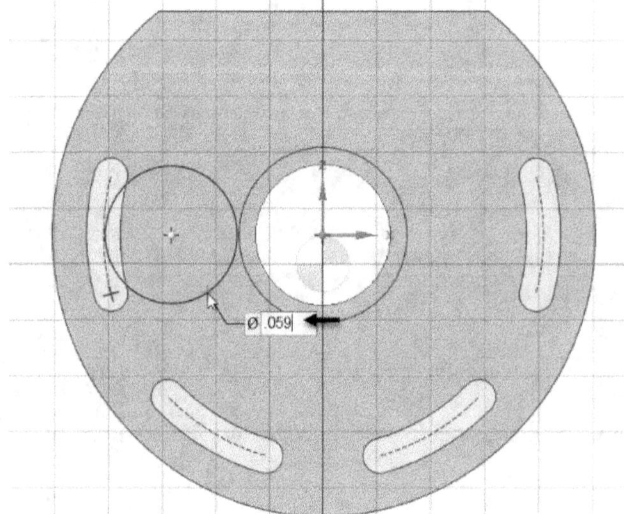

34. Select the centerpoint of the newly created circle.

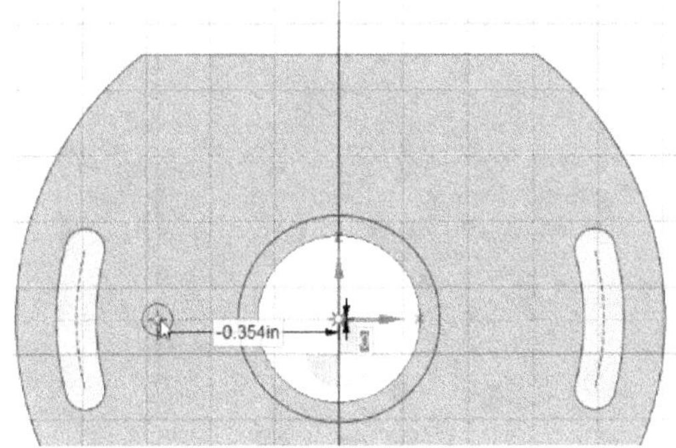

35. Type 0.118 and press ENTER; another circle is created.

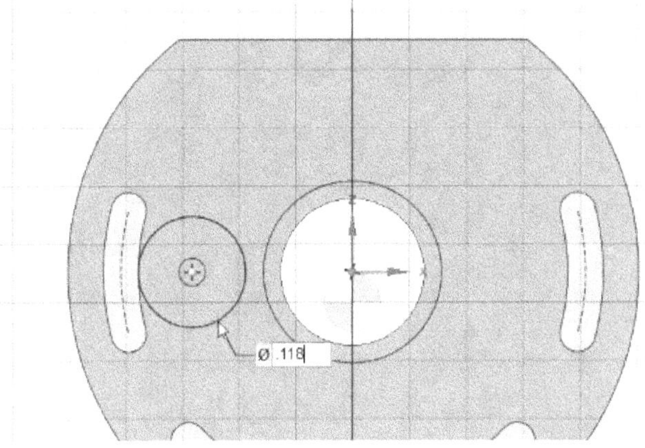

36. Click **Design > Mode > 3D Mode** on the ribbon.
37. Click **Design > Orient > Home** on the ribbon.
38. Click **Design > Edit > Pull** on the ribbon.
39. Click in the region enclosed by the small circle.

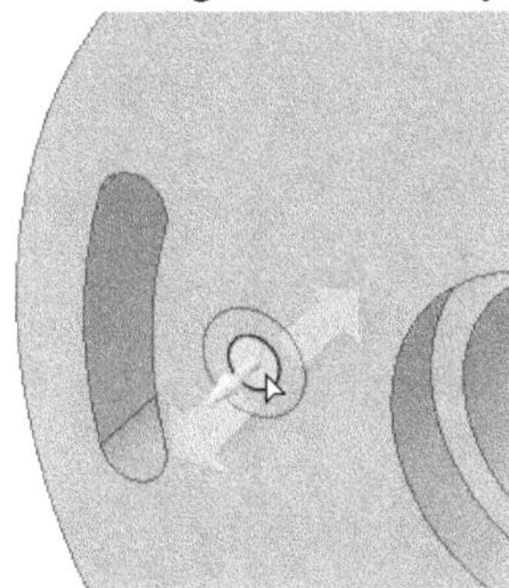

40. Click the **Cut** icon on the **Options – Pull** panel.
41. Click and drag the left mouse button toward the right.
42. Type 0.236, and press ENTER.

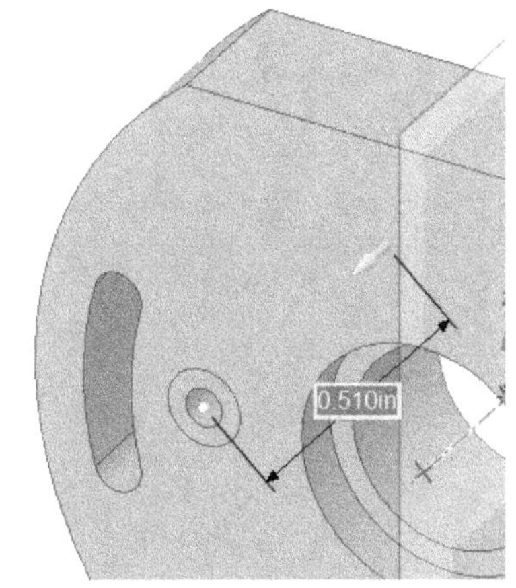

43. Click in the graphics area
44. Click in the region enclosed by the small circle.

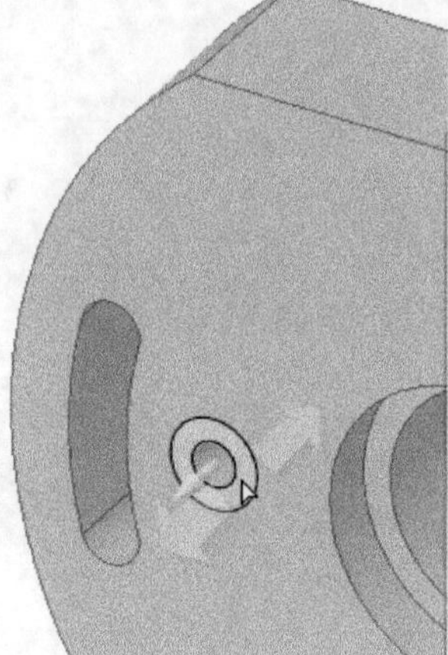

45. Click the **Cut** icon on the **Options – Pull** panel.
46. Click and drag the left mouse button toward the right.
47. Type 0.04 and press ENTER.

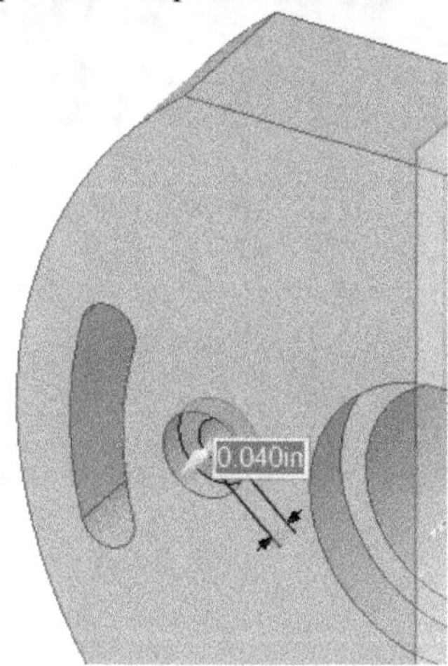

48. Click in the graphics area.

Creating a Circular Pattern

1. On the ribbon, click **Design > Edit > Move**.
2. Select the face of the hole, as shown.

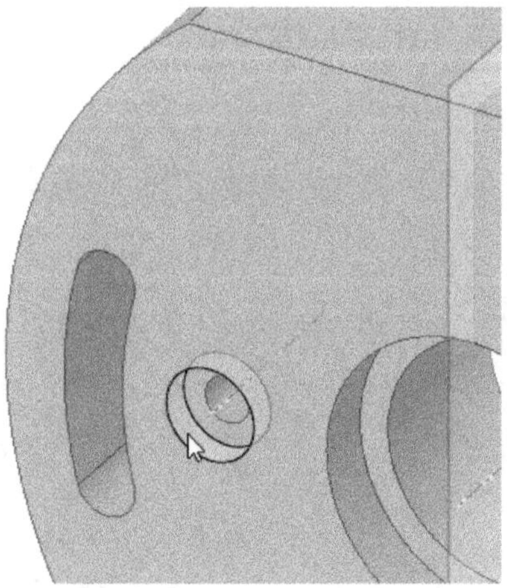

3. On the **Options** panel, click the **Selection** tab.
4. Select **Coaxial Face > Coaxial surfaces**.

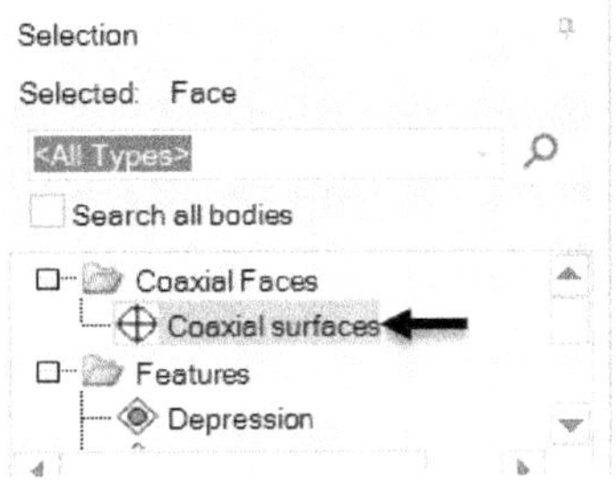

5. Click the **Options – Move** tab.
6. Check the **Create patterns** option.

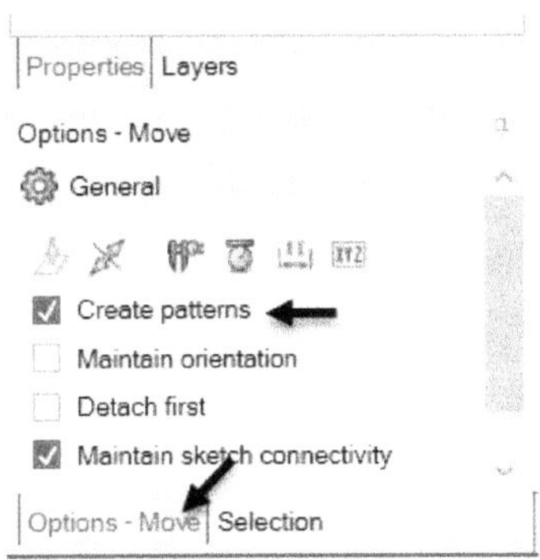

7. Click the **Anchor** icon on the top-left corner of the graphics window.

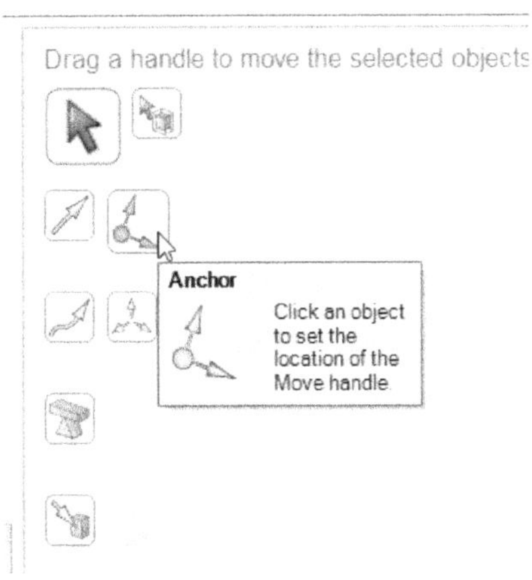

8. Select the circular edge of the hole, as shown.

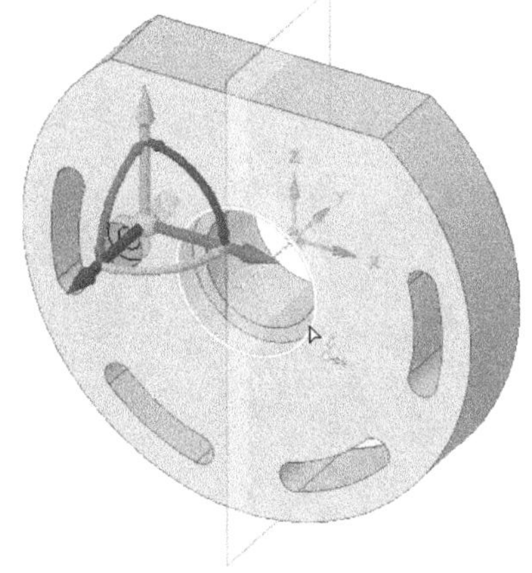

9. Click and drag the blue color rotate handle of the triad.

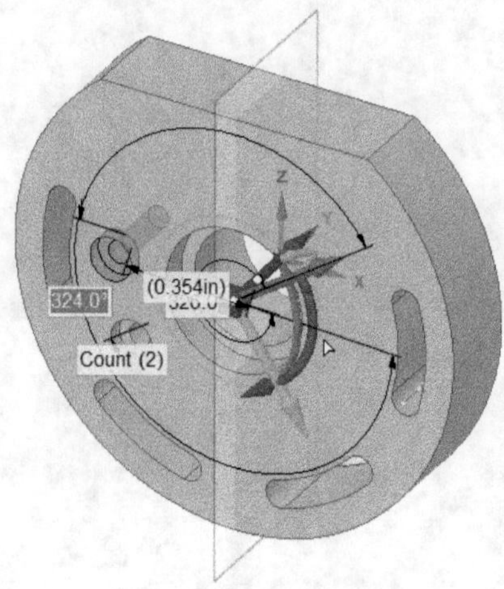

10. Release the mouse button, and then click in the graphics area.
11. Select the **Pattern** from the **Structure** panel.
12. Enter 60 and 6 in the **Angle** and **Count** boxes of the **Properties** panel.

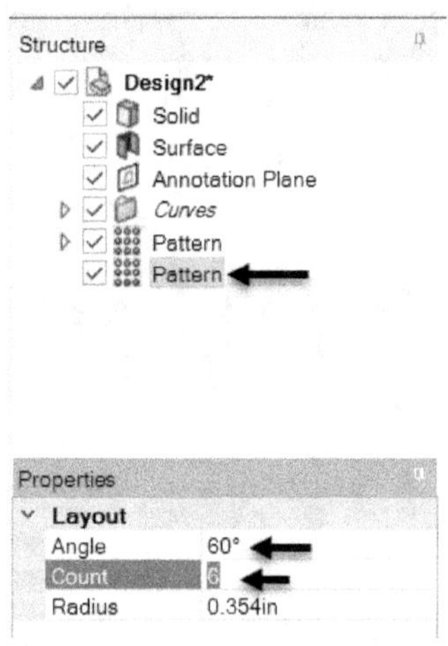

13. Click in the graphics area to create a circular pattern.

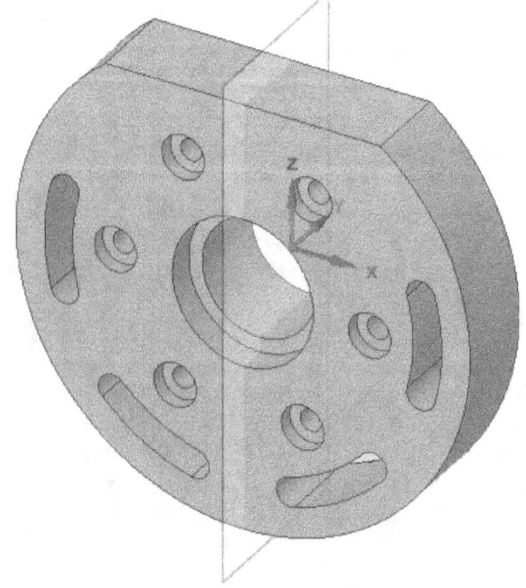

Creating Chamfers

1. Click **Design > Edit > Pull** on the ribbon.

2. Select the circular edge of the counterbore hole.

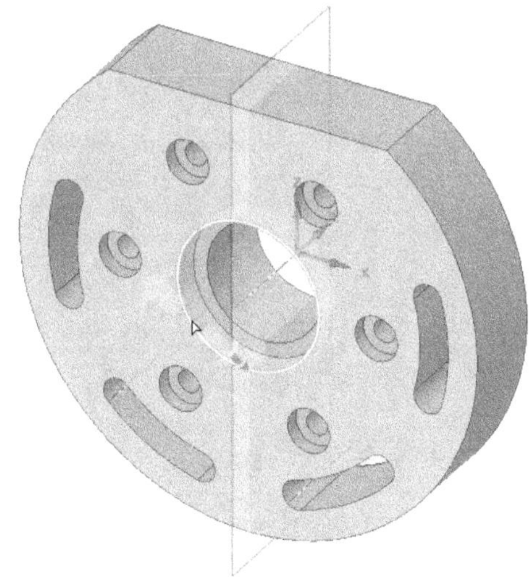

3. Click the **Chamfer** icon on the **Options – Pull** panel.

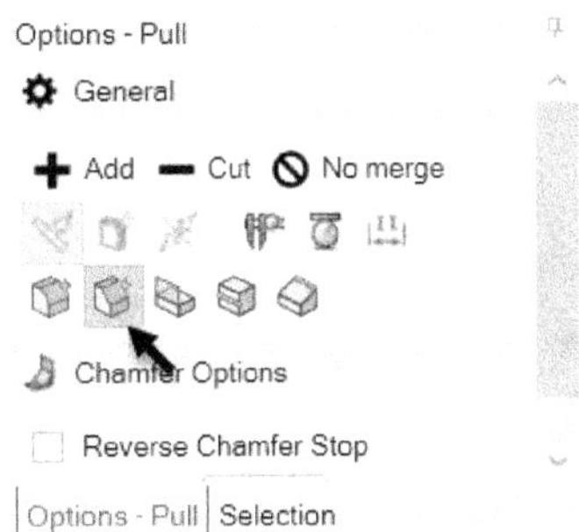

4. Click and drag the left mouse button and then release it.
5. In the **Properties** panel, enter 0.022 in the **Setback#1** box.

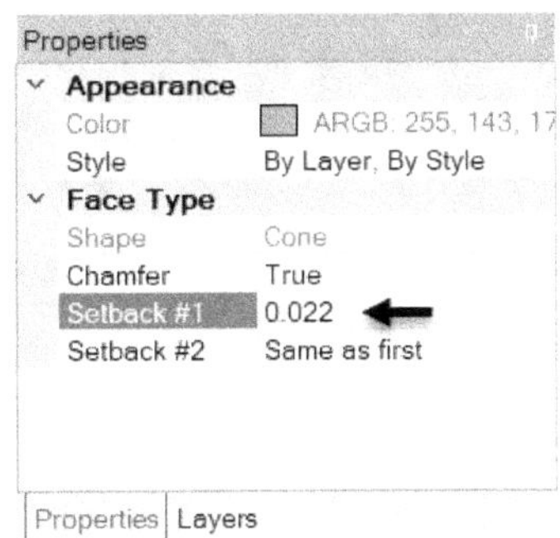

6. Click in the graphics area.

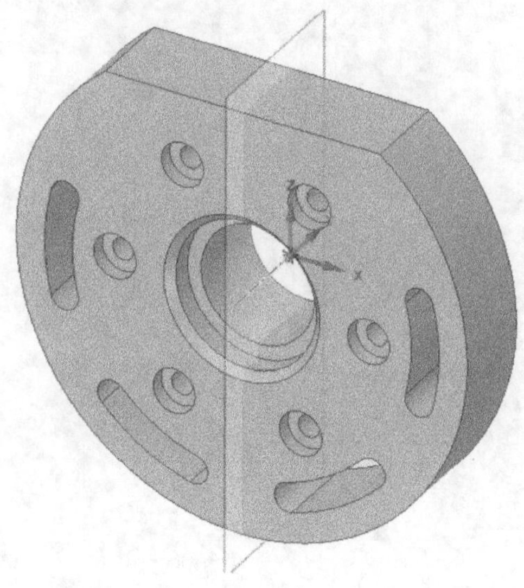

Saving the Part

1.   Click **Save** on the **Quick Access Toolbar**.
2.   On the **Save As** dialog, type-in Ch5_tut1 in the **File name** box.
3.   Click **Save** to save the file.
4.   Click the **Close** icon on the file tab.

TUTORIAL 2

In this tutorial, you create the model shown in the figure.

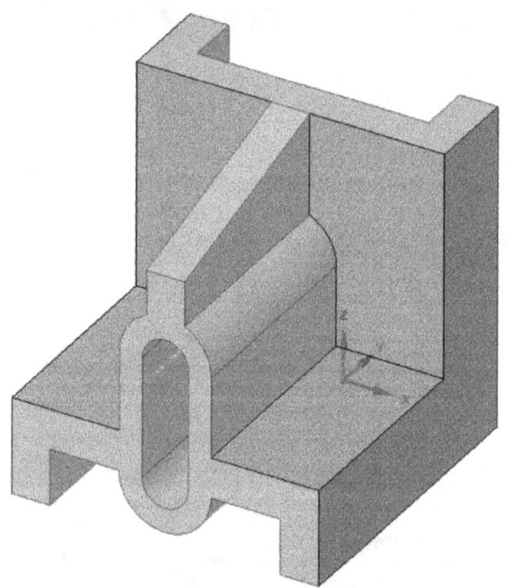

Creating the Base

1.   Click **File > New > Design** on the ribbon.

2.   Click the **Select New Sketch Plane** icon on the Toolbar located at the bottom of the graphics area.
3.   Click on the second quadrant to select the YZ plane.

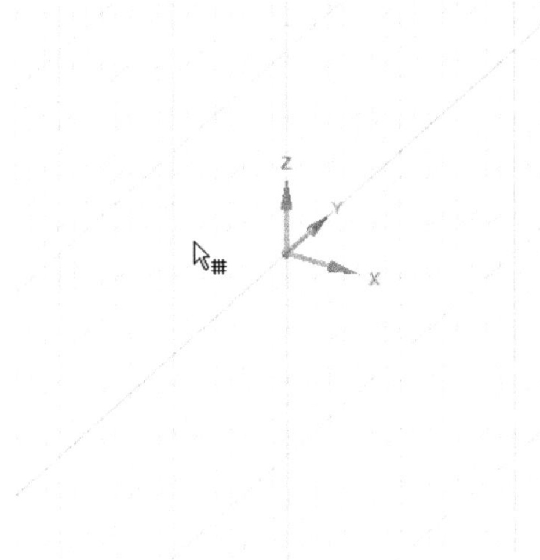

4. On the ribbon, click **Design > Orient > Plan View** to change the view orientation to the sketch plane.

5. Draw an L-shaped sketch using the **Line** tool, as shown (do not add dimensions).

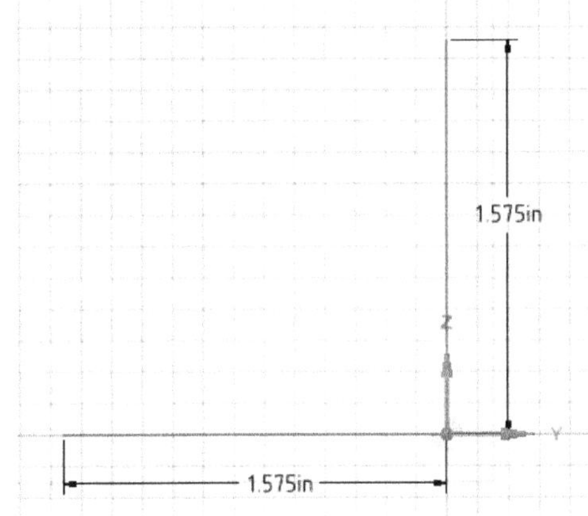

6. On the ribbon, click **Design > Sketch > Offset Curve**.

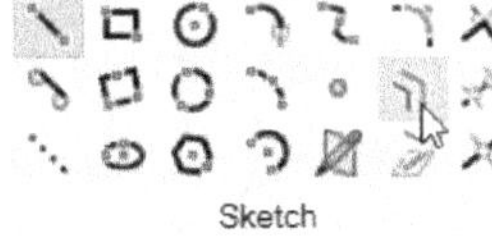

7. Select the horizontal line and move the mouse pointer upward.
8. Type-in **0.472** in the box attached and press Enter.

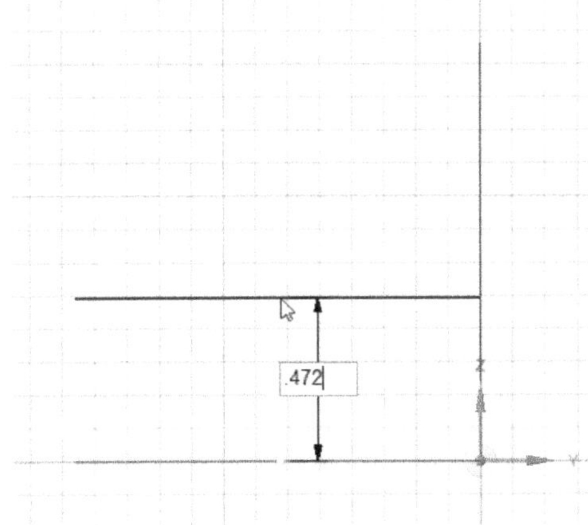

9. Likewise, offset the vertical line up to a distance of 0.472.
10. Click **Design > Sketch > Trim Away** on the ribbon.
11. Click on the portions of the sketch to trim, as shown.

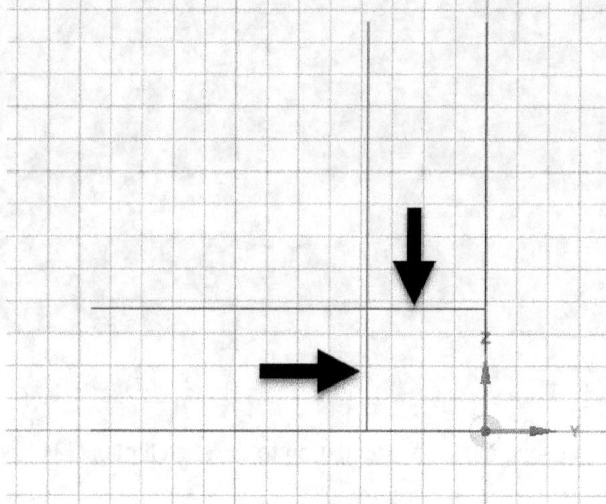

12. Click the **Line** tool and draw lines closing the offset sketch, as shown.

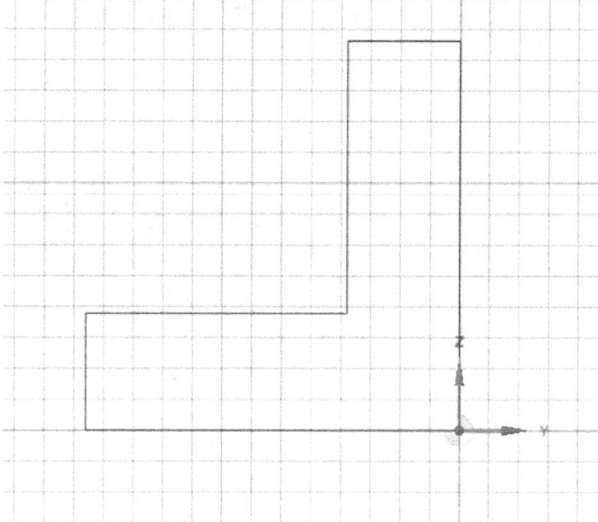

13. Click **Design > Mode > 3D Mode** on the ribbon.
14. Click **Design > Orient > Home** on the ribbon.

15. Click **Design > Edit > Pull** on the ribbon.
16. Click in the region enclosed by the sketch.
17. Click the **Pull Both Sides** icon on the **Options – Pull** panel.
18. Click and drag the left mouse button and then release it.
19. Type-in 0.787 in the box attached to it and press Enter.
20. Press Esc.

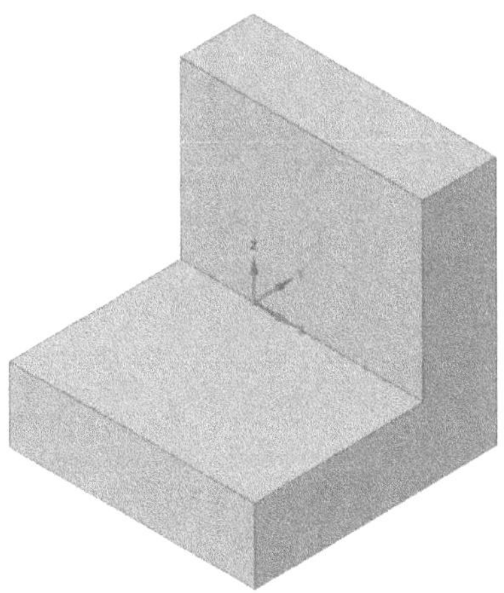

Creating the Shell

You can create a shell by removing the face of the model and applying thickness to other faces.

1. Click **Design > Insert > Shell** on the ribbon.

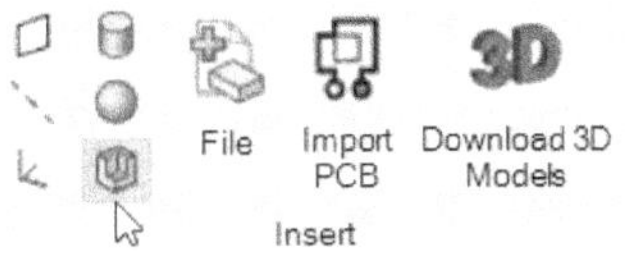

Now, you need to select the faces to remove.

2. Press and hold the Ctrl key and select the faces of the model, as shown.

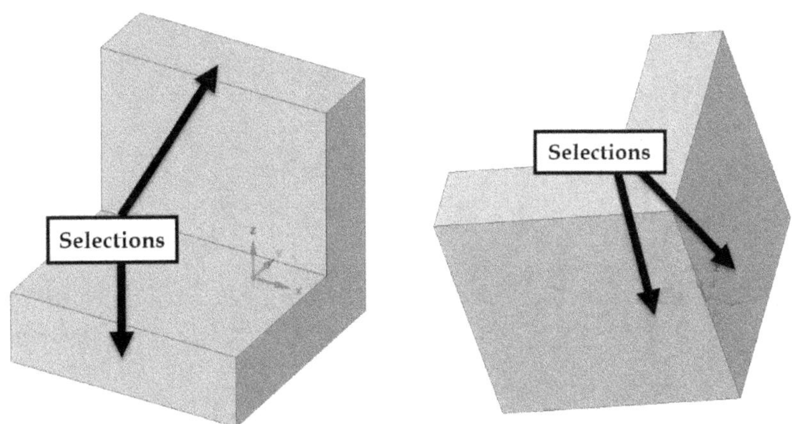

3. Type 0.197 in the thickness box. Next, press ENTER.

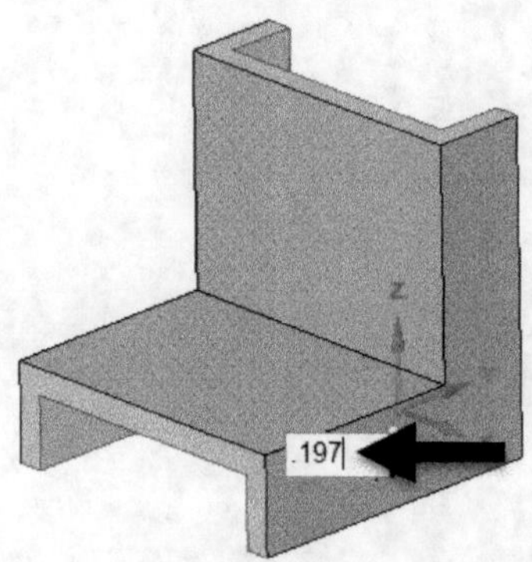

4. Click the **Complete** icon on the top left corner of the graphics area.

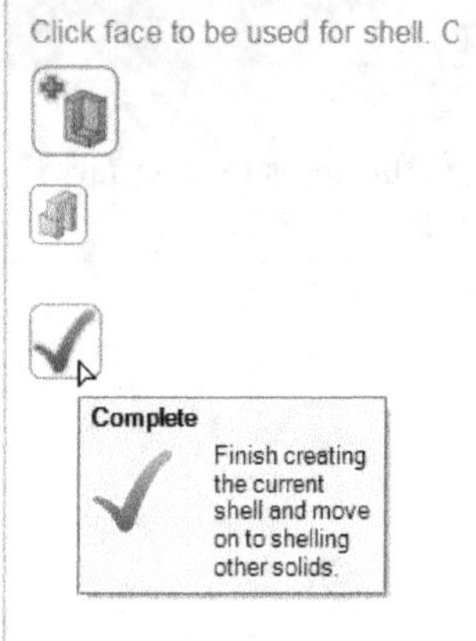

Creating the Third extrusion

1. Click **Design > Mode > Sketch Mode** icon on the ribbon.
2. Select the front face of the model.

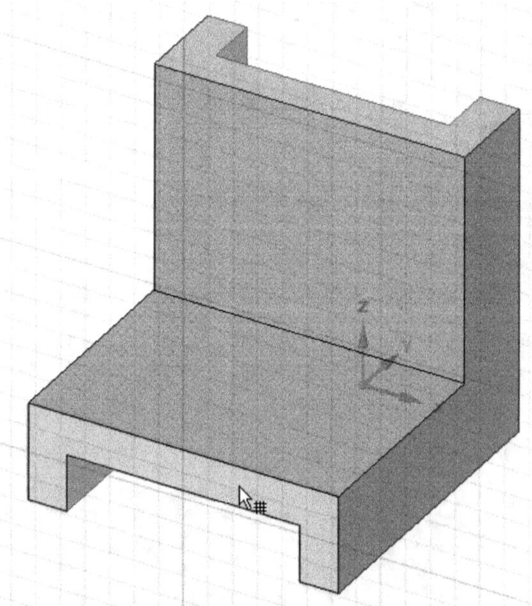

3. Select the midpoint of the horizontal edge of the model, as shown.
4. Move the pointer horizontally toward the right.
5. Type 0.472, and press ENTER.

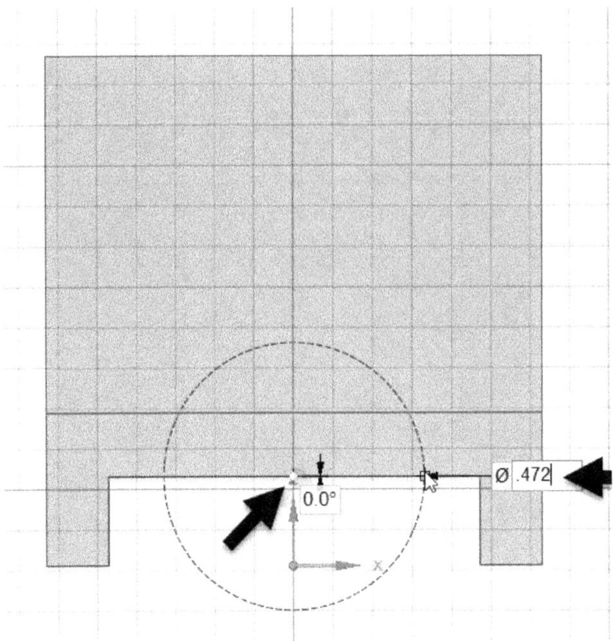

6. Move the pointer horizontally toward right and type 0.472 in the diameter box.
7. Press ENTER.
8. Move the pointer horizontally toward left and click to create an arc.

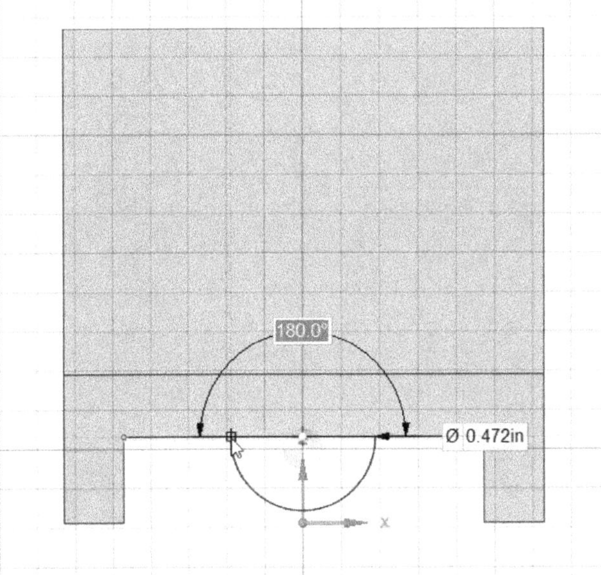

9. Click **Design > Sketch > Tangent Line** on the ribbon.
10. Select the endpoint of the arc, and then move the pointer vertically upward.
11. Type 0.59 and press ENTER.

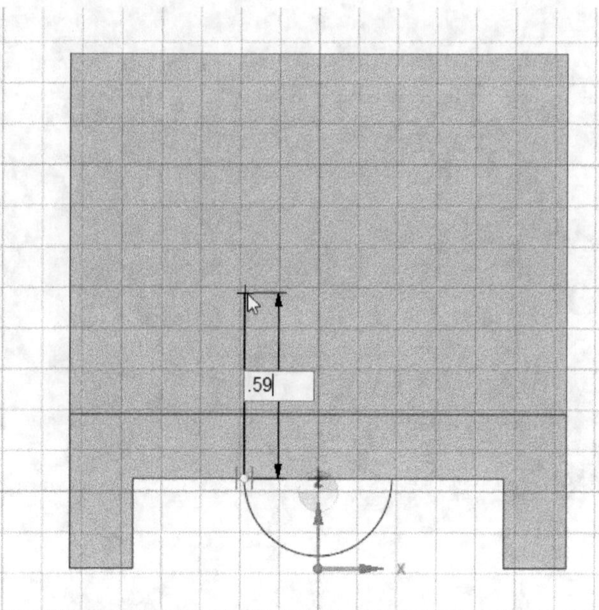

12. Select another endpoint of the arc.
13. Move the pointer upward and type 0.59.

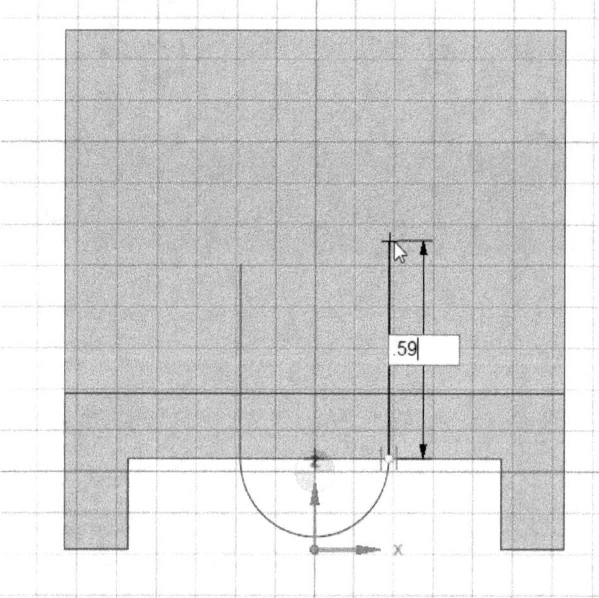

14. On the ribbon, click **Design > Sketch > Tangent Arc**.

15. Select the endpoint of the left line.
16. Move the pointer toward the right and select the endpoint of the right line.

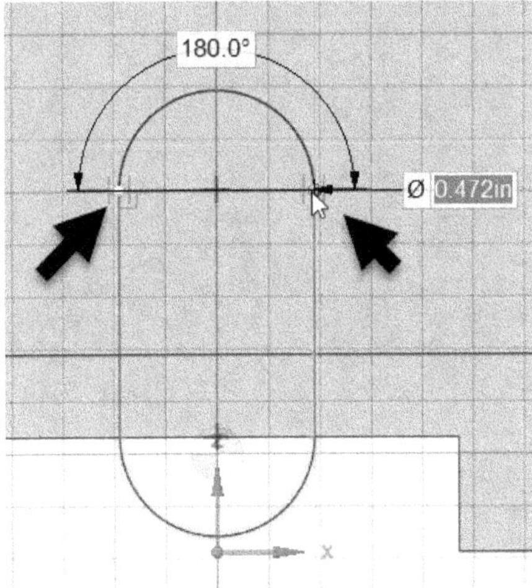

17. Click **Design > Edit > Pull** on the ribbon.
18. Click the **Add** icon on the **Options – Pull** panel.
19. Press and hold the Ctrl key.
20. Click in the three regions of the sketch.

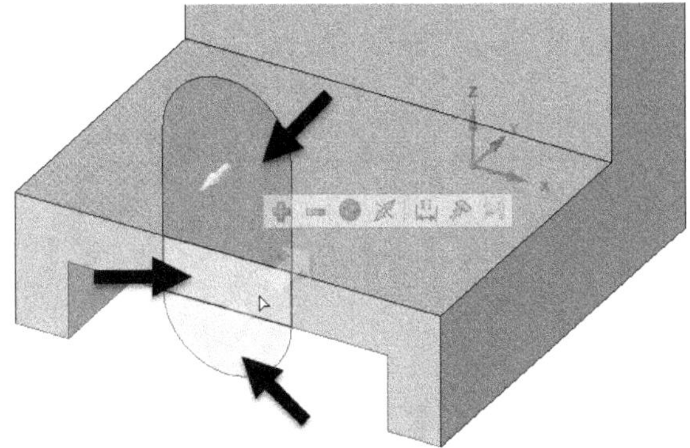

21. Click the **Up To** icon on the top-left corner of the graphics area.

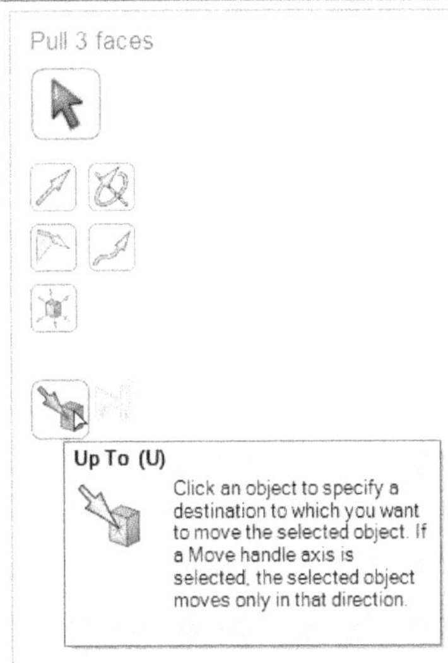

22. Press and hold the middle mouse button, and then drag the pointer.
23. Select the back face.

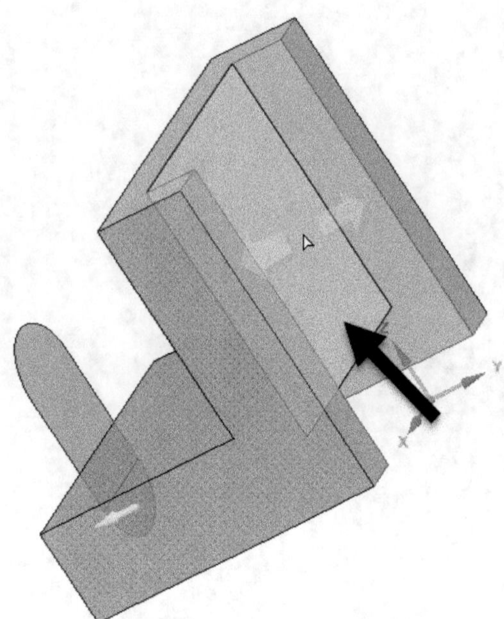

Creating a Cutout

1. Start a sketch on the front face of the model.

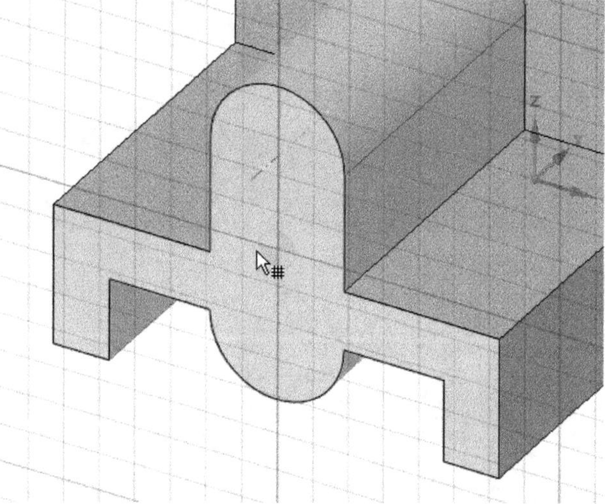

2. Create a vertical slot.

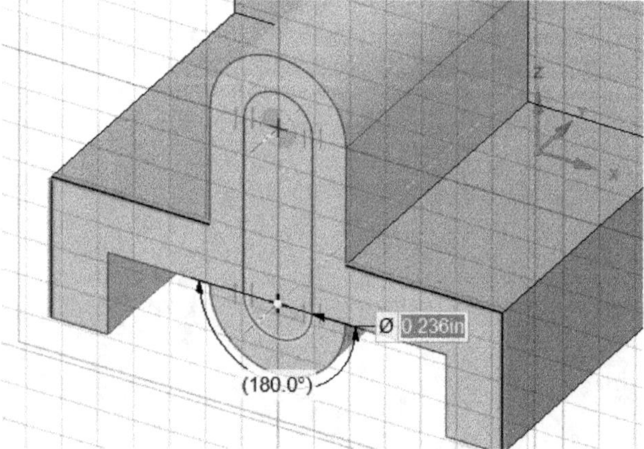

3. Click **Design > Edit > Pull** on the ribbon.
4. Click in the region enclosed by the sketch.
5. Select the **Cut** option from the toolbar.

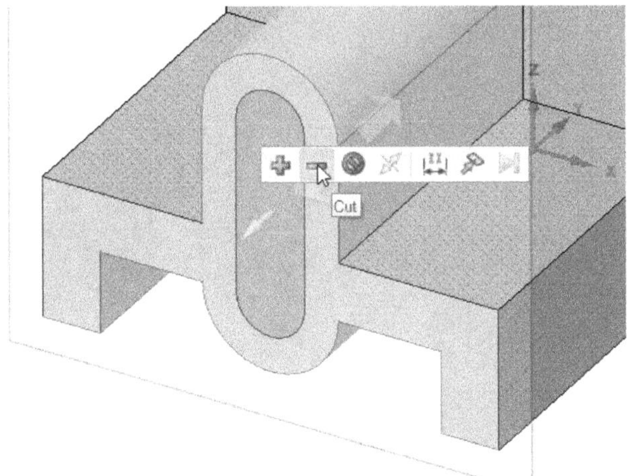

6. Click and drag the left mouse button into the model.
7. Release the left mouse button.

Creating the Rib

In this section, you create a rib in the middle of the model.

1. Click **Design > Mode > Sketch Mode** on the ribbon
2. Select the Z-axis of the coordinate system.

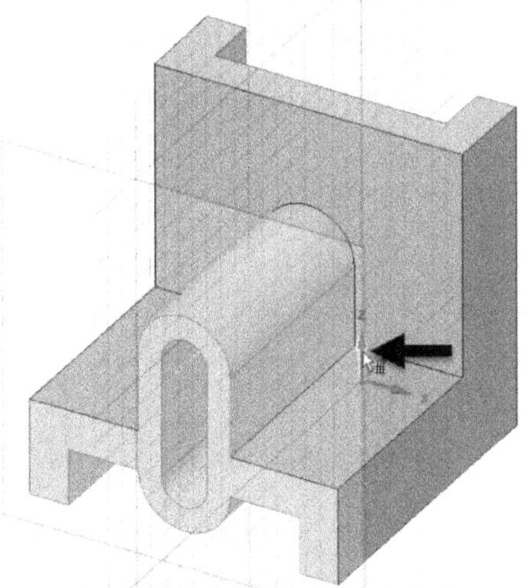

3. Click **Design > Sketch > Line** on the ribbon.
4. Draw the sketch, as shown below.

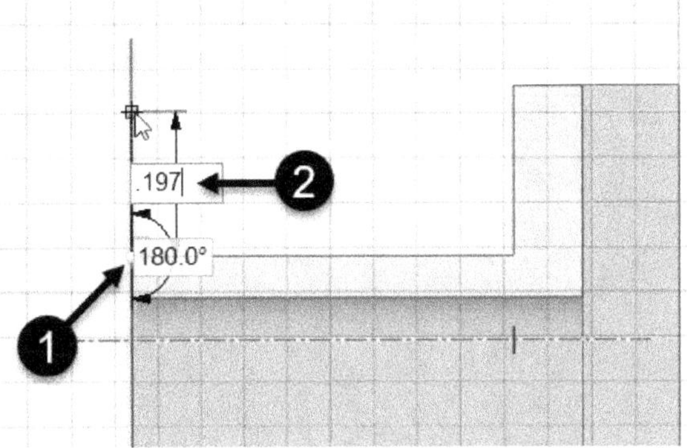
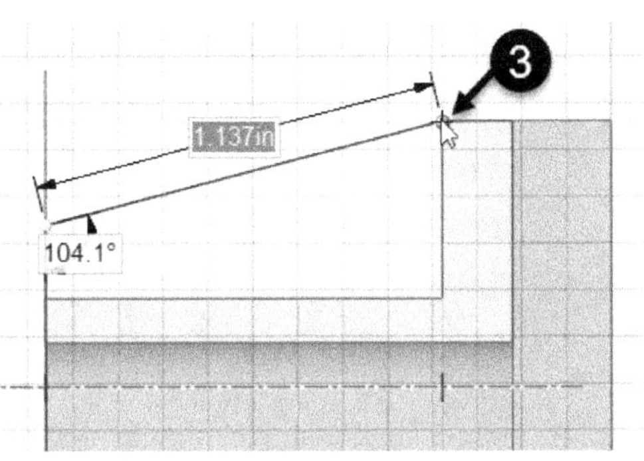

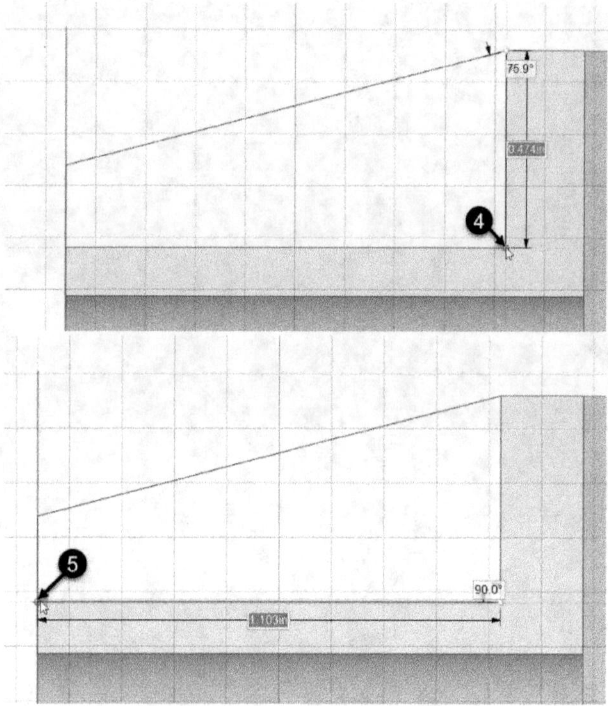

5. Click **Design > Mode > 3D Mode** on the ribbon.
6. Click **Design > Edit > Pull** on the ribbon.
7. Click in the region enclosed by the sketch.

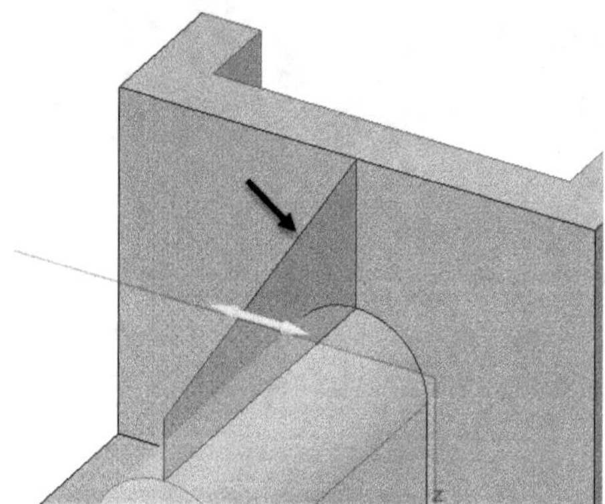

8. Click the **Pull Both Sides** icon on the **Options – Pull** panel.
9. Press and hold the left mouse button, and then drag the pointer.
10. Release the pointer.
11. Type **0.197,** and press ENTER.

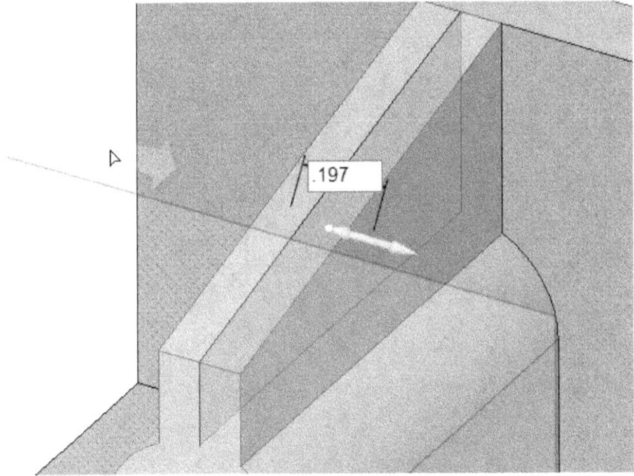

12. Click in the graphics area.

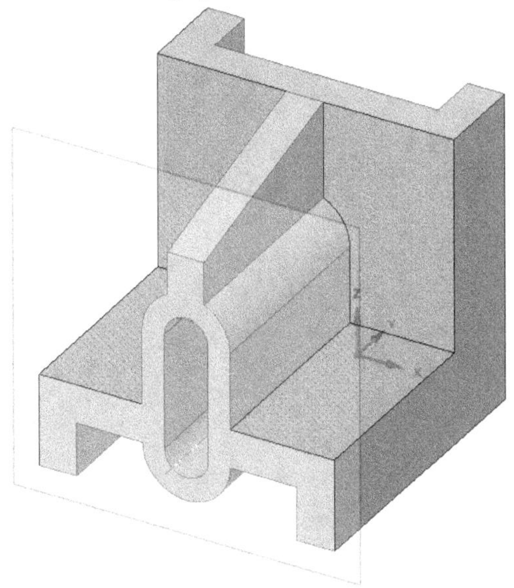

13. Save the model and close it.

TUTORIAL 3

In this tutorial, you create a shampoo bottle using the **Blend** and **Pull** tools.

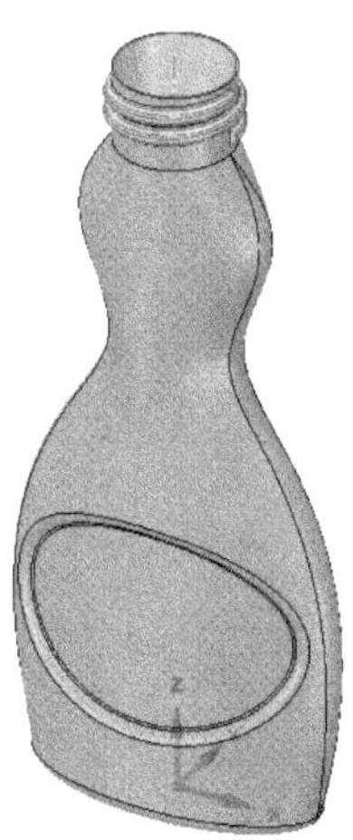

Creating the First Section and Guide curves

To create a loft, you need to create sections and guide curves.

1. Click **File > New > Design** on the ribbon.
2. Click the **Select New Sketch Plane** icon on the toolbar.

3. Click in the third quadrant to select the XY plane.

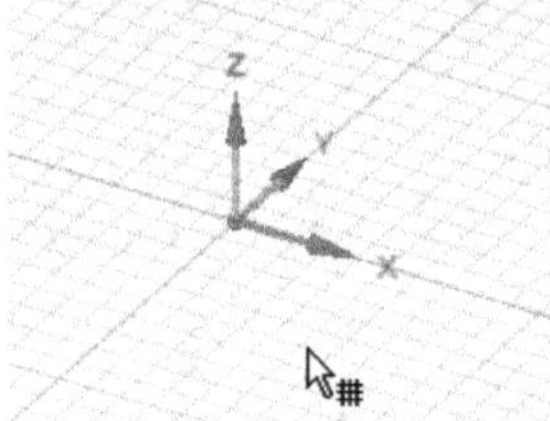

4. Click **Design > Orient > Plan View** on the ribbon.
5. Click **Design > Sketch > Ellipse** on the ribbon.
6. Select the origin point of the sketch.
7. Move the pointer horizontally toward the right.
8. Type 3.936, and press ENTER.

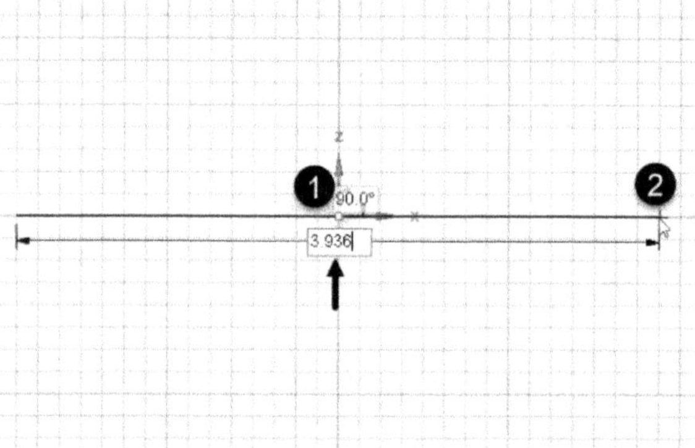

9. Move the pointer vertically upward.
10. Type 1.968, and press ENTER.

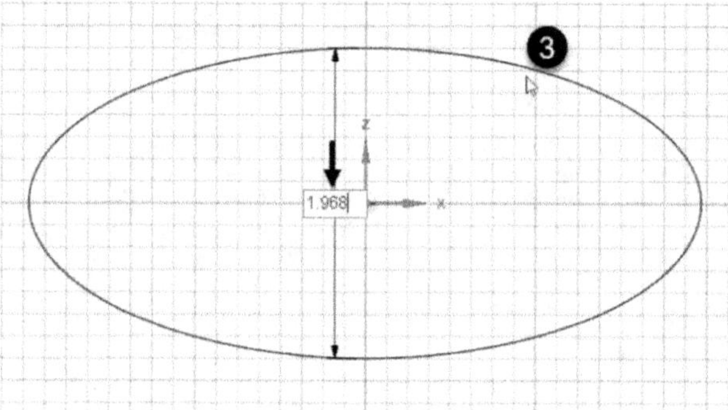

11. Click **Design > Mode > 3D Mode** on the ribbon.

12. Click **Design > Orient > Home** on the ribbon
13. Click **Design > Mode > Sketch Mode** on the ribbon.
14. Select the X-axis of the coordinate system.
15. Click **Design > Orient > Plan View** on the ribbon.
16. Click **Design > Sketch > Point** on the ribbon.

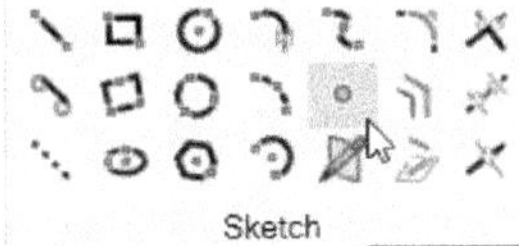

17. On the **Options - Sketch** panel, scroll to the **Dimensions** section and then select the **Cartesian dimension** option.

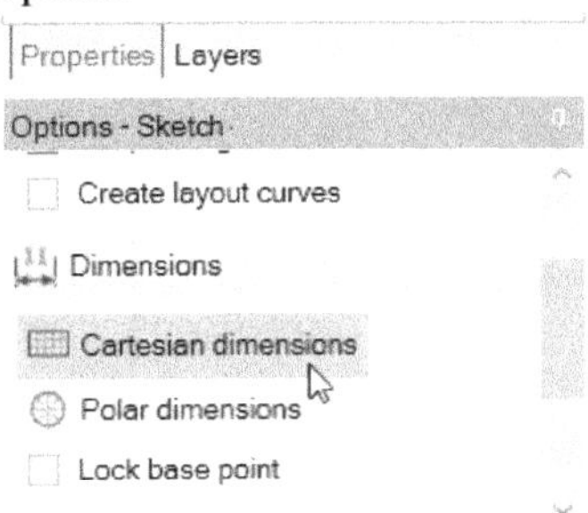

18. Check the **Lock base point** option in the **Options – Sketch** panel.
19. Select the origin point of the sketch; the base point is defined.
20. Move the pointer toward left.
21. Type -2.362 in the vertical and horizontal distance boxes, respectively.

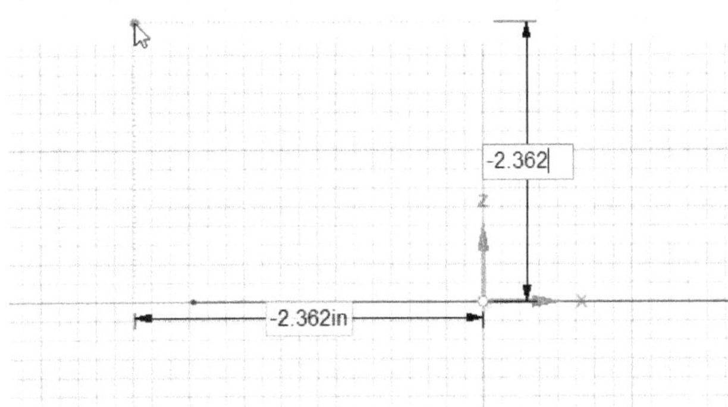

22. Likewise, create the other points, as shown.

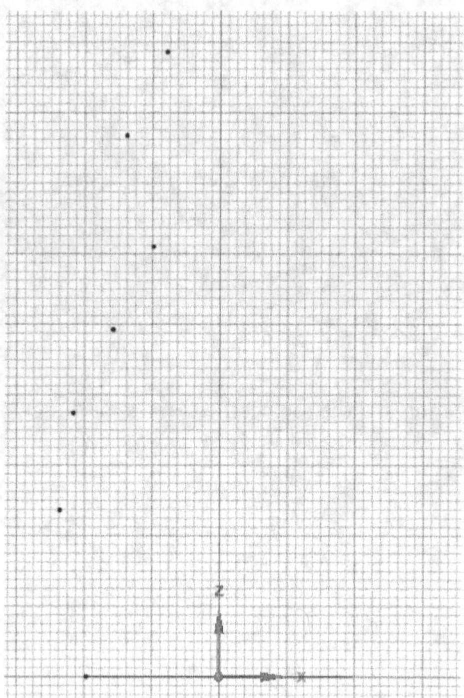

The vertical and horizontal distances of the points are given below.

Third point:
Vertical distance -3.74
Horizontal distance -2.165

Fourth point:
Vertical distance -4.921
Horizontal distance -1.575

Fifth point:
Vertical distance -6.102
Horizontal distance -0.984

Sixth point:
Vertical distance -7.677
Horizontal distance -1.378

Seventh point:
Vertical distance -8.858
Horizontal distance -0.787

23. Press Esc.
24. Click **Design** > **Sketch** > **Spline** on the ribbon.

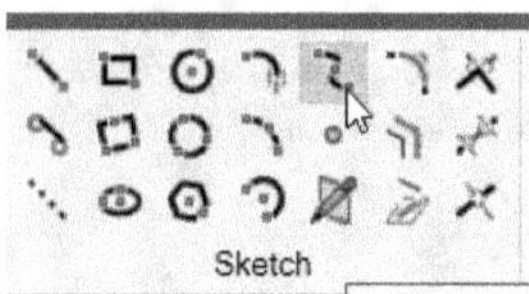

25. Select the quadrant point of the ellipse, as shown.

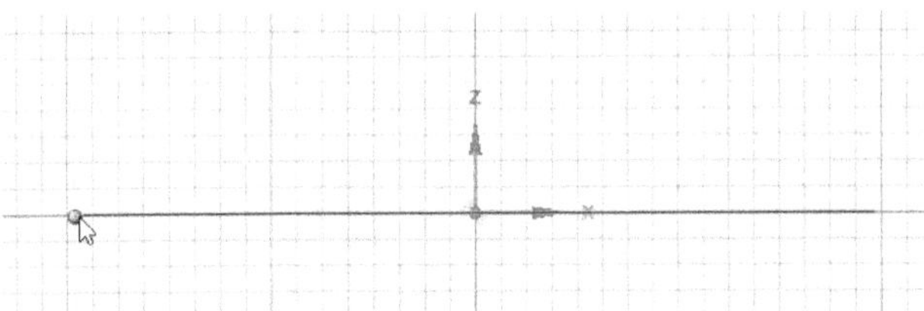

26. Move the cursor up, and then select the points one-by-one.

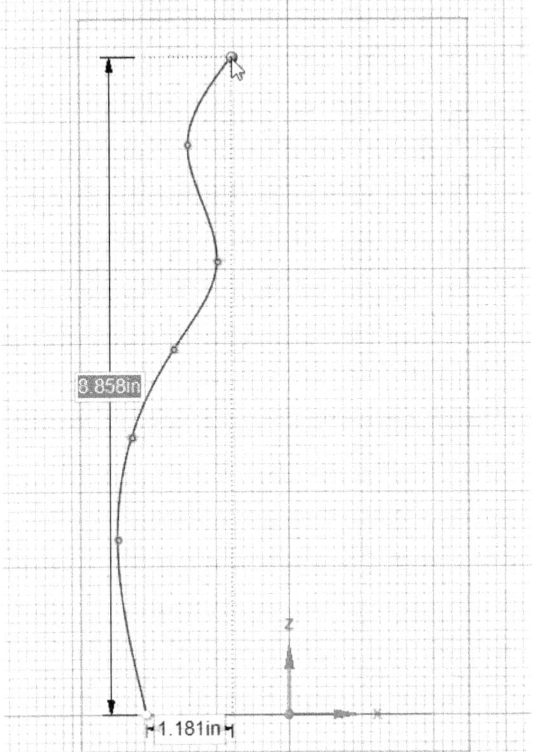

27. Press Esc.
28. Click **Design > Mode > 3D Mode** on the ribbon.
29. Click **Design > Edit > Move** on the ribbon.
30. Select the curve from the graphics area.
31. Check the **Create patterns** option on the **Options – Move** panel.

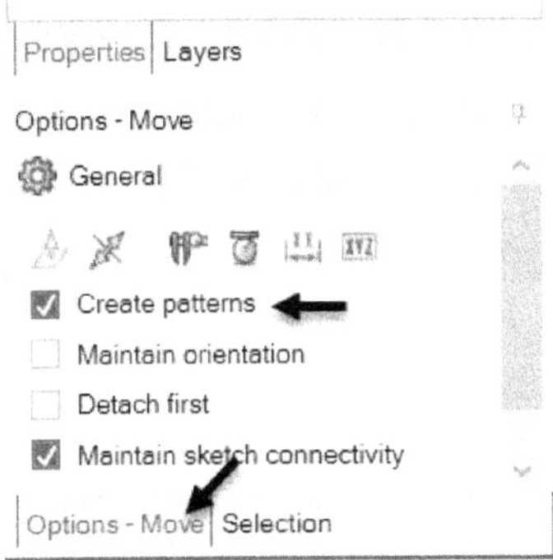

32. Click the **Anchor** icon on the top-left corner of the graphics area.

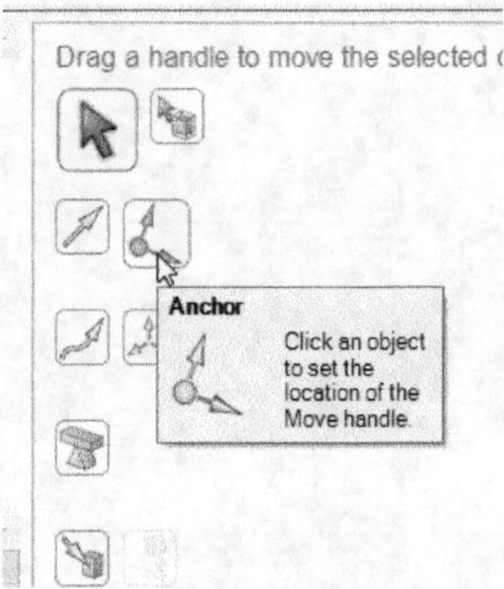

33. Select the coordinate system from the graphics area; the triad is moved to the coordinate system.

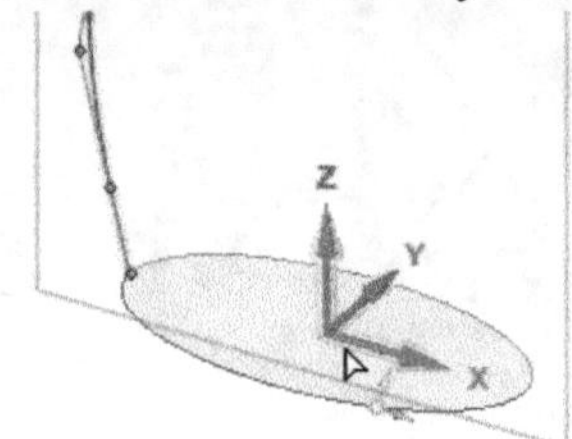

34. Click and drag the green rotate handle of the triad.

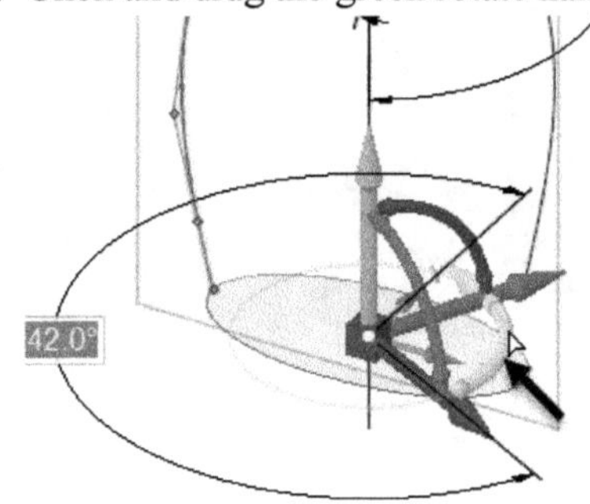

35. Type **180** in the Angle box and press ENTER.

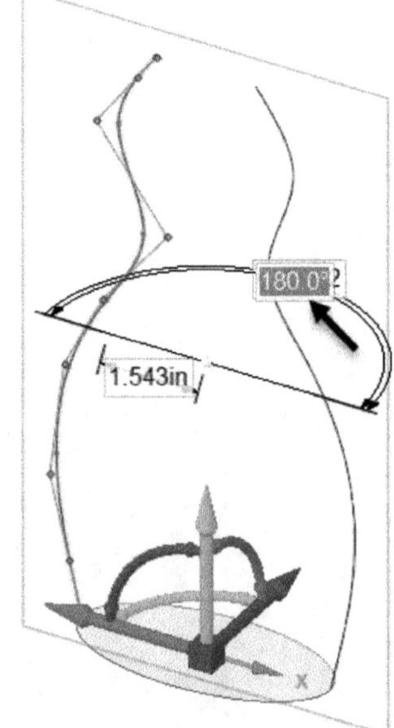

36. Click in the graphics area.
37. Click **Design > Insert > Plane** on the ribbon.
38. Select the ellipse located at the bottom.

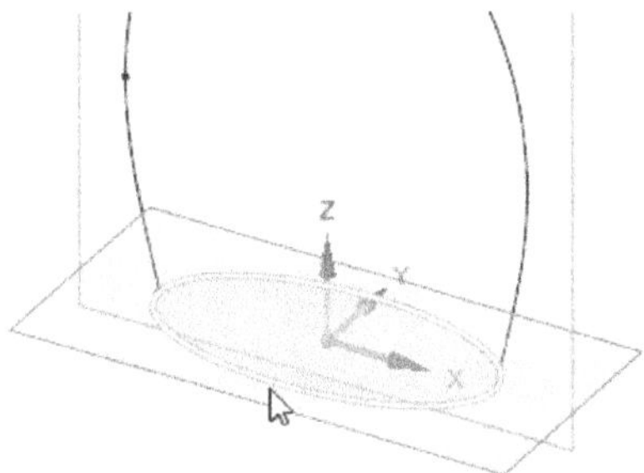

39. Click **Design > Edit > Move** on the ribbon.
40. Select the horizontal plane.
41. Click and drag the blue arrow of the triad.
42. Move the pointer upward, and then release.
43. Type **8.858** in the distance box, and then press ENTER.

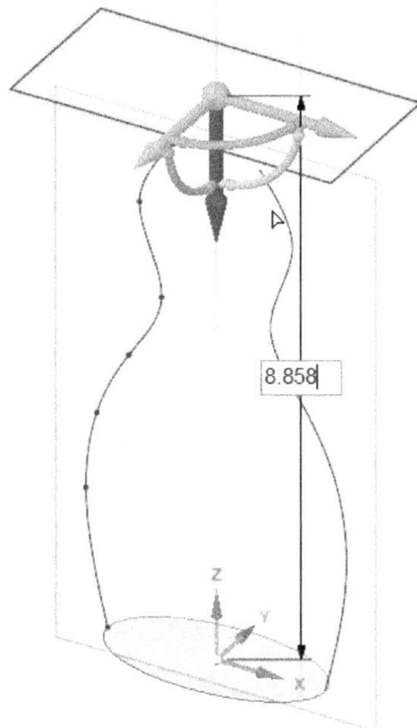

44. Click **Design > Mode > Sketch Mode**.
45. Select the horizontal plane, as shown.

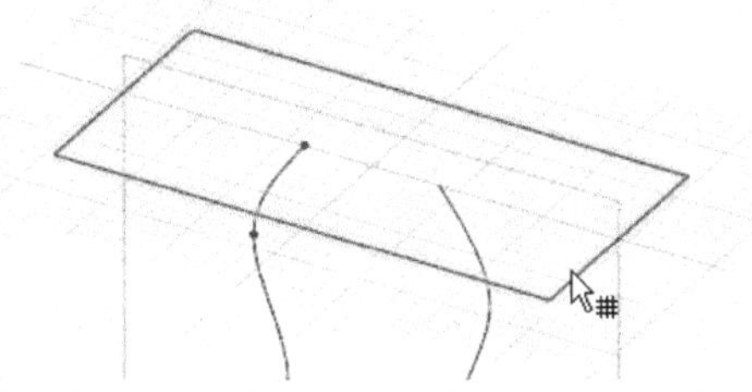

46. Click **Design > Sketch > Circle** on the ribbon.
47. Specify the centerpoint of the circle, as shown.

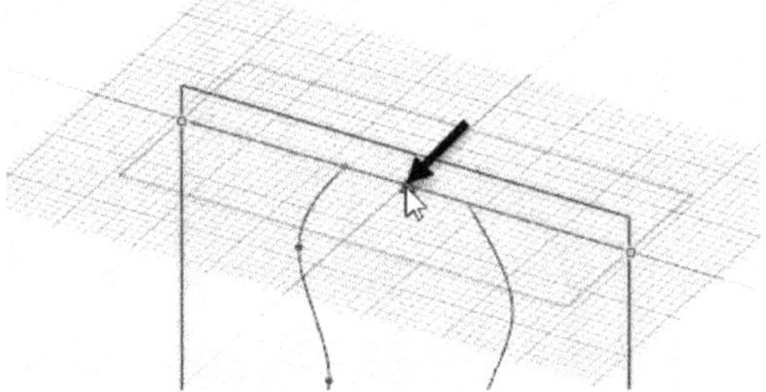

48. Select the endpoint of the curve, as shown.

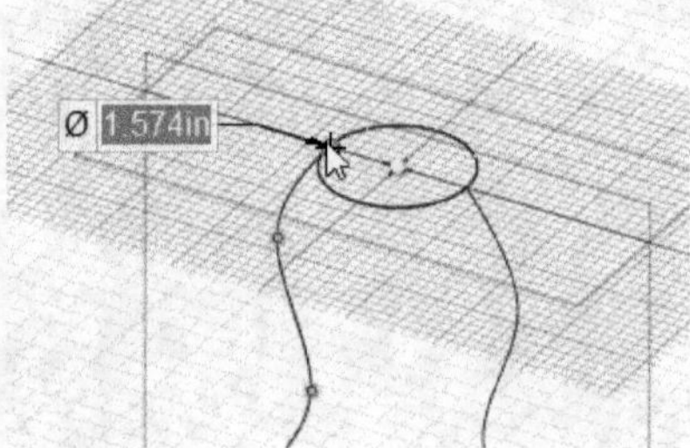

49. Press Esc.
50. Click **Design > Mode > 3D Mode** on the ribbon.
51. Click **Design > Edit > Blend** on the ribbon.

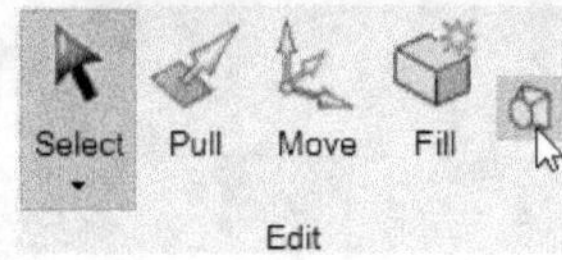

52. Press and hold the Ctrl key and select the ellipse and the circle.

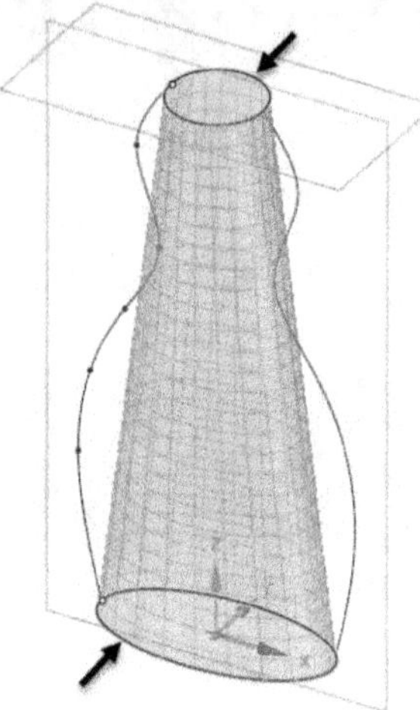

53. Click the **Select Guides** icon on the top-left corner of the graphics area.

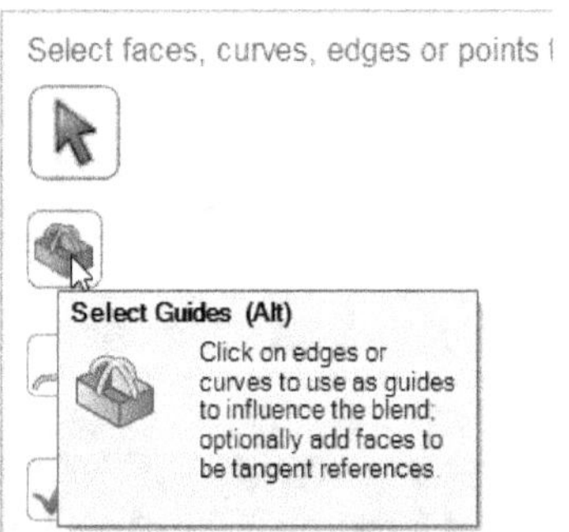

54. Press and hold the Ctrl key and select the two curves.

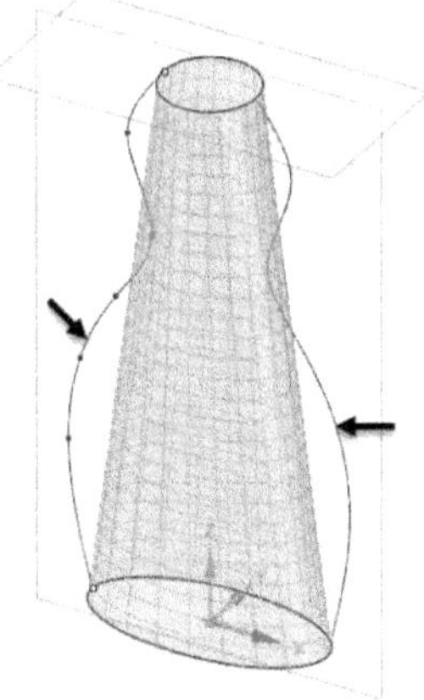

55. On the **Options- Blend Options** panel, click the down arrow next to the **Show UV grid** option.

56. Click and drag the slider to the right.

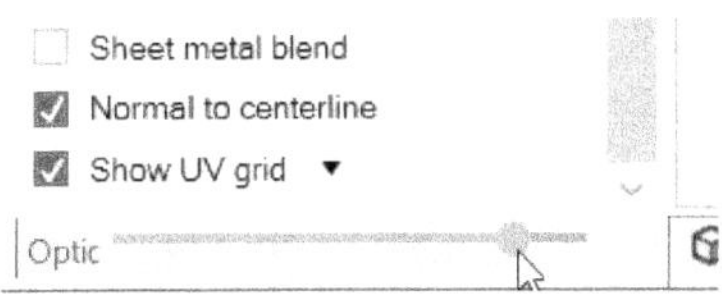

The UV grid spacing is changed.

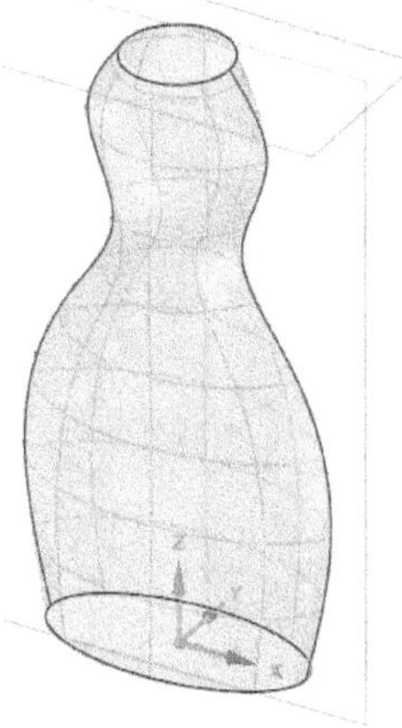

57. Click **Complete** on the top-left corner of the graphics area.

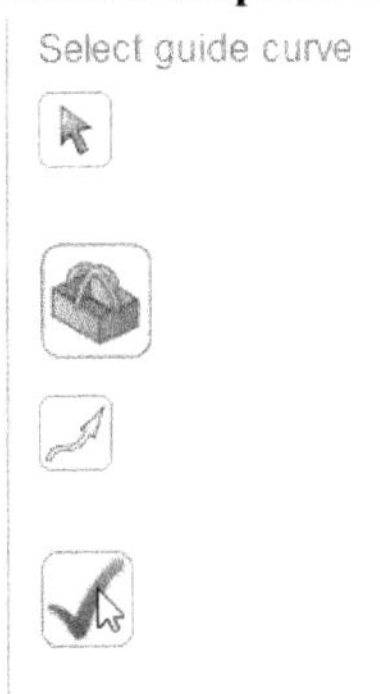

58. Deselect the checkboxes next to the elements in the **Structure** panel, as shown.

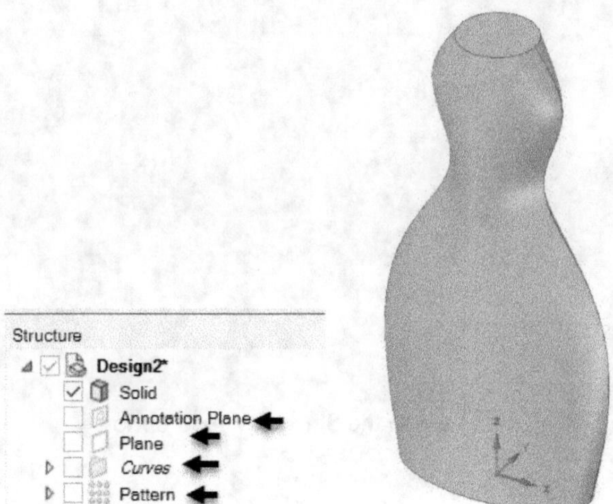

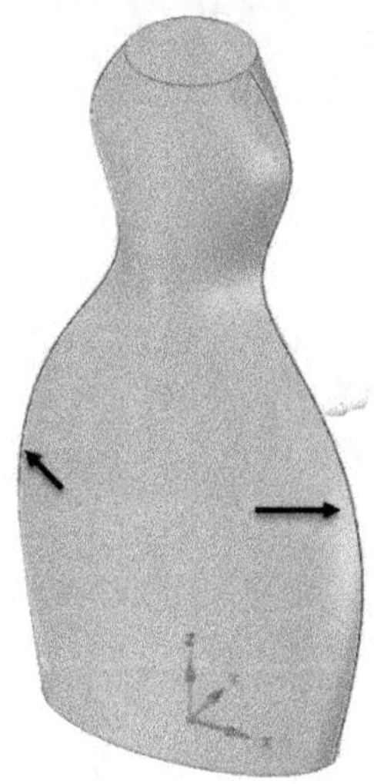

59. Click **Design > Edit > Pull** on the ribbon.
60. Select the edges of the model, as shown.

61. Click on the **Round** icon on the **Options – Pull** panel.

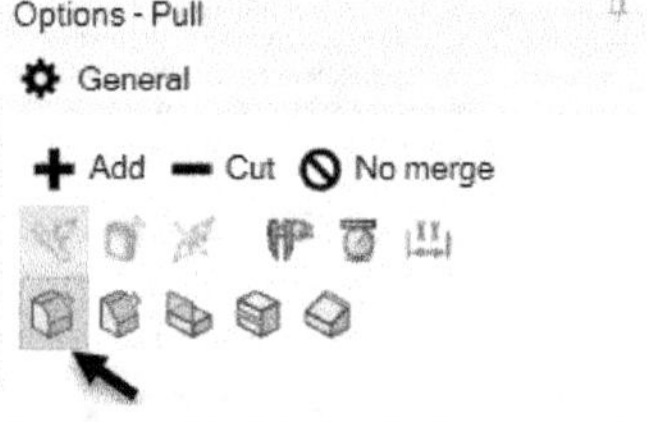

62. Press and hold the left mouse button.
63. Drag the pointer toward the left and release it.
64. Type **0.3** in the radius box, and press ENTER.

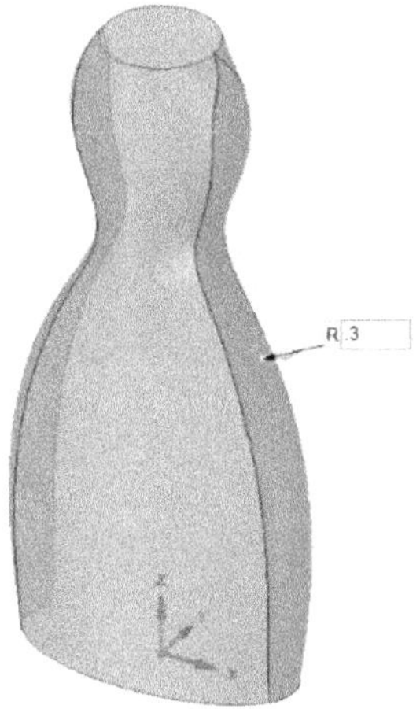

65. Click in the graphics area.

Creating the Extrusion

1. Click **Design > Edit > Pull** on the ribbon.
2. Select the top face of the loft.

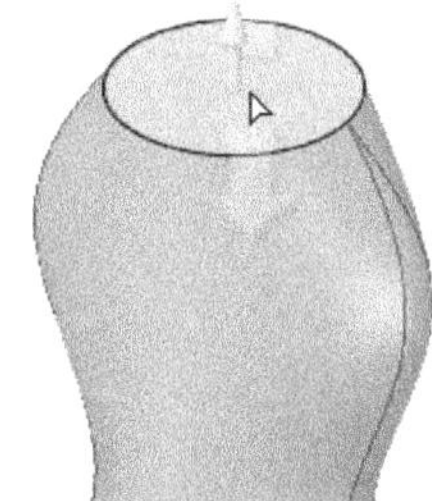

3. Press and hold the left mouse button.
4. Drag the pointer upward.
5. Type 1 and press Enter.

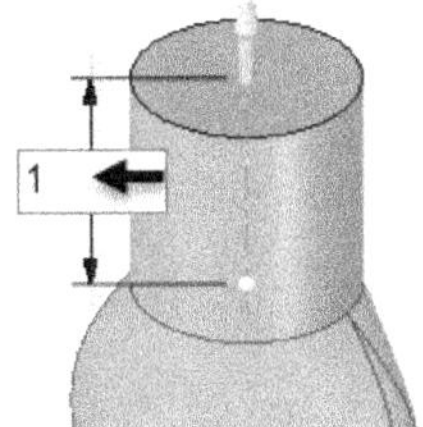

6. Click in the graphics area.

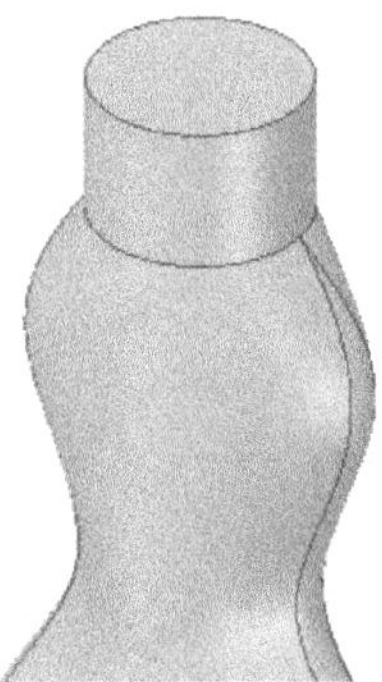

Creating an Emboss

1. Click **Design > Insert > Plane** on the ribbon.

2. Select the X-axis from the coordinate system.
3. Click **Design > Edit > Move** on the ribbon.
4. Click and drag the blue axis of the triad.
5. Next, release it.

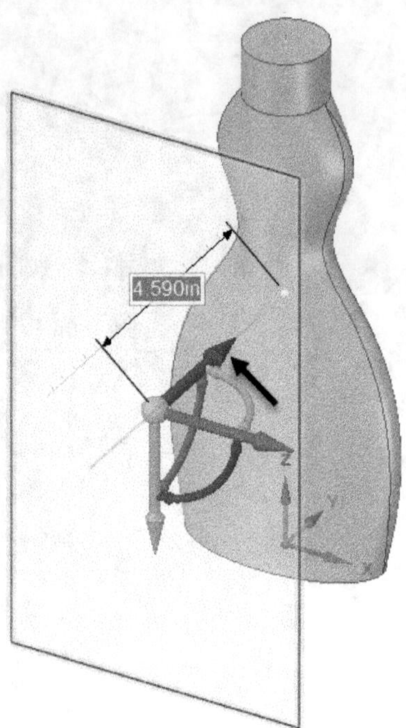

6. Click in the graphics area.
7. Click **Design > Mode > Sketch Mode** on the ribbon.
8. Select the newly created plane.

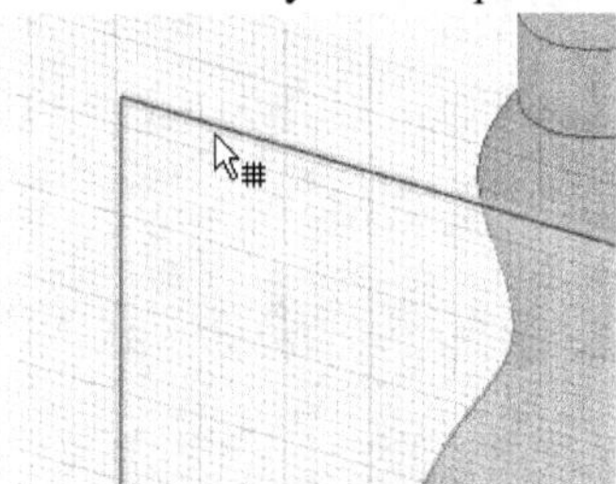

9. Click **Design > Orient > Plan View** on the ribbon.
10. Click **Design > Sketch > Ellipse** on the ribbon.
11. On the **Options - Sketch** panel, scroll to the **Dimensions** section and then select the **Cartesian dimension** option.

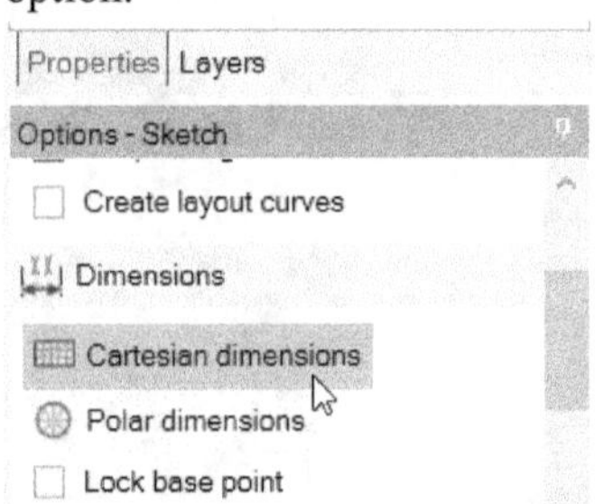

12. Select the origin point of the sketch; the base point is defined.
13. Move the pointer vertically along the Z-axis.
14. Type 0 and press the Tab key.
15. Type -2.55 in the dimension box. Next, press ENTER.

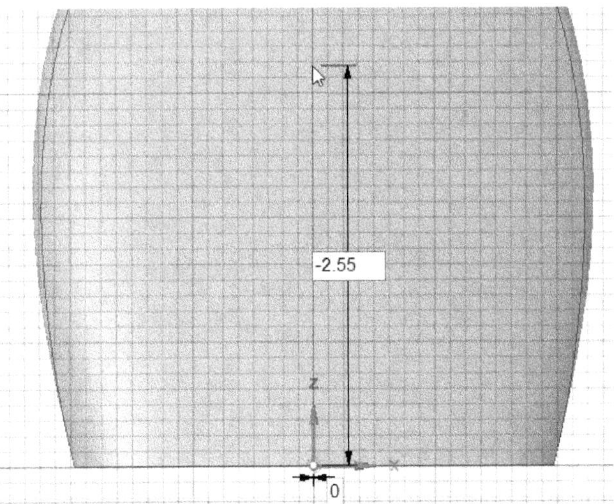

16. Move the pointer horizontally toward the right.
17. Type 4 and press ENTER.

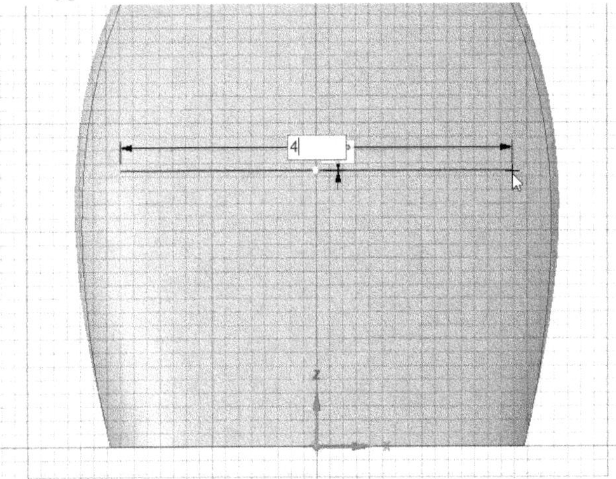

18. Move the pointer vertically.
19. Type 2.7 and press ENTER.

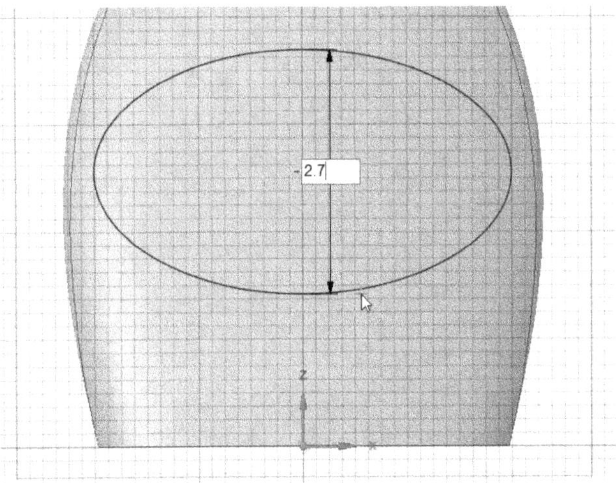

20. Click **Design > Mode > 3D Mode** on the ribbon.
21. Click **Design > Orient > Home** on the ribbon.
22. Click **Design > Edit > Pull** on the ribbon.
23. Click in the region enclosed by the sketch.

24. Click the **No merge** icon on the **Options – Pull** panel.

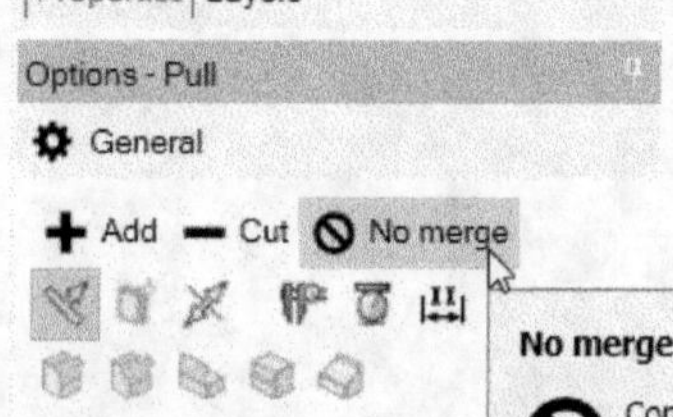

25. Click the **Up To** icon in the top-left corner of the graphics area.

26. Click on the surface of the loft.

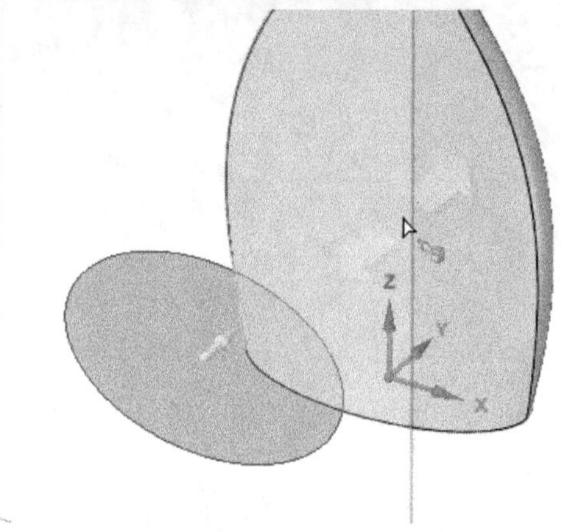

27. Press and hold the left mouse button.
28. Drag the pointer in the forward direction.
29. Next, release it.
30. Type 0.125, and press ENTER.

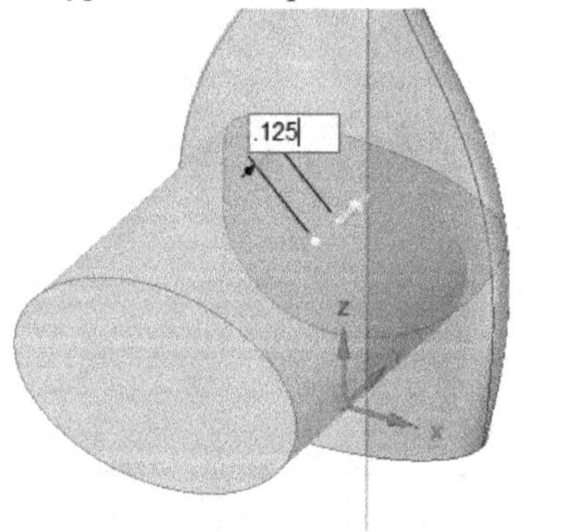

31. Click in the graphics area.
32. Click **Design > Intersect > Combine** on the ribbon.

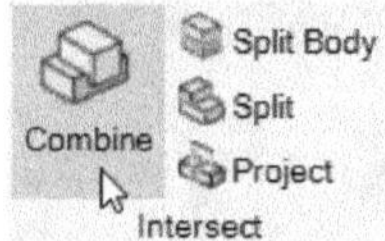

33. Select the Target and cutter bodies, as shown.

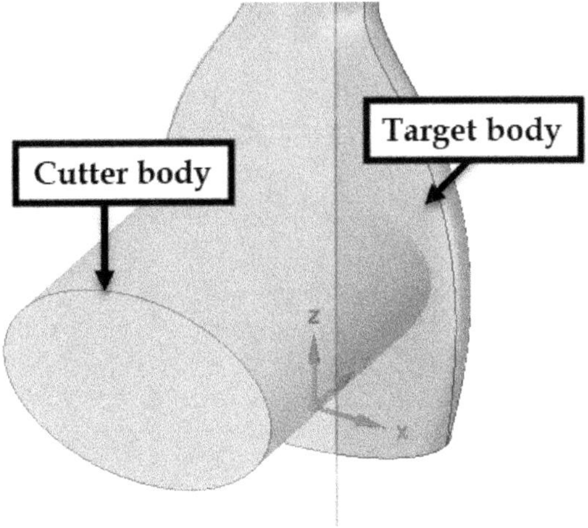

34. Place the pointer on the intersecting portion.
35. Click to select it.

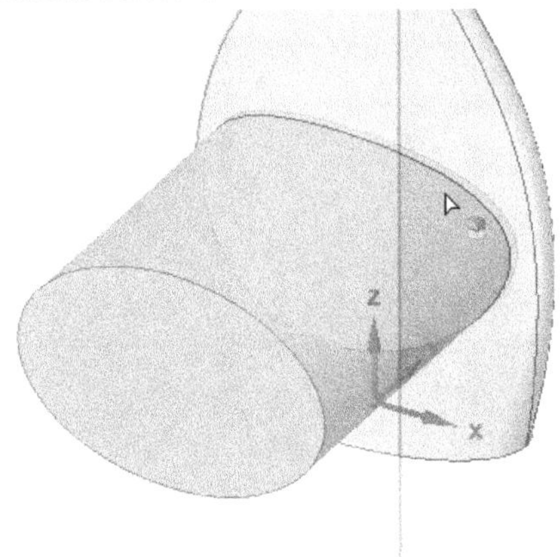

36. Click in the graphics area, and then press Esc.
37. Deselect the checkbox next to the second **Solid** in the **Structure** panel.

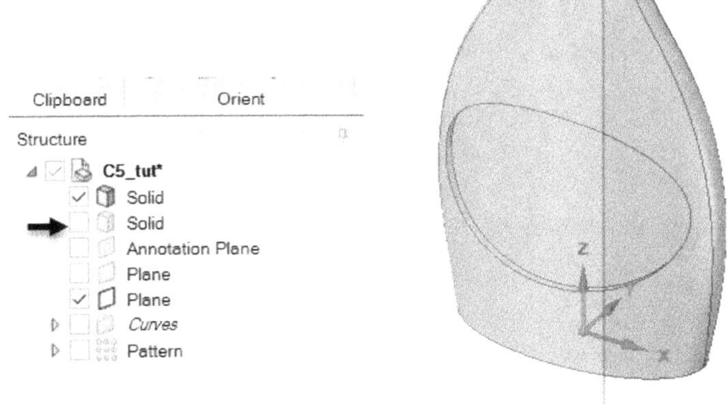

Creating Fillets

1. Click **Design > Edit > Pull** on the ribbon.
2. Press and hold the Ctrl key and select the bottom edges of the loft.

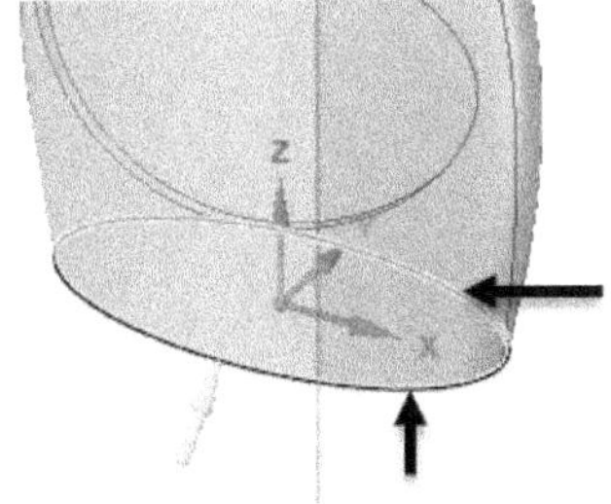

3. Click the **Round** icon on the **Options – Pull** panel.
4. Press and hold the left mouse button, and then drag the pointer upward.
5. Next, release the pointer.
6. Type 0.2 in the radius box, and then press ENTER.

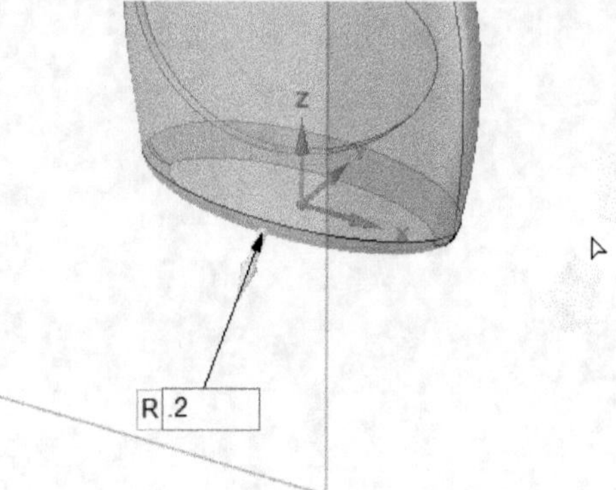

7. Click in the graphics area.
8. Press and hold the Ctrl key and select the edges of the emboss.

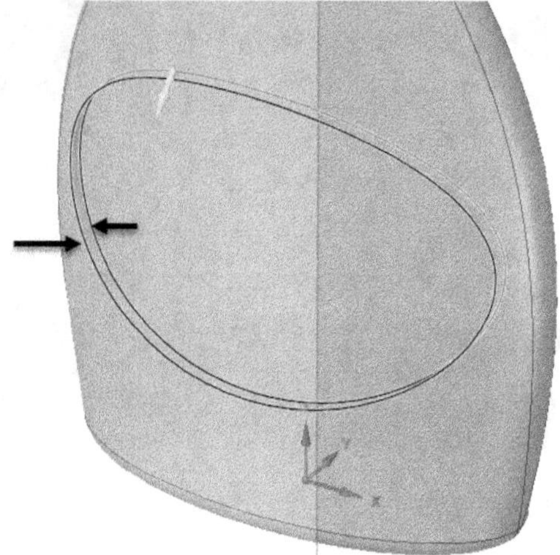

9. Press hold the left mouse button and drag the pointer downward.
10. Next, release the pointer.
11. Type 0.04 and press ENTER.
12. Click in the graphics area.

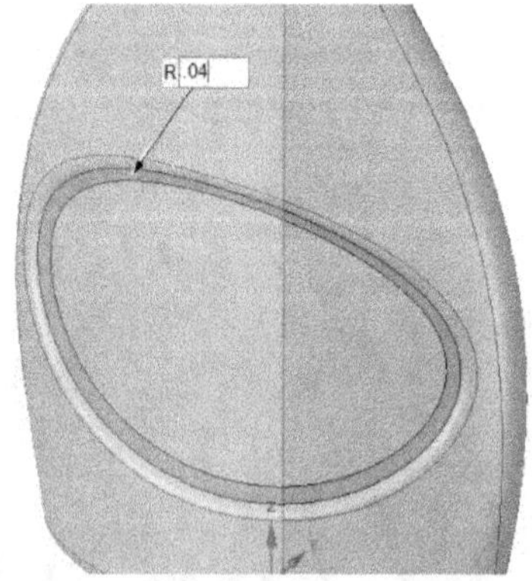

Shelling the Model

1. Click **Design > Insert > Shell** on the ribbon.

2. Select the top face of the cylinder.

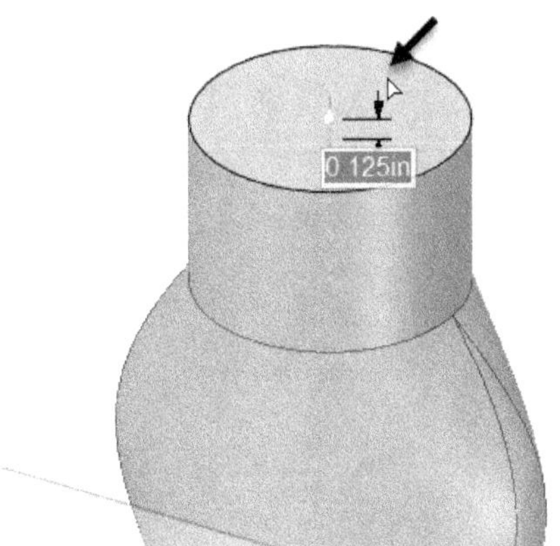

3. Type 0.03 and press ENTER.
4. Click **Complete** to create the shell.

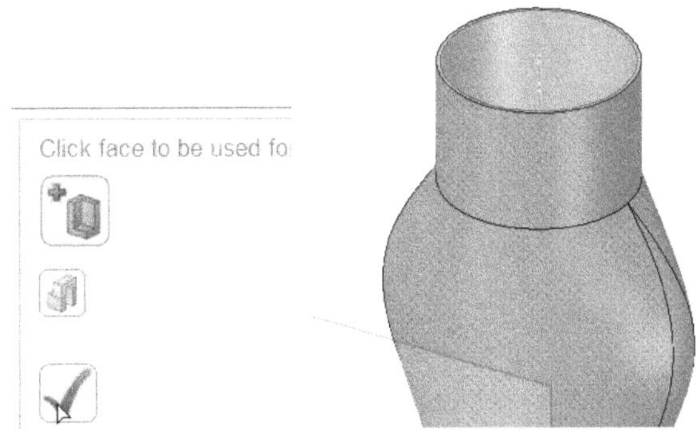

Adding Threads

1. Click **Design > Mode > Sketch Mode** on the ribbon.
2. Select the X-axis from the coordinate system.

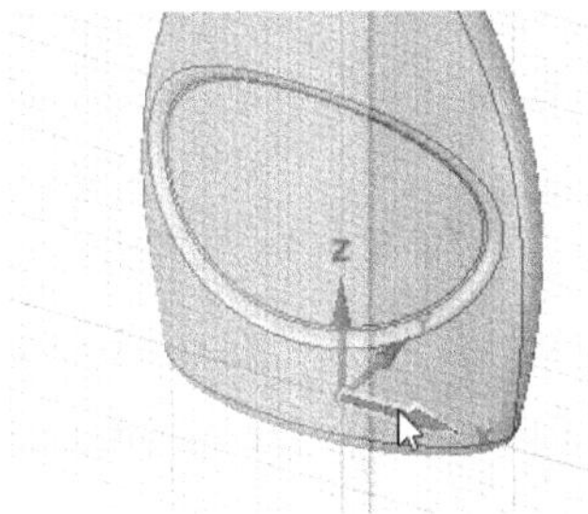

3. Click **Design > Orient > Plan View** on the ribbon.
4. Click **Design > Sketch > Line** on the ribbon.
5. Click in the **Polar Dimensions** icon on the **Options-Sketch** panel.

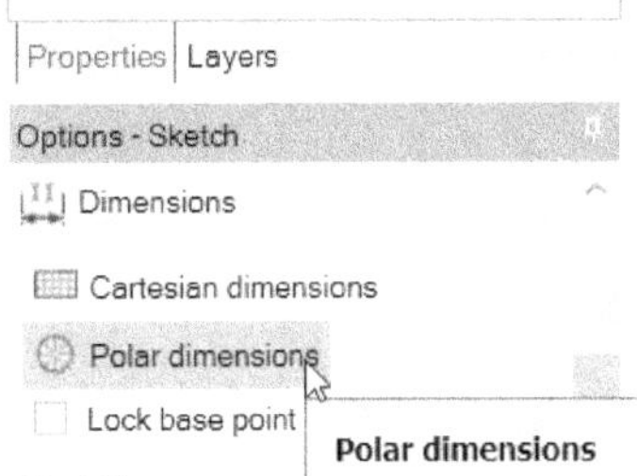

6. Zoom to the top portion of the model.
7. Select the top vertex of the inner edge, as shown.

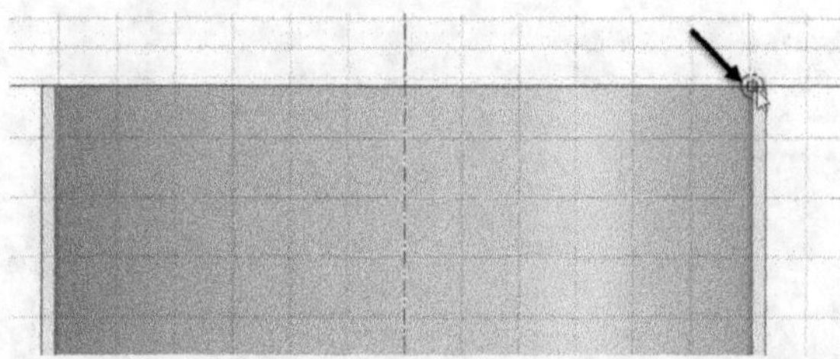

8. Move the pointer downward and type 0.086 and 90 in the distance and angle boxes, respectively.

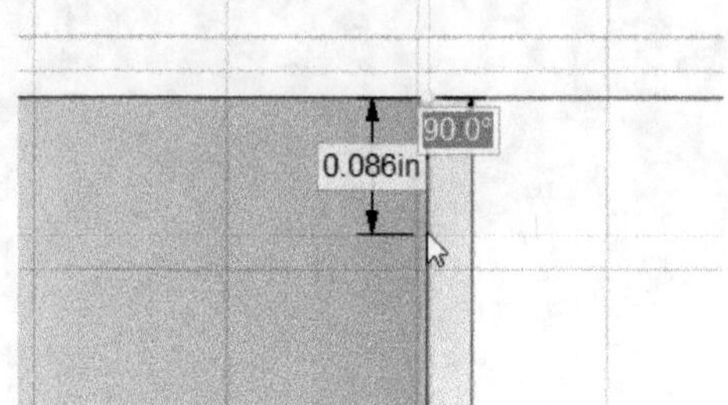

9. Press Enter.
10. Move the pointer vertically downward.
11. Type 0.22 and press ENTER.

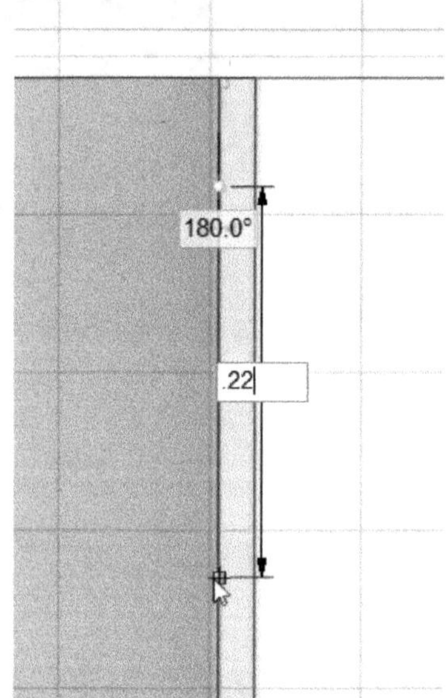

12. Move the pointer toward the right.
13. Type 80 and 0.127 in the Angle and distance boxes, respectively.

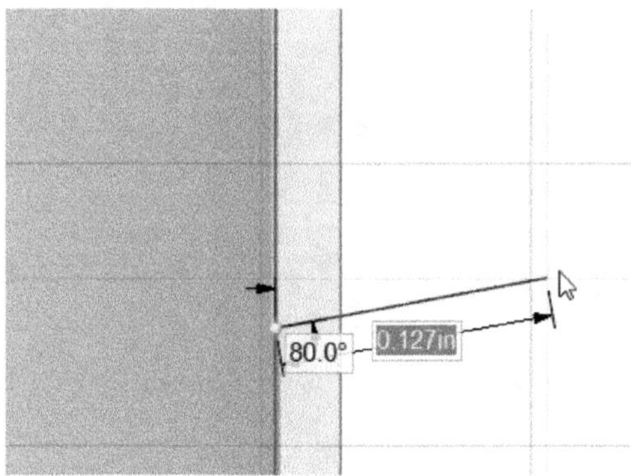

14. Press ENTER.
15. Move the pointer vertically upward.
16. Type 0.12 and press ENTER.

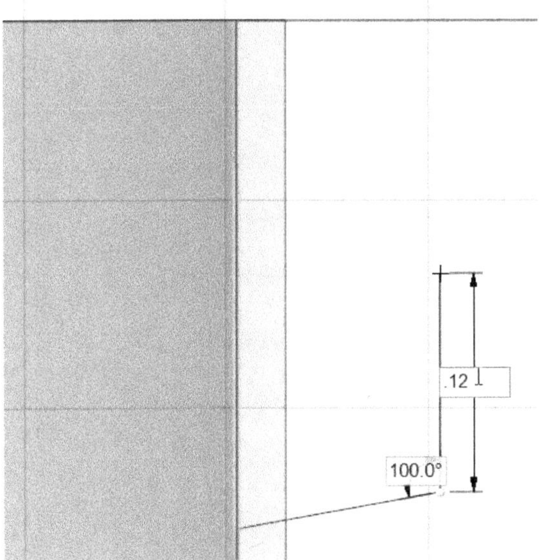

17. Move the pointer toward the left and select the start point of the sketch.

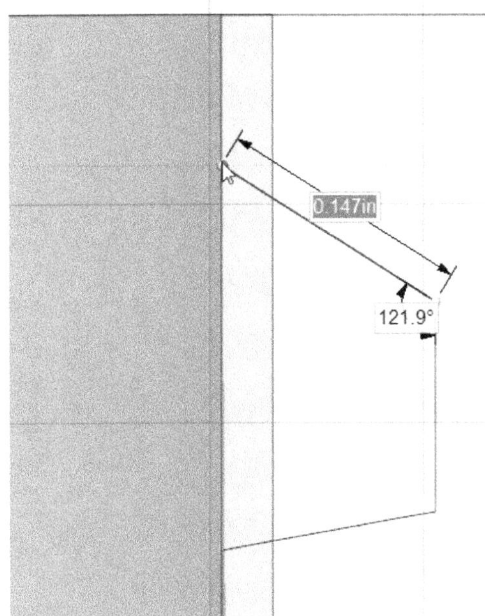

18. Click in the graphics area.
19. Click **Design > Model > 3D Mode** on the ribbon.
20. Click **Design > Orient > Home**.
21. Click **Design > Edit > Pull** on the ribbon.
22. Click in the region enclosed by the sketch.

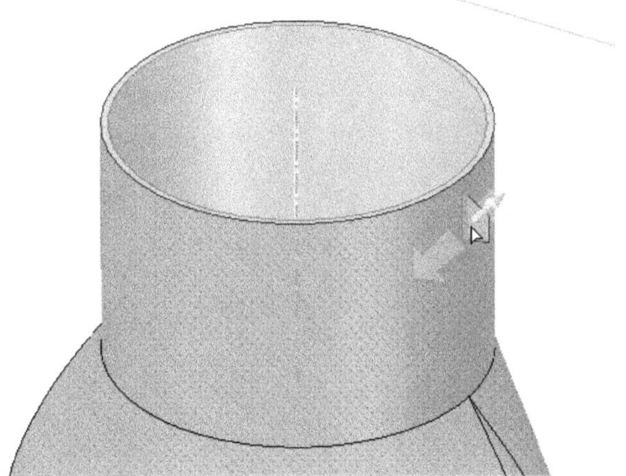

23. Click the **Revolve** icon on the top-left corner of the graphics area.

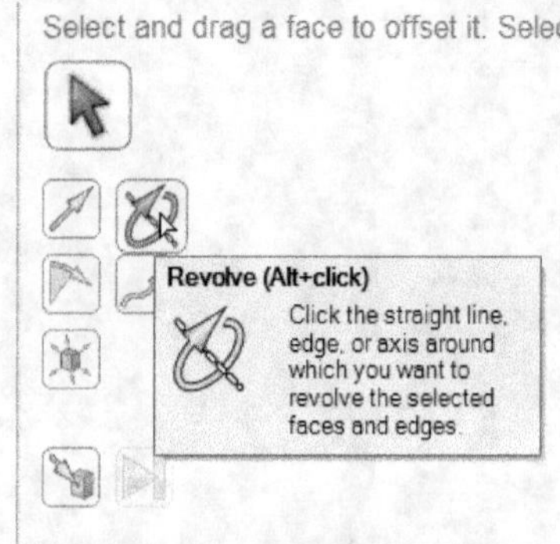

24. Select the axis, as shown.

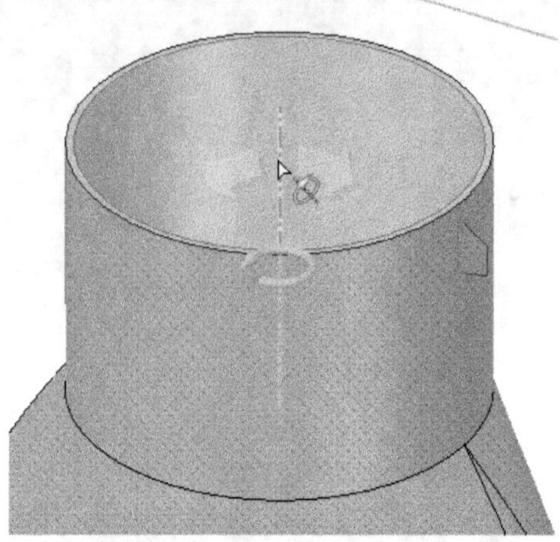

25. Check the **Revolve Helix** option from the **Options – Pull** panel.

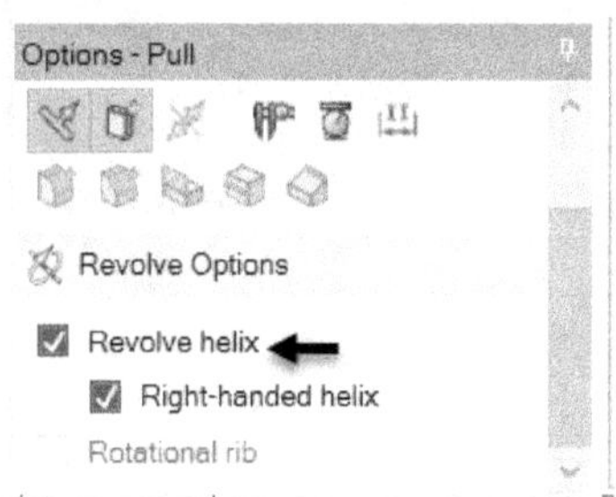

26. Type **-0.55** in the **Height** box, and then press TAB.
27. Type **0.275** in the **Pitch** box.

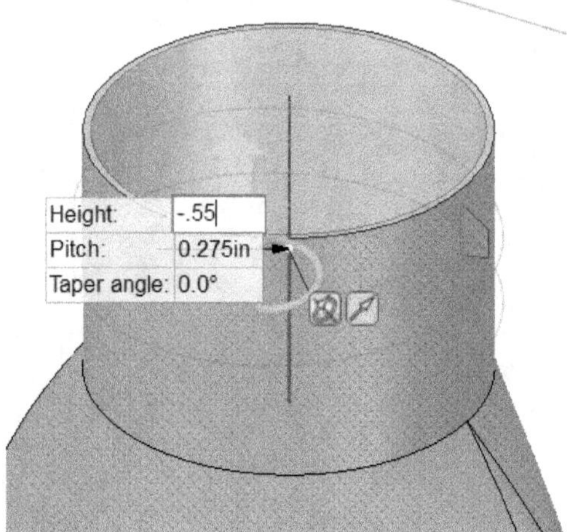

28. Press Esc.

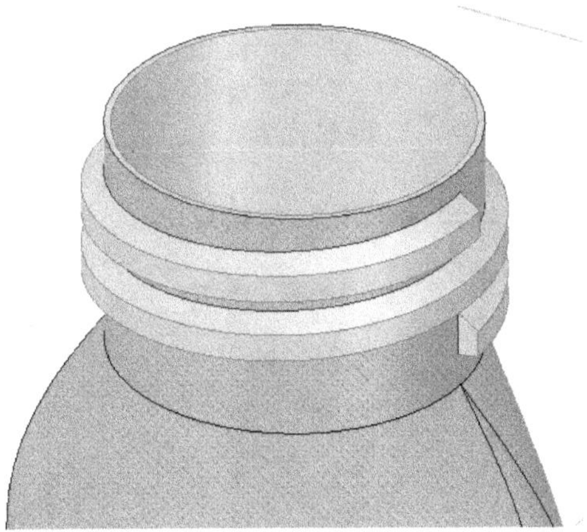

29. Press and hold the Ctrl key and select the edges of the helical solid.
30. Click **Design > Edit > Pull**.
31. Click the **Round** icon on the **Options – Pull** panel.
32. Press and hold the left mouse button and drag the pointer.
33. Release the mouse button and type **0.04** in the radius box.
34. Press ENTER; the selected edges are rounded.

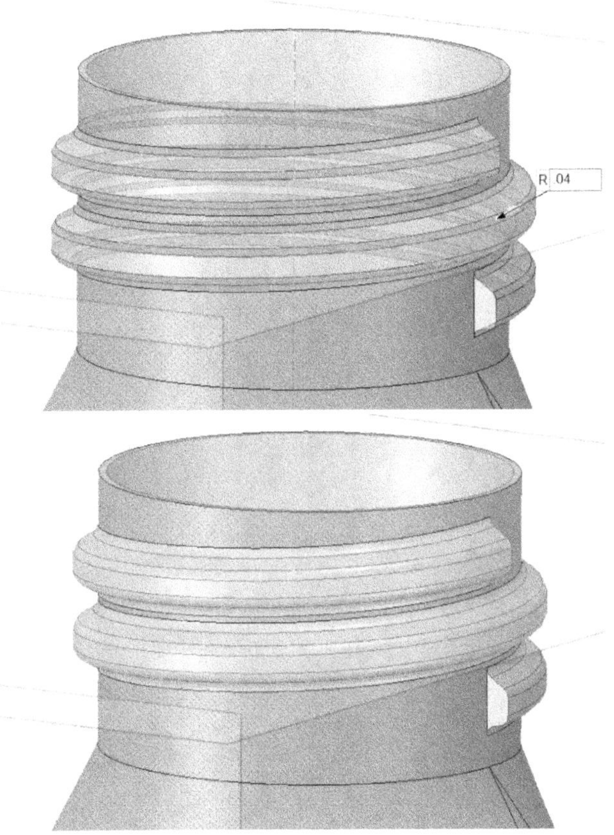

35. Press Esc.
36. Save the model and close it.

TUTORIAL 4

In this tutorial, you create a plastic casing.

Creating the Base

1. Click **File > New >Design** on the ribbon.
2. Click the **Select New Sketch Plane** icon on the toolbar and select the XY plane.
3. Click **Design > Orient > Plan View** on the ribbon.
4. Uncheck the **Snap grid** option on the **Options – Sketch** panel located at the bottom left corner

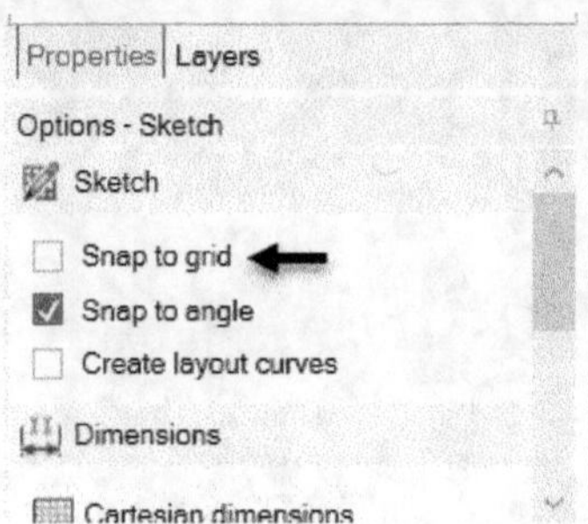

5. Click **Design > Sketch > Line** on the ribbon.
6. On the **Options - Sketch** panel, scroll to the **Dimensions** section and then select the **Cartesian dimensions** option.

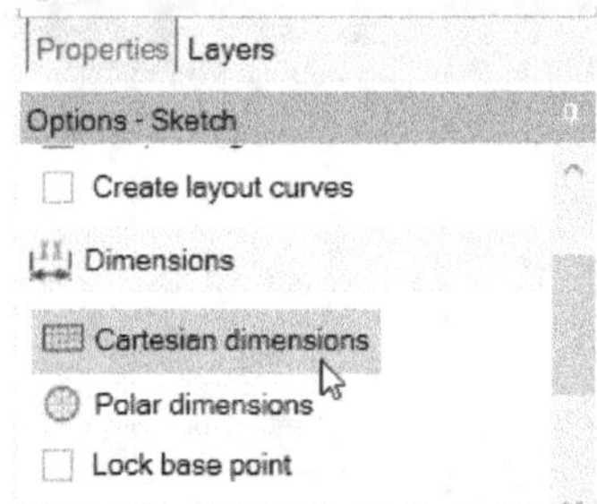

7. Select the sketch origin as the base point.
8. Move the pointer toward the right.
9. Type 7 in the horizontal distance box.
10. Press TAB and type 10 in the vertical distance box.

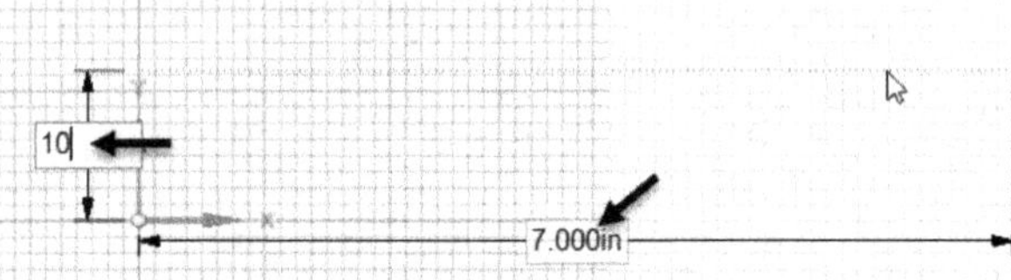

11. Press ENTER; the start point of the line is specified.
12. Move the pointer toward left.
13. Type -14 and press ENTER.

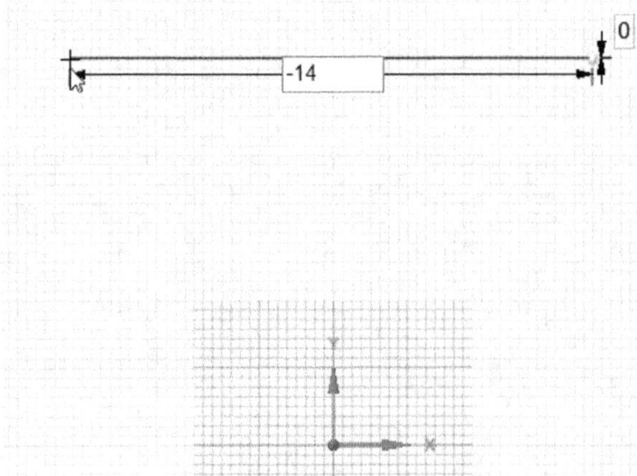

14. Right click and select **Finish Line (Esc).**

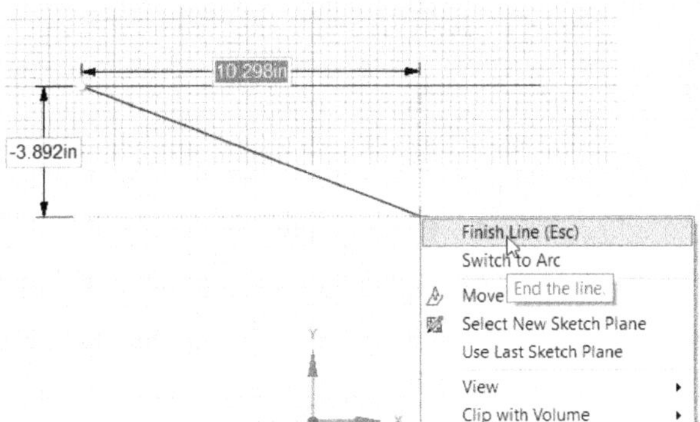

15. On the ribbon, click **Design > Sketch > Offset Curve**.

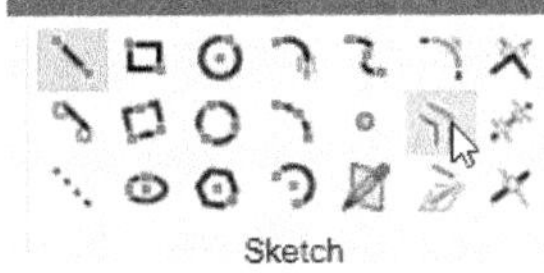

16. Select the horizontal line and move the pointer downward.
17. Type **20** and press Enter.

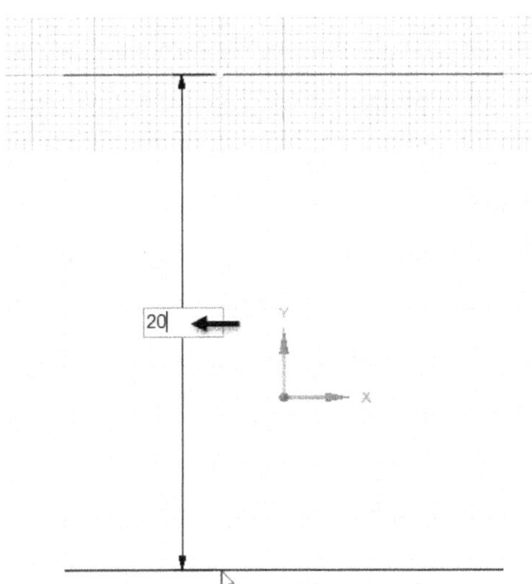

18. On the ribbon, click **Design > Sketch > Three-Point Arc**.
19. Select the right endpoints of the two horizontal lines.
20. Move the pointer, type 30 in the **Radius** box, and then press ENTER.

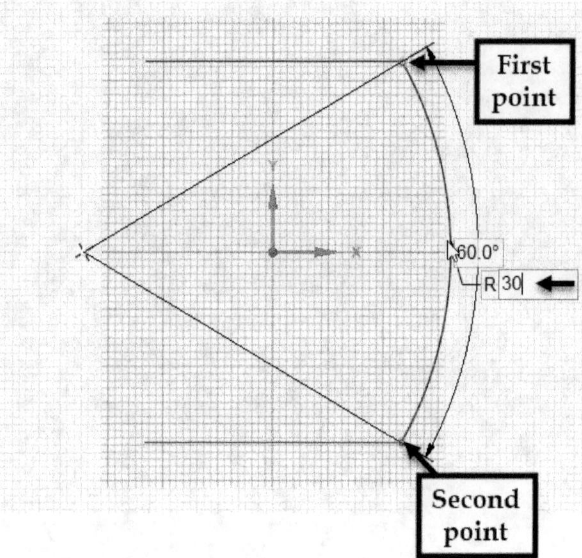

21. Likewise, create another three-point arc.

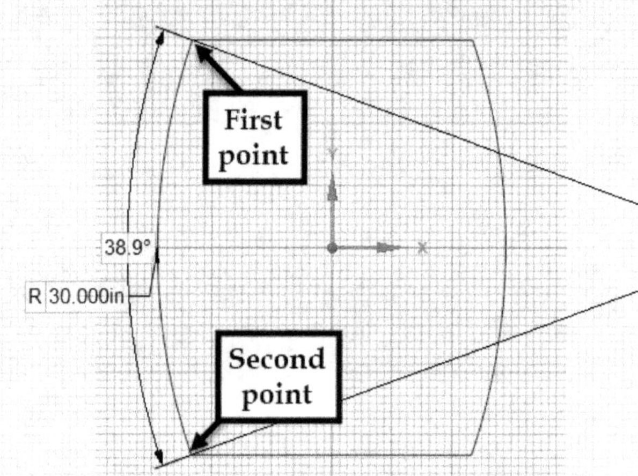

22. On the ribbon, click **Design > Mode > 3D Mode**.
23. Click **Design > Orient > Home** on the ribbon to change the view orientation.
24. On the ribbon, click **Design > Edit > Pull**.
25. Click on the sketch surface.
26. Press and hold the left mouse button and drag the pointer upward.
27. Release the left mouse button.
28. Type 3.15 and press Enter.

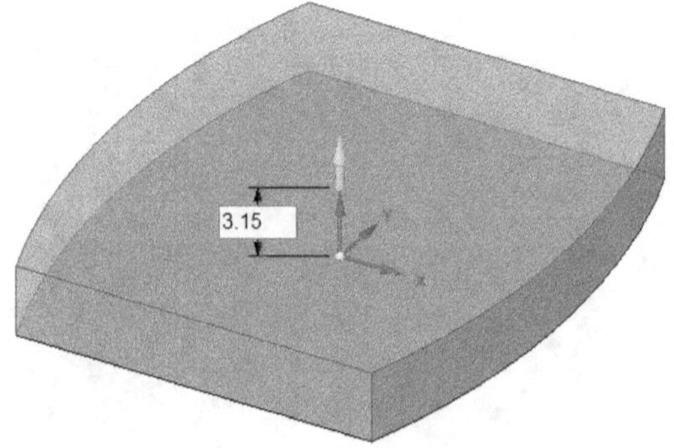

29. Click in the graphics area.
30. On the ribbon, click **Design > Edit > Pull**.
31. Click the **Draft** icon on the top-left corner of the graphics area.

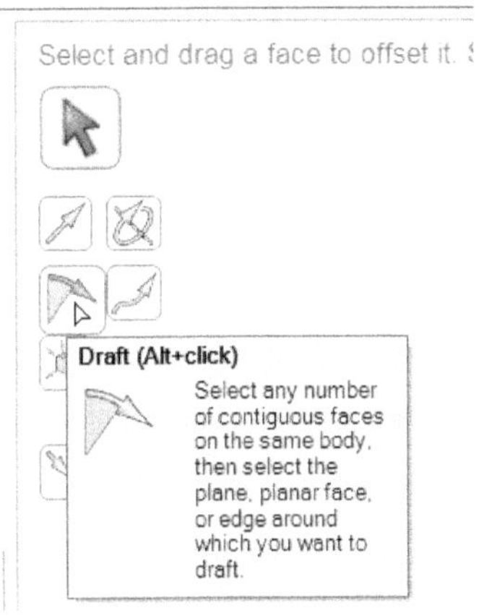

32. Select the top face of the model.

33. Press and hold the Ctrl key and select the side faces of the model.

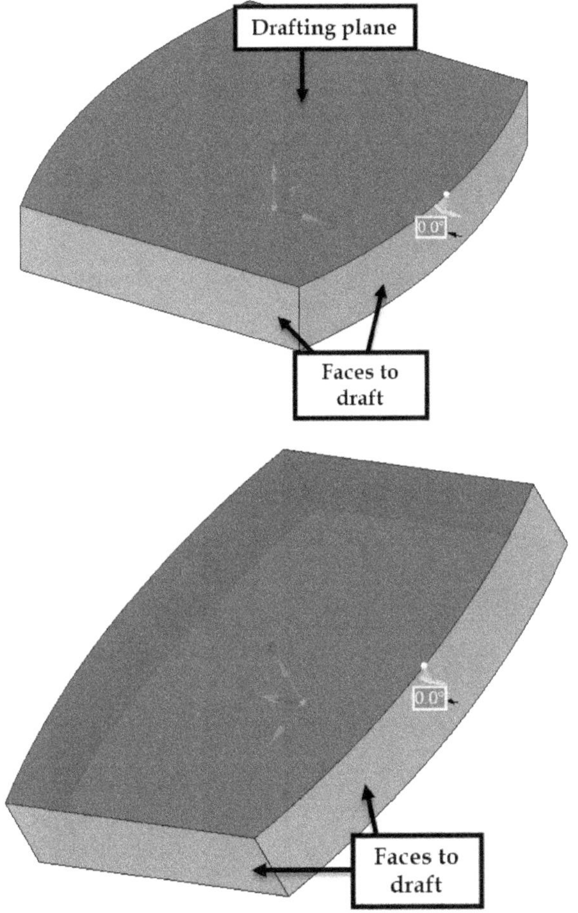

34. Type 10 and press ENTER.

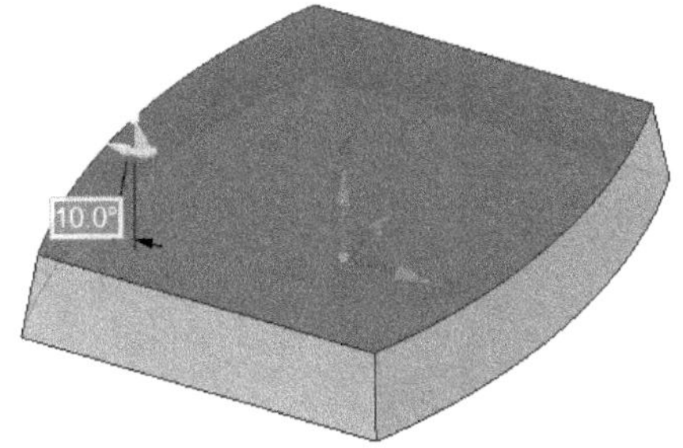

35. Click in the graphics area.

Creating the Extruded surface

1. Click **Design > Mode > Sketch Mode** on the ribbon, and then select the Z-axis.

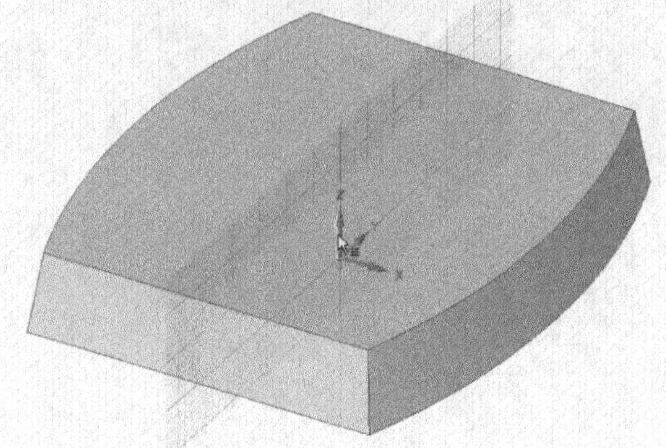

2. Click **Design > Orient > Plan view**.
3. Click **Design > Sketch > Spline** on the ribbon.

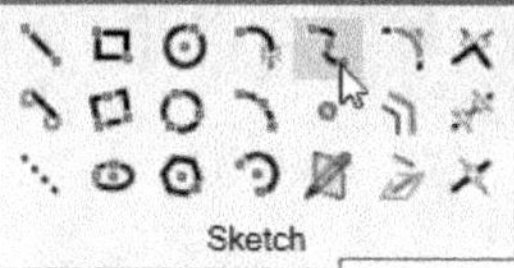

4. On the **Options - Sketch** panel, scroll to the **Dimensions** section and then select the **Cartesian dimensions** option.

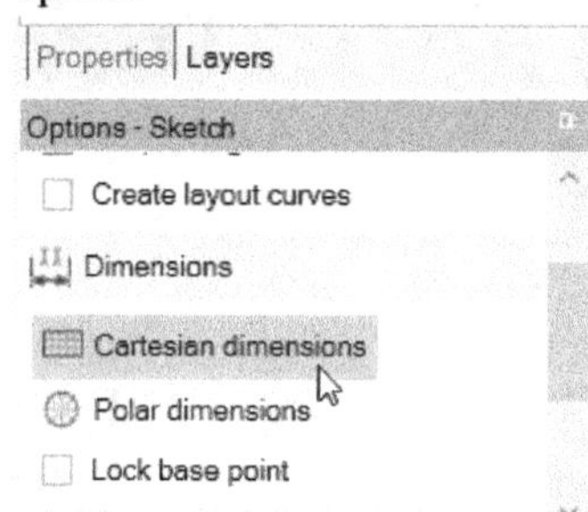

5. Select the sketch origin to define the base point.

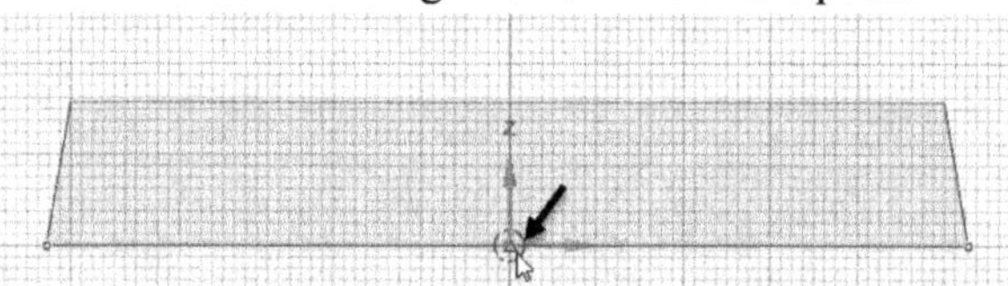

6. Move the pointer toward left.
7. Type 10.5 in the horizontal distance box.
8. Press Tab and type 1.375 in the vertical distance box.

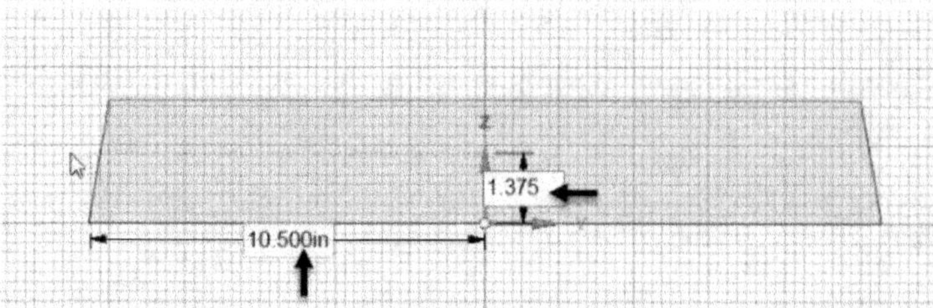

9. Press Enter to specify the start point of the spline.
10. Specify the other points of the spline by moving the pointer and clicking.

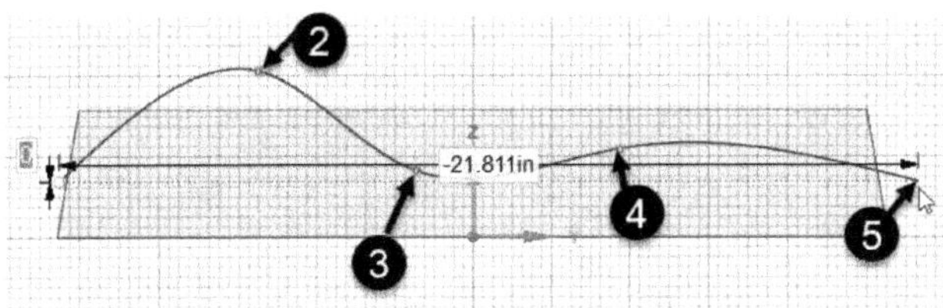

11. Right-click and select **Finish Spline (Esc)**.
12. Press Esc.
13. Select the spline, and then click on its second point.

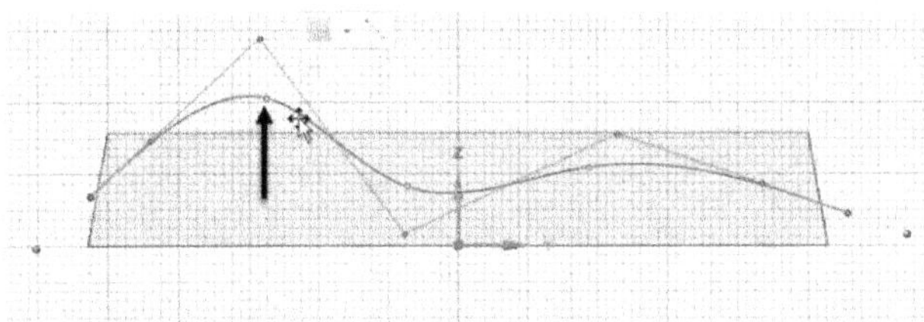

14. Type 4 in the horizontal distance box.
15. Press Tab and type 1.625 in the vertical distance box.

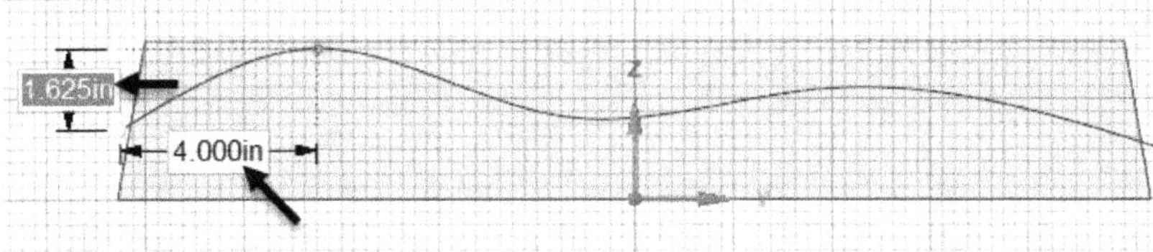

16. Click in the graphics area.
17. Select the third point.

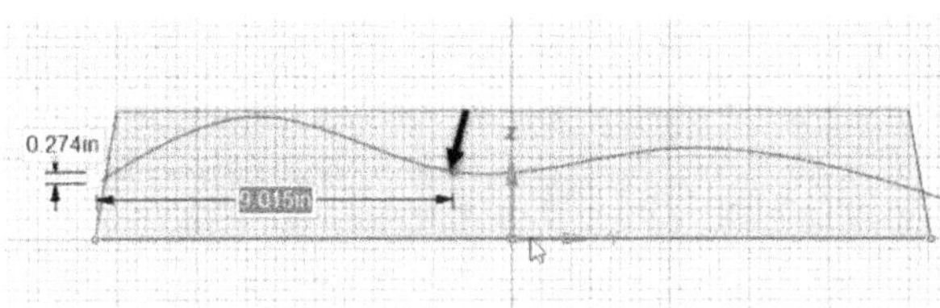

18. Type 8 in the horizontal distance box.
19. Press Tab and type 0.775 in the vertical distance box.

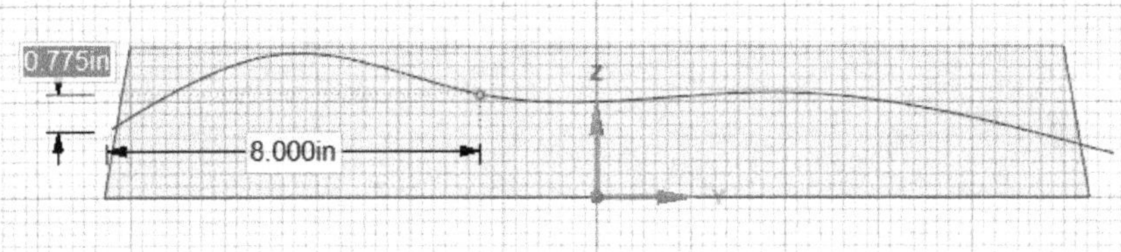

20. Click in the graphics area.
21. Select the fourth point.
22. Specify the values in the horizontal and vertical distances boxes, as shown in the figure.

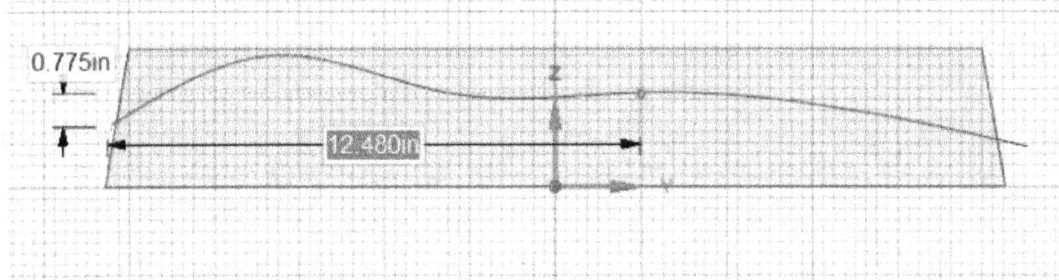

23. Click in the graphics area.

24. Select the fifth point.
25. Specify the values in the horizontal and vertical distance boxes, as shown in the figure.

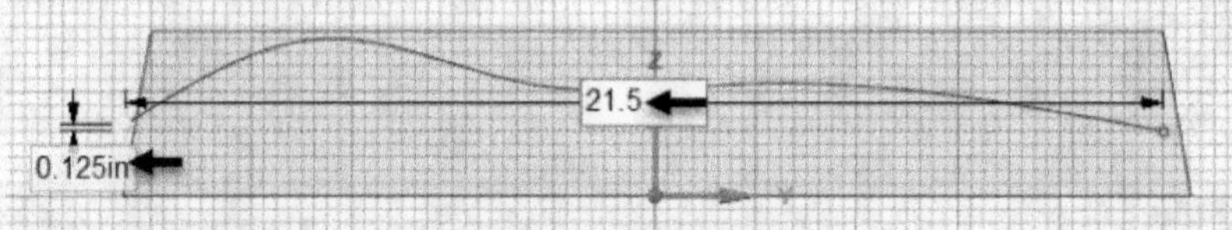

26. On the ribbon, click **Design > Mode > 3D Mode**.
27. Click **Design > Orient > Home** on the ribbon to change the view orientation.
28. On the ribbon, click **Design > Edit > Pull**.
29. Select the spline from the **Structure** panel.

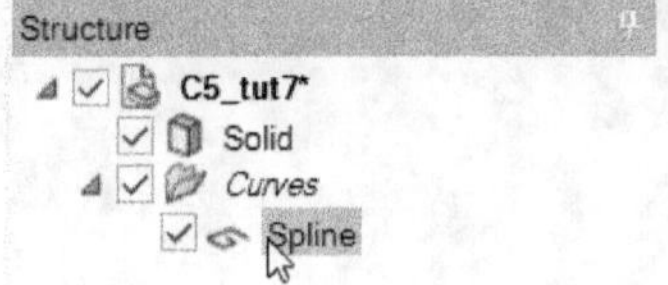

30. Click the **Pull Both Sides** icon on the **Options-Pull** panel.

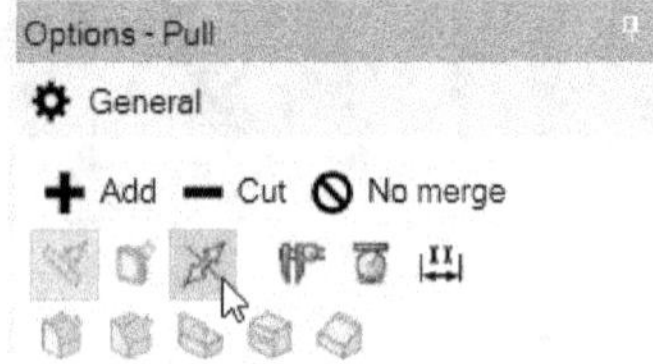

31. Press and hold the left mouse button and drag it.
32. Release the left mouse button.
33. Type 19 and press ENTER.
34. Click in the graphics area.

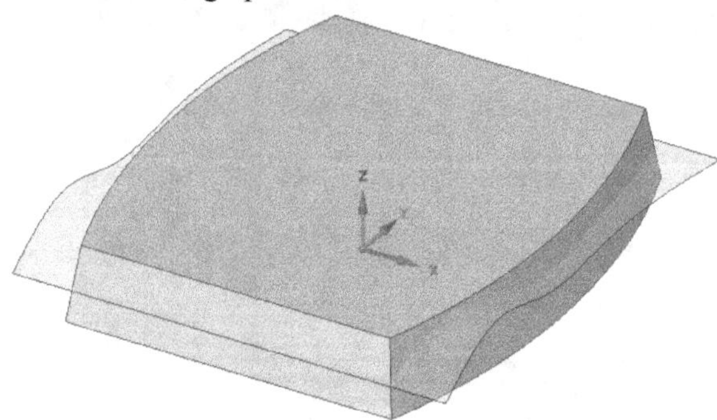

35. On the ribbon, click **Design > Intersect > Split Body**.

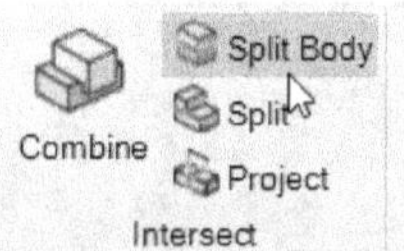

36. Select the solid and the surface bodies; the target and the cutter objects are specified.
37. Select the top portion to remove it.

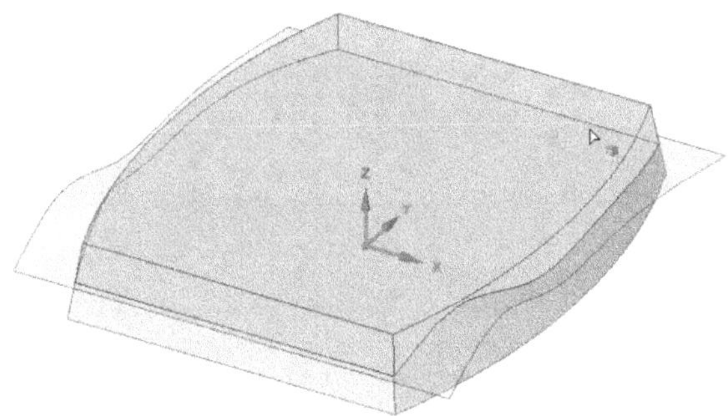

38. Click in the graphics area.
39. Press Esc.
40. Hide the extruded surface by clicking the right mouse button on it and then select **Hide**.

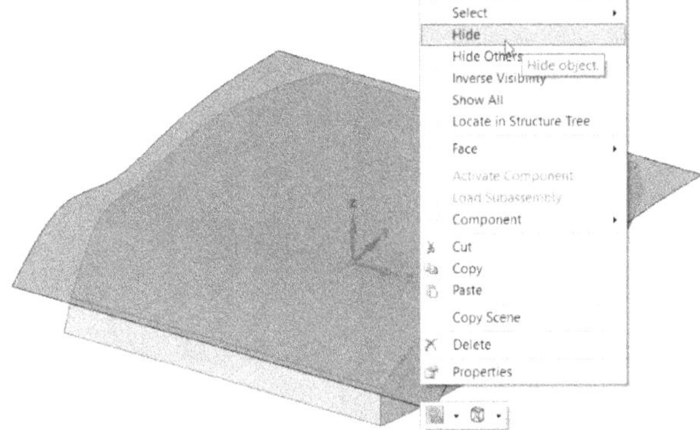

Creating Rounds

1. On the ribbon, click **Design > Edit > Pull**.
2. Press and hold the Ctrl key and click on the two edges of the model, as shown.

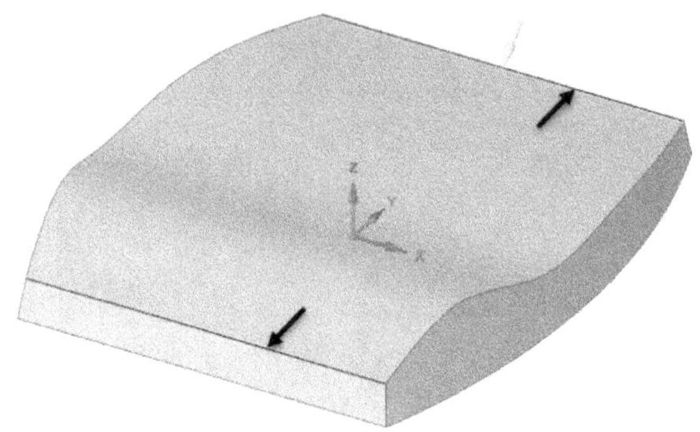

3. Click the **Round** icon on the **Options-Pull** panel.

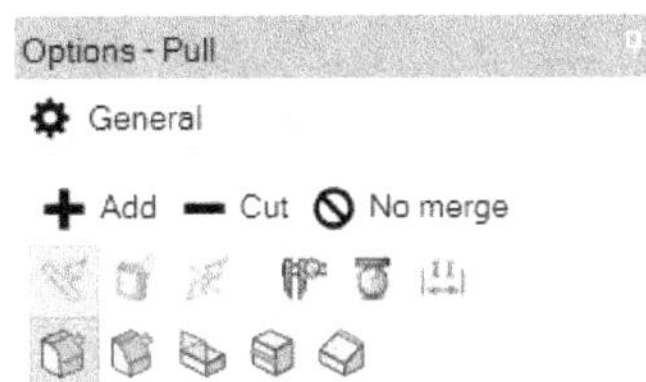

4. Click and drag the left mouse button.
5. Type **1.5** in the **Radius** box.
6. Press ENTER.

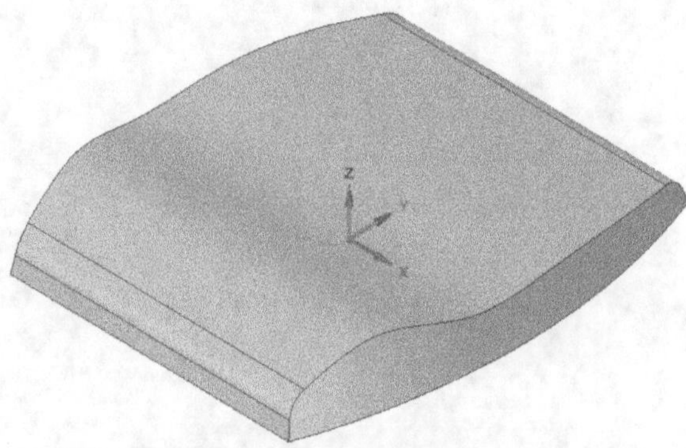

7. Select the curved edge on the model.

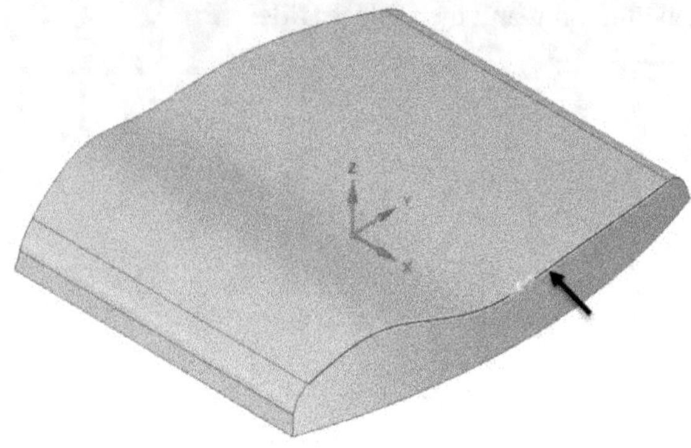

8. Right click and select **Select > Select Tangent Edge Loop**.
9. Press and hold the left mouse button and drag the pointer.
10. Type 0.8 and press ENTER.

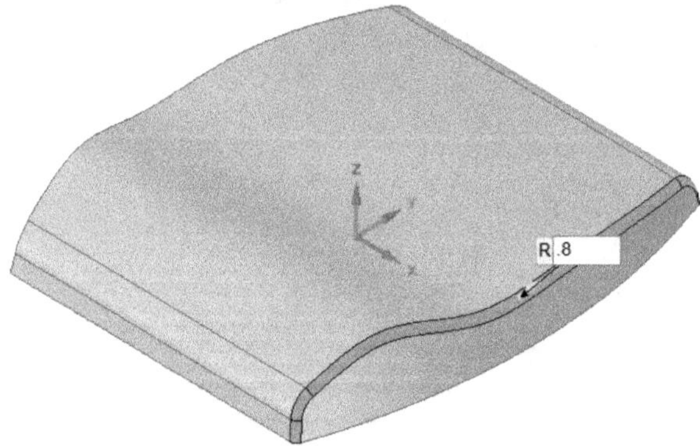

11. Click in the graphics area.

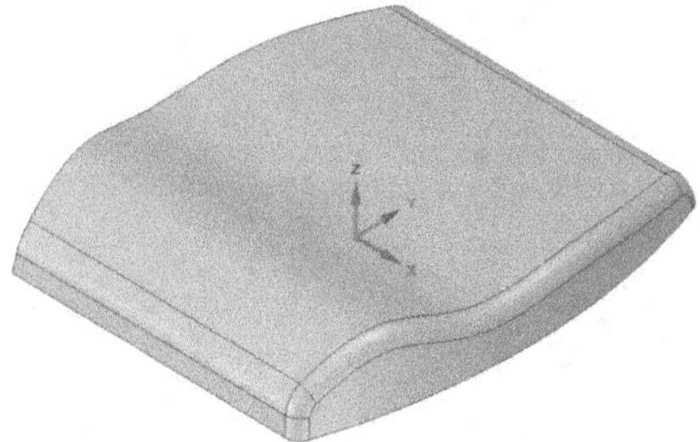

12. Likewise, create another round on the other side.

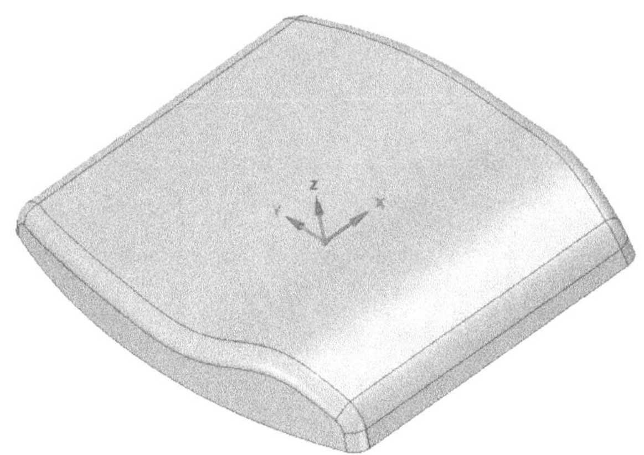

Shelling the Model

1. On the ribbon, click **Design > Insert > Shell**.

2. Rotate the model and select the bottom face.

3. Type **0.2** in the Thickness box, and then press ENTER.

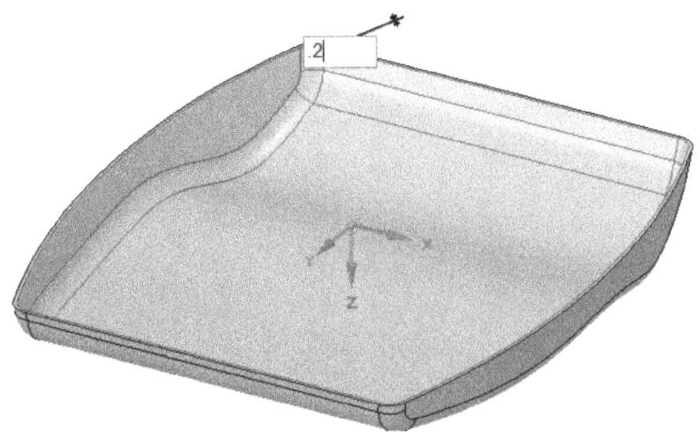

4. Click **Complete**.

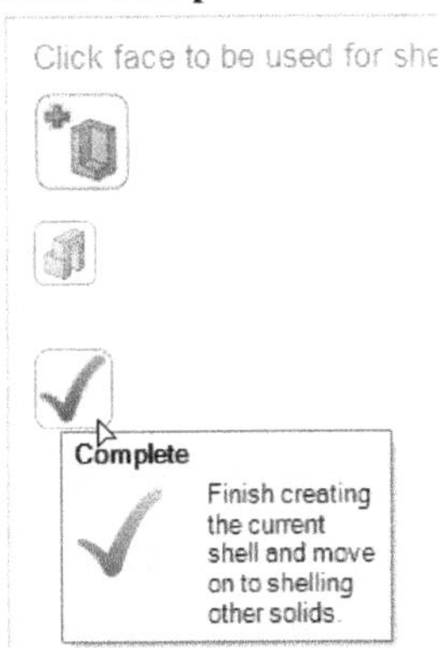

5. Save and close the model.

TUTORIAL 5

In this tutorial, you construct a patterned cylindrical shell.

Constructing a cylindrical shell

1. Click **File > New > Design** on the ribbon.

2. Click the **Select New Sketch Plane** on the Toolbar.

3. Place the pointer on the fourth quadrant of the Coordinate system.
4. Click to select the XY plane.

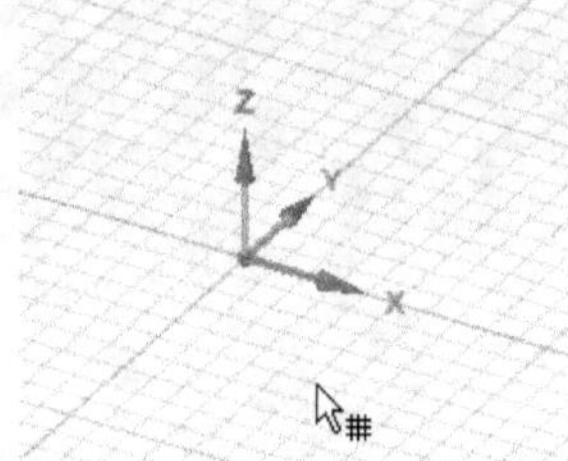

5. Click **Design > Orient > Plan View** on the ribbon.

6. Click **Design > Sketch > Circle** on the ribbon.

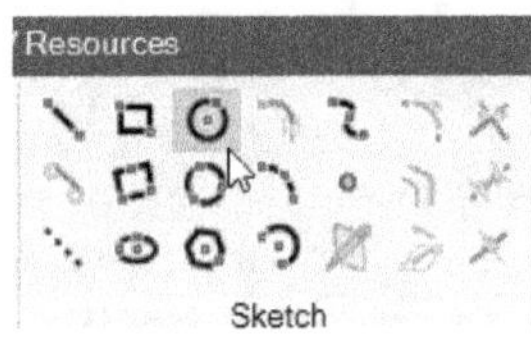

7. Click on the origin point and type-in **1.85** in the box attached. Press Enter.

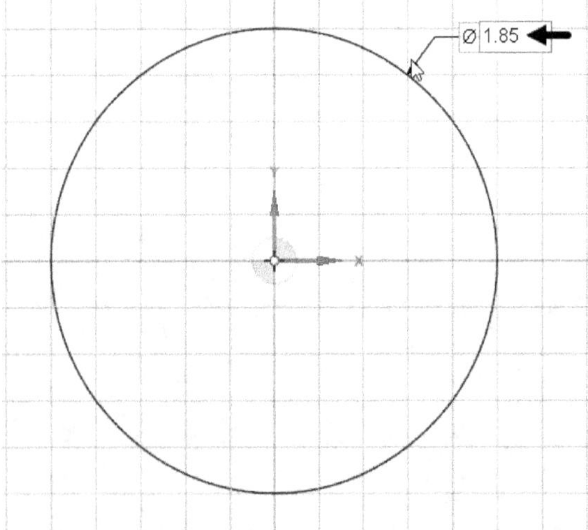

8. Select the origin point and then type-in 1.96 in the box attached. Press Enter.

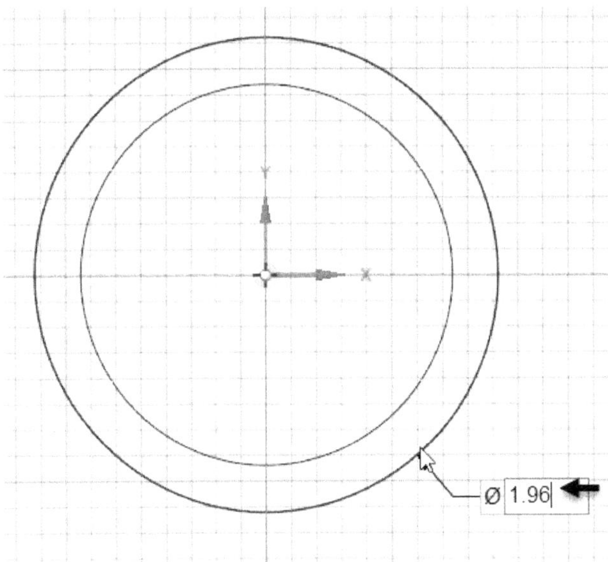

9. Press Esc to deactivate the tool.
10. Click the **Return to 3D Mode** icon on the Toolbar.

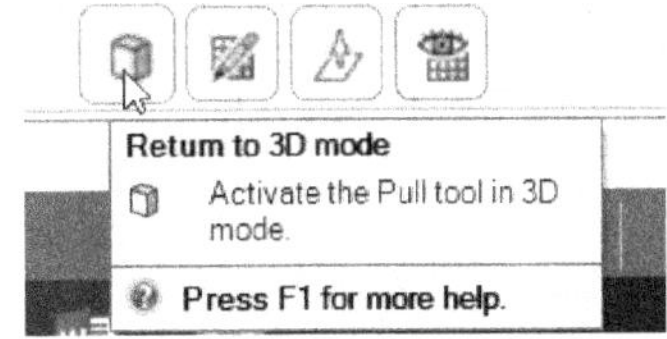

11. Click **Design > Orient > Home** on the ribbon to change the view orientation.

12. Click **Design > Edit > Pull** on the ribbon and click in the enclosed region of the sketch, as shown.

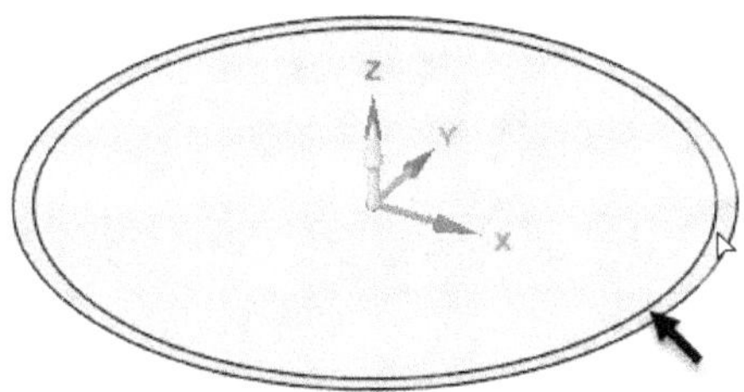

13. Press and hold the left mouse button and drag the pointer upward.
14. Type-in 3.93 in the box attached and then press Enter.
15. Press Esc.

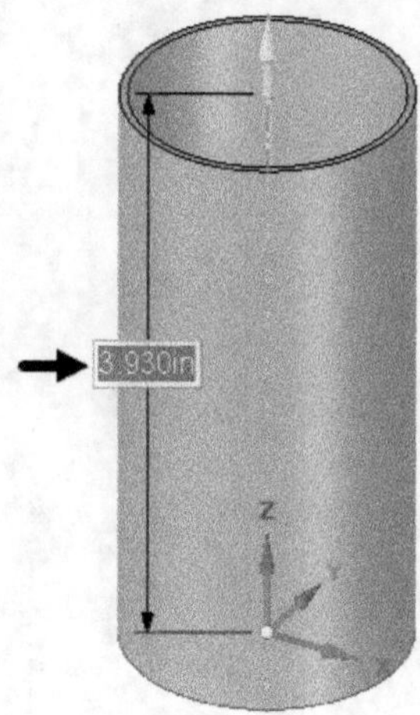

Adding a Slot

1. On the ribbon, click **Design > Mode > Sketch Mode**.
2. Select the X-axis of the Coordinate system.

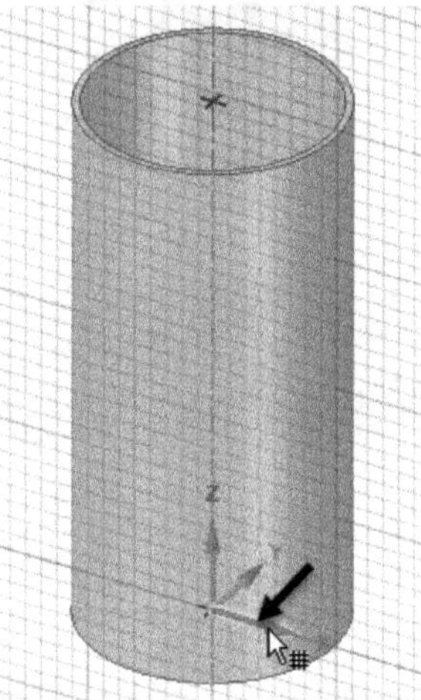

3. On the ribbon, click **Design > Orient > Plan view**.
4. Uncheck the **Snap grid** option on the **Options – Sketch** panel located at the bottom left corner.

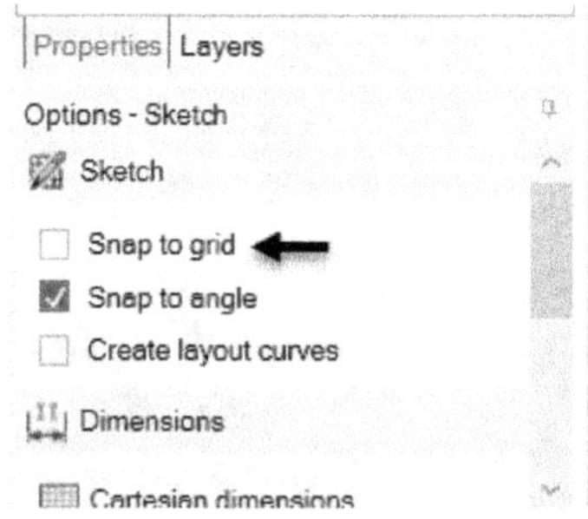

5. On the ribbon, click **Design > Sketch > Circle**.
6. On the **Options - Sketch** panel, scroll to the **Dimensions** section and then select the **Cartesian dimensions** option.

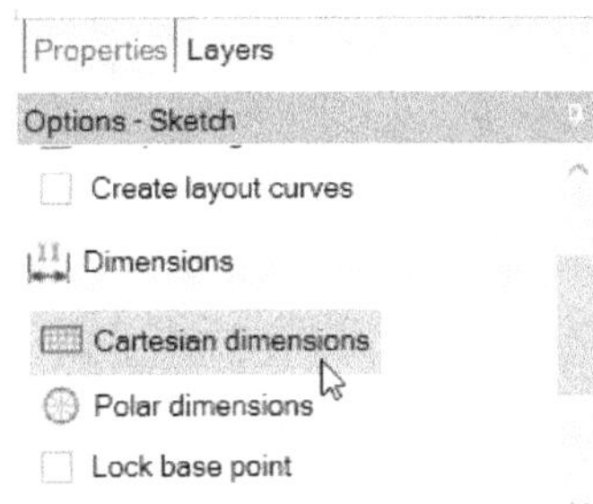

7. Select the origin point of the sketch; the base point is defined.

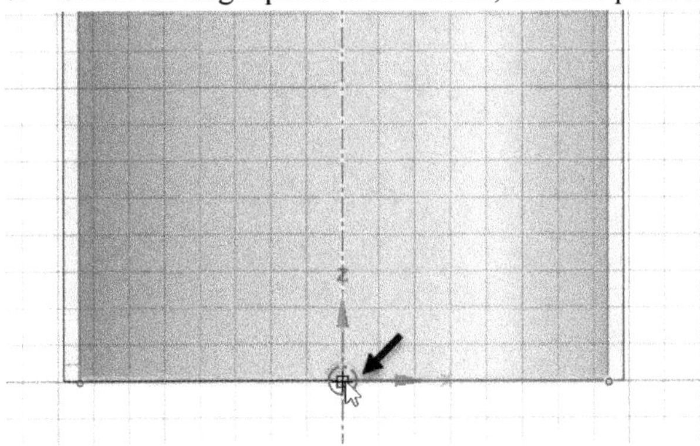

8. Move the pointer vertically along the Z-axis.
9. Press the Tab key and type -0.28 in the dimension box. Next, press ENTER.
10. Type 0.16 and press ENTER; the circle is created.

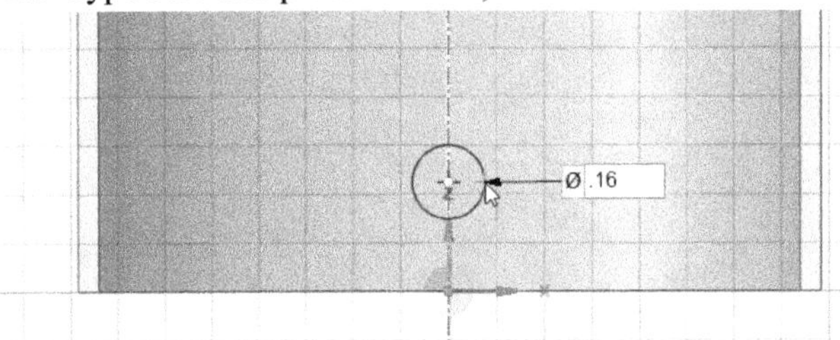

11. Move the pointer vertically upward.
12. Press the Tab key and type -0.32. Next, press ENTER.

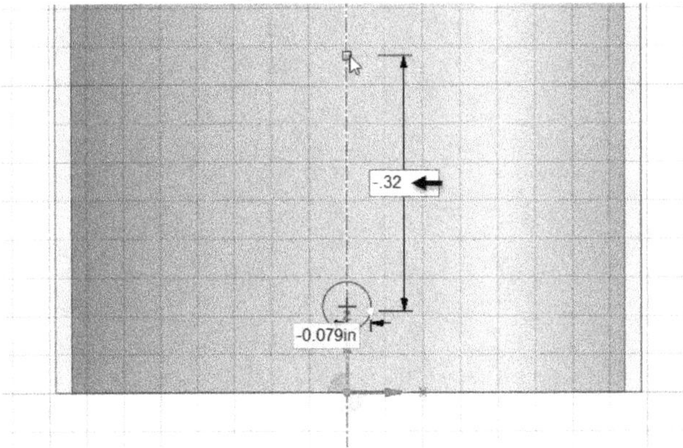

13. Type 0.16 and press ENTER; another circle is created.

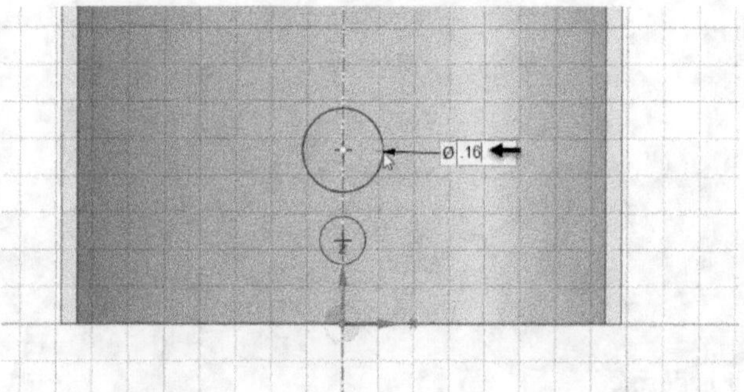

14. On the ribbon, click **Design > Sketch > Tangent Line**.

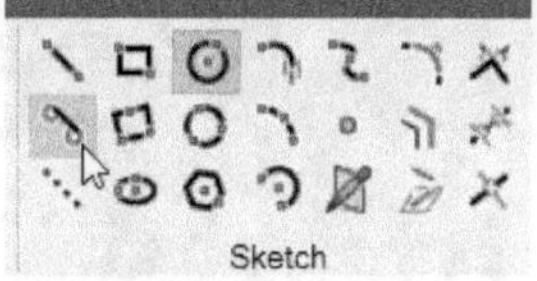

15. Select the upper circle.
16. Move the pointer downward and select the lower circle.

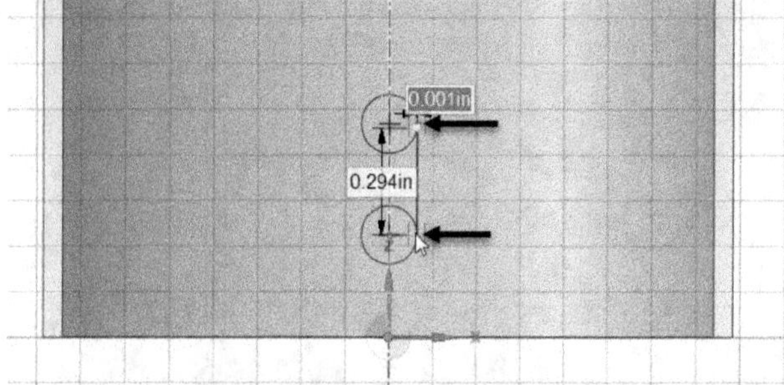

17. Again, select the two circles to create a line tangent to them.

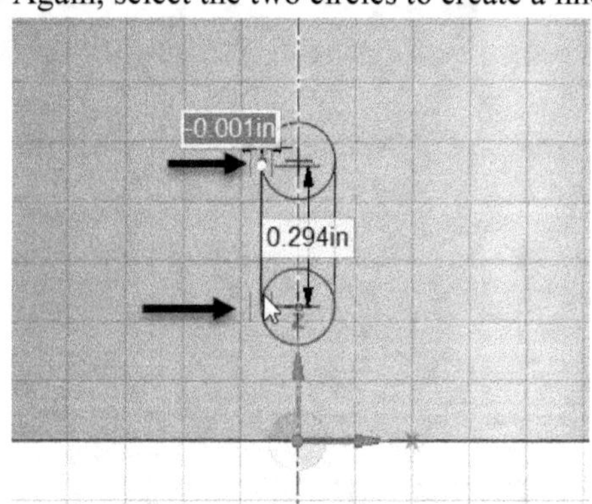

18. On the ribbon, click **Design > Sketch > Trim away**.

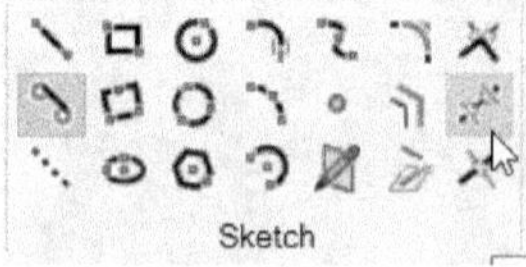

19. Select the portions of the circles, as shown; the circles are trimmed.

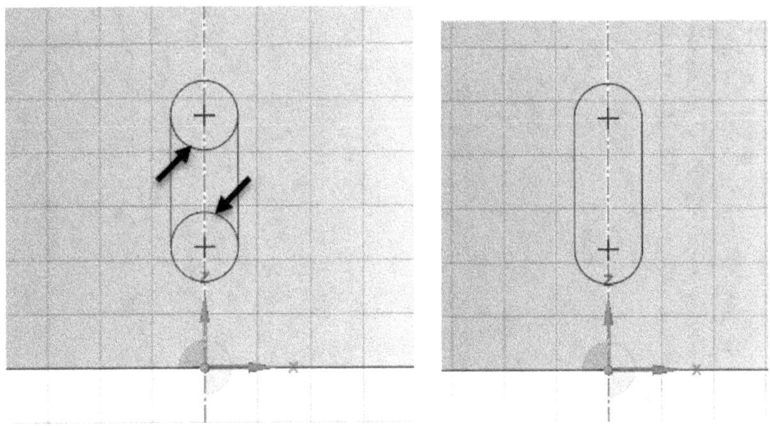

20. On the ribbon, click **Design > Mode > 3D Mode**.

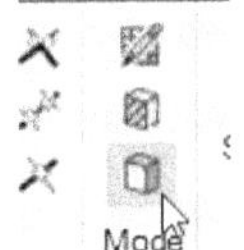

21. Click **Design > Orient > Home** on the ribbon to change the view orientation.
22. Click **Design > Edit > Pull** on the ribbon.
23. Select the Surface from the Structure panel, as shown.

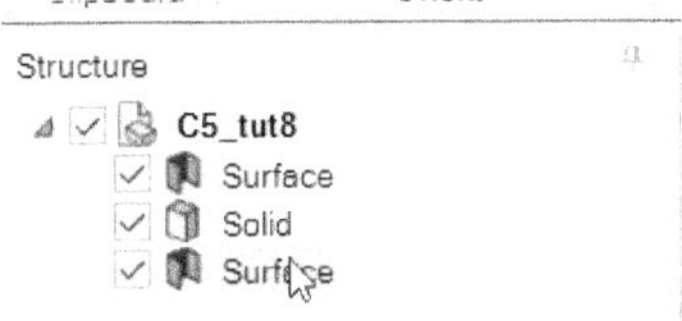

24. Click the **Cut** icon on the **Options –Pull** panel.

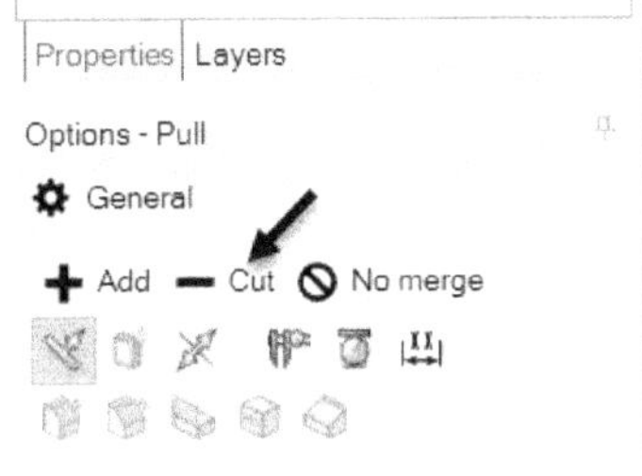

25. Press and hold the left mouse button and drag the pointer toward left.
26. Release the pointer; the cutout is created on the model.

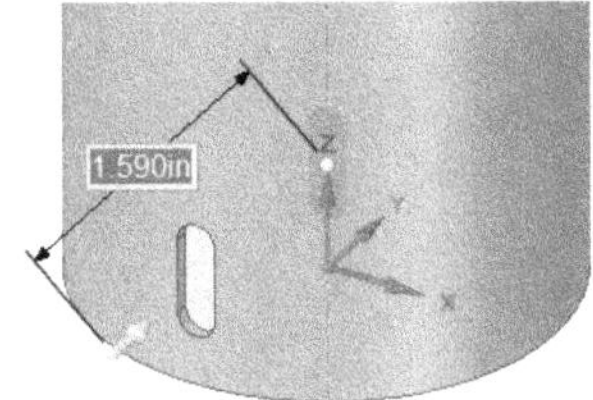

Constructing the Linear pattern

1. On the ribbon, click **Design > Edit > Move**.
2. Select the face of the cut-out, as shown.

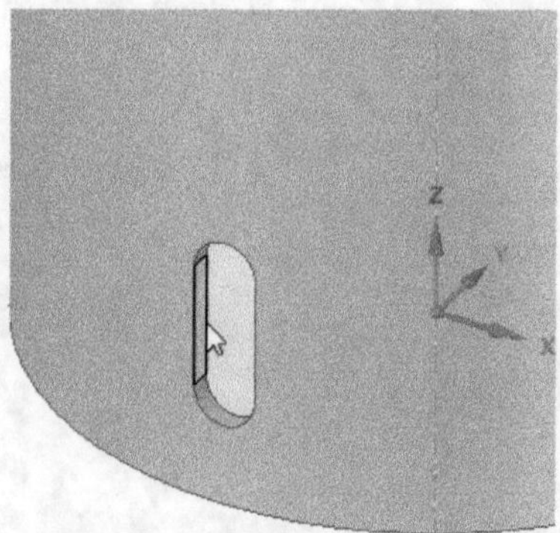

3. On the **Options** panel, click the **Selection** tab.
4. Select **Features > Depression**.

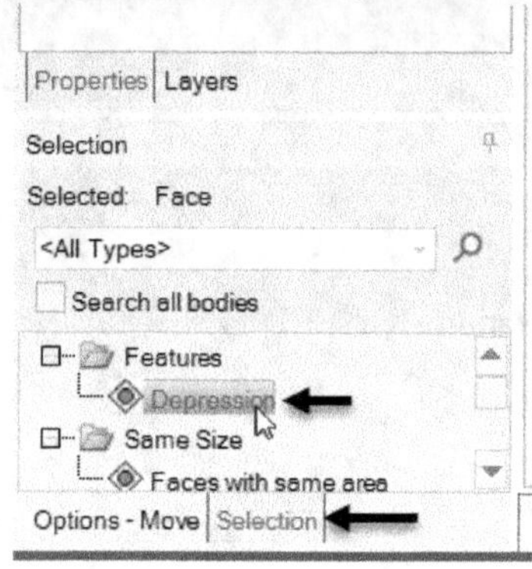

5. Click the **Options – Move** tab.
6. Check the **Create patterns** option.

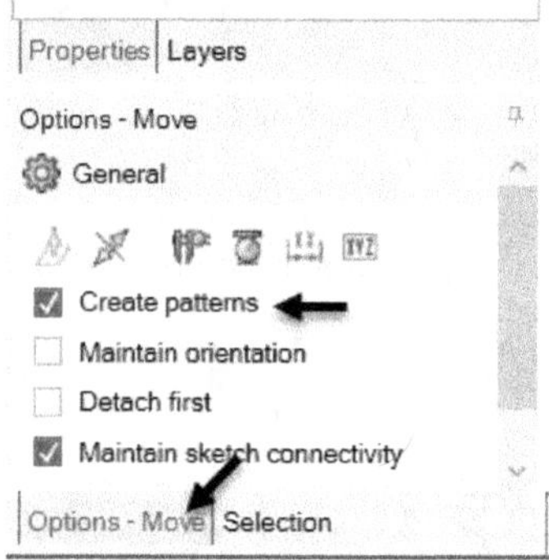

7. Click the **Move Direction** icon on the top-left corner of the graphics area.

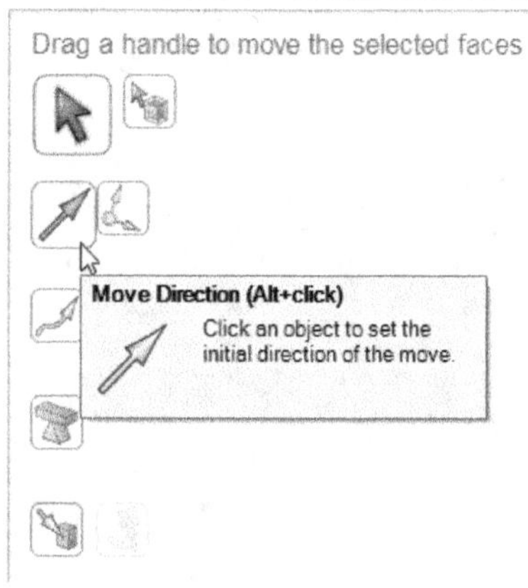

8. Select the Z-axis of the triad.

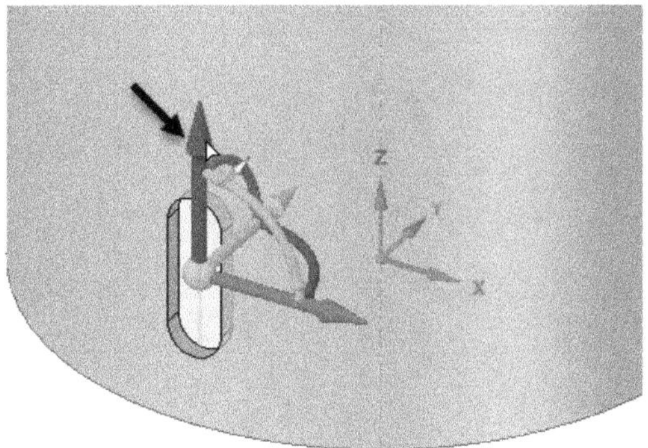

9. Press and hold the left mouse button on the Z-axis.
10. Drag the pointer upward.

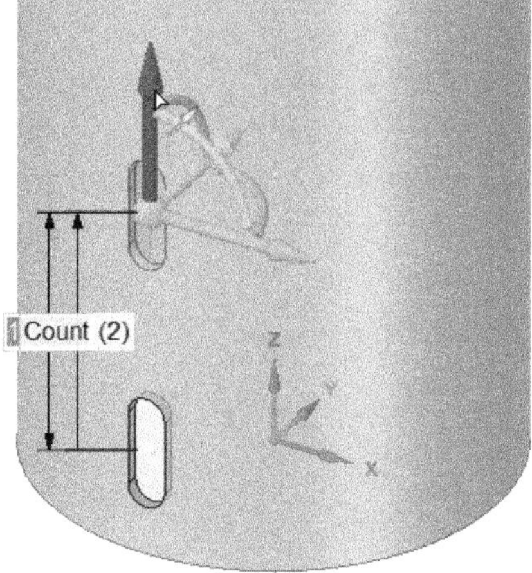

11. Type 3.05 in the spacing box displayed between the occurrences.

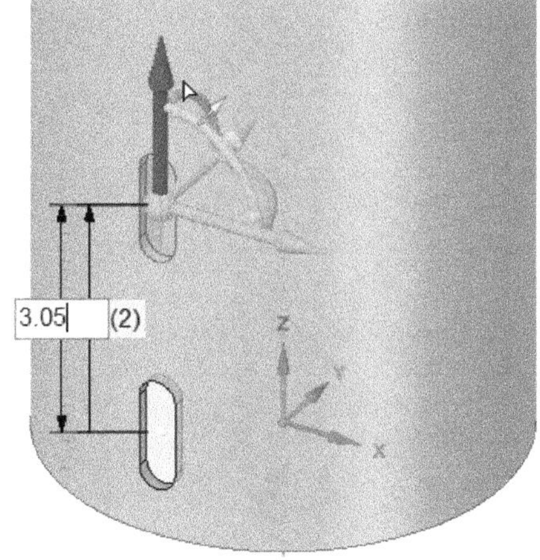

12. Press TAB to update the spacing.
13. Press TAB to switch to the Count box.
14. Type 6 and press ENTER.
15. Release the left mouse button, and then click in the graphics area.

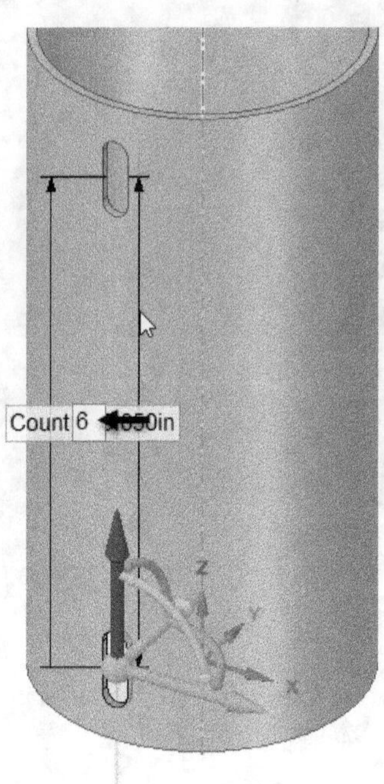

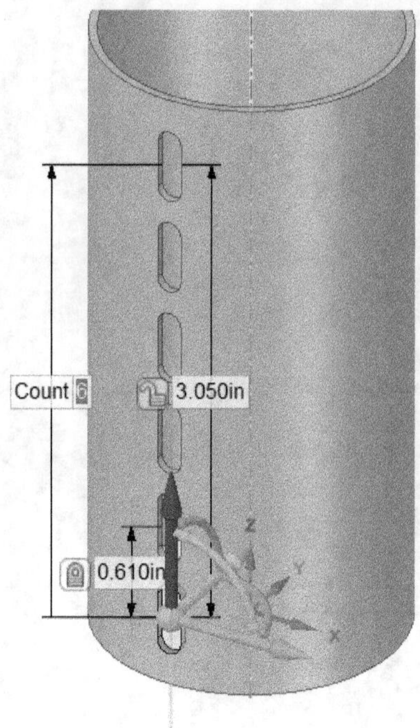

Creating the Circular Pattern

1. Select the **Pattern** from the **Structure** panel.
2. Check the **Create patterns** option in the **Options-Move** panel.

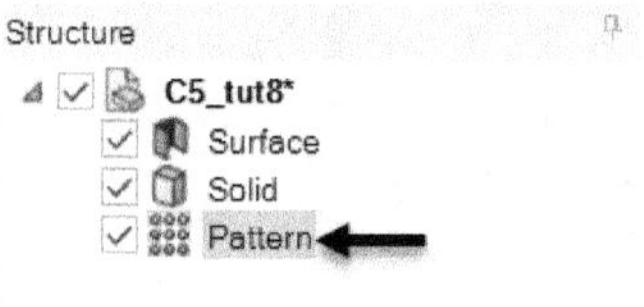

3. Click the **Anchor** icon on the top-left corner of the graphics window.
4. Select the coordinate system from the graphics area.

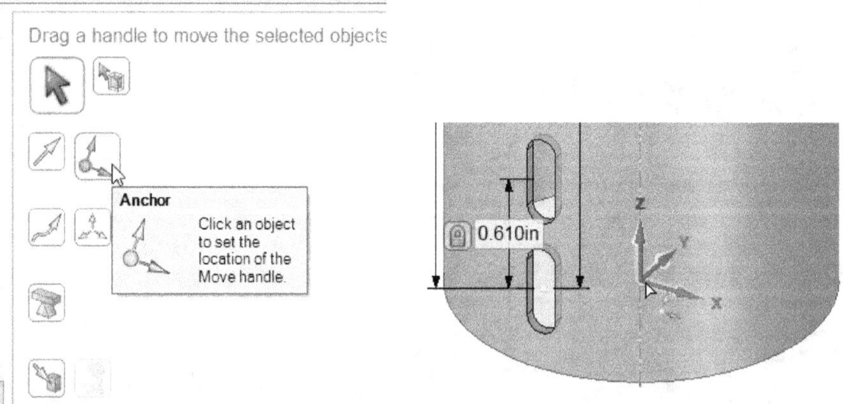

5. Click the **Move radially about axis** option.
6. Click and drag the blue color rotate handle of the triad.

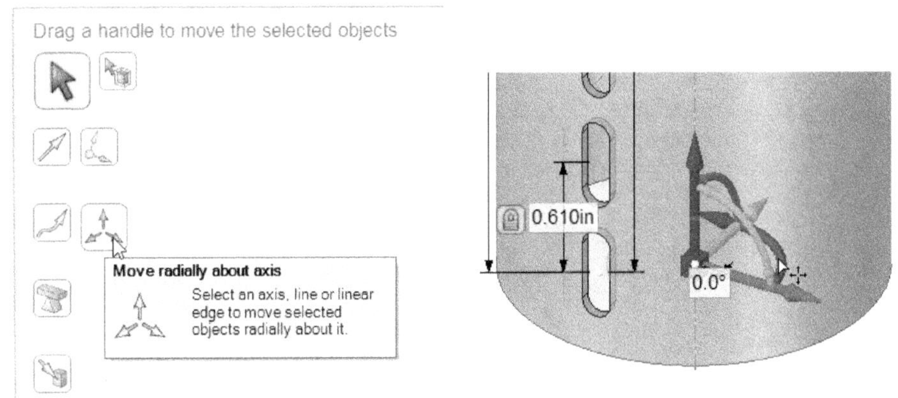

7. Release the mouse button, and then click in the graphics area.

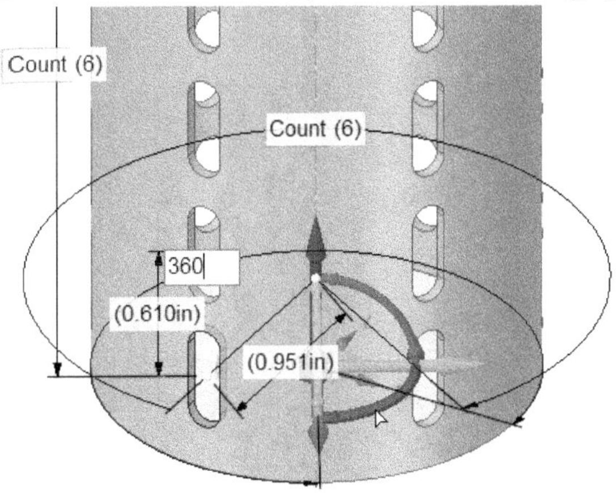

8. Select the **Pattern** from the **Structure** panel.
9. Enter 30 and 12 in the **Angle** and **Count** boxes of the **Properties** panel.
10. Click in the graphics area to create a circular pattern.

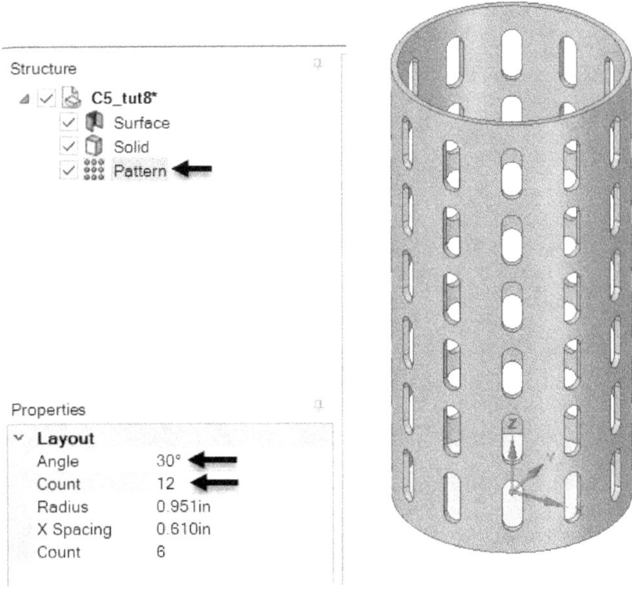

11. Save and close the model.